Relief and Rehabilitation for a Post-war World

Histories of Internationalism

Series Editors: Jessica Reinisch, Professor of Modern History at Birkbeck, University of London, UK, and David Brydan, Senior Lecturer of 20th Century History and International Relations at King's College London, UK.

Editorial Board: Tomoko Akami, Australian National University, Australia
Martin Conway, University of Oxford, UK
Adom Getachew, University of Chicago, USA
Sandrine Kott, University of Geneva, Switzerland
Stephen Legg, University of Nottingham, UK
Su Lin Lewis, University of Bristol, UK
Erez Manela, Harvard University, USA
Samuel Moyn, Yale University, USA
Alanna O'Malley, Leiden University, The Netherlands
Kiran Patel, Ludwig Maximilian University Munich, Germany
Tehila Sasson, Emory University, USA
Frank Trentmann, Birkbeck University, USA
Heidi Tworek, University of British Columbia, Canada

This new book series features cutting-edge research on the history of international cooperation and internationalizing ambitions in the modern world. Providing an intellectual home for research into the many guises of internationalism, its titles draw on methods and insights from political, social, cultural, economic and intellectual history. It showcases a rapidly expanding scholarship which has begun to transform our understanding of internationalism.

Cutting across established academic fields such as European, World, International and Global History, the series will critically examine historical perceptions of geography, regions, centres, peripheries, borderlands and connections across space in the history of internationalism.

It will include both monographs and edited volumes that shed new light on local and global contexts for international projects; the impact of class, race and gender on international aspirations; the roles played by a variety of international organisations and institutions; and the hopes, fears, tensions and conflicts underlying them.

The series is published in association with Birkbeck's Centre for the Study of Internationalism.

Published:
Organizing the 20th-Century World, ed. by Karen Gram-Skjoldager, Haakon Andreas Ikonomou, Torsten Kahlert
Placing Internationalism: International Conferences and the Making of the Modern World, ed. by Stephen Legg, Mike Heffernan, Jake Hodder, and Benjamin Thorpe
Inventing the Third World: In Search of Freedom for the Postwar Global South, ed. by Jeremy Adelman and Gyan Prakash
Internationalists in European History: Rethinking the Twentieth Century, ed. by Jessica Reinisch and David Brydan
International Cooperation in Cold War Europe, Daniel Stinsky
Socialist Internationalism and the Gritty Politics of the Particular, ed. by Kristin Roth-Ey
Relief and Rehabilitation for a Postwar World, ed. by Samantha K. Knapton and Katherine Rossy
Cosmopolitan Elites and the Making of Globality, Leonie Wolters

Forthcoming:
Informing Interwar Internationalism: The Information Strategies of the League of Nations, Emil Eiby Seidenfaden
Socialism, Internationalism, and Development in the Third World: Envisioning Modernity in the Era of Decolonization, ed. by Su Lin Lewis and Nana Osei-Opare
Dam Internationalism: Rethinking Power, Expertise and Technology in the Twentieth Century, ed. by Vincent Lagendijk and Frederik Schulze

Relief and Rehabilitation for a Post-war World

Humanitarian Intervention and the UNRRA

Edited by Samantha K. Knapton and Katherine Rossy

BLOOMSBURY ACADEMIC
LONDON • NEW YORK • OXFORD • NEW DELHI • SYDNEY

BLOOMSBURY ACADEMIC

Bloomsbury Publishing Plc, 50 Bedford Square, London, WC1B 3DP, UK
Bloomsbury Publishing Inc, 1385 Broadway, New York, NY 10018, USA
Bloomsbury Publishing Ireland, 29 Earlsfort Terrace, Dublin 2, D02 AY28, Ireland

BLOOMSBURY, BLOOMSBURY ACADEMIC and the Diana logo
are trademarks of Bloomsbury Publishing Plc

First published in Great Britain 2024
This paperback edition published in 2025

Copyright © Samantha K. Knapton and Katherine Rossy, 2024

Samantha K. Knapton and Katherine Rossy have asserted their right under the Copyright, Designs and Patents Act, 1988, to be identified as Editors of this work.

For legal purposes the Acknowledgements on p. xi constitute an extension of this copyright page.

Series design by Tjaša Krivec
Cover image: Victims of war, far removed from light and air in one of the Naples caves, put their simple faith in UNRRA and the promise on the poster on the wall: 'Food, health and hope' [1945]. UN Photo

All rights reserved. No part of this publication may be: i) reproduced or transmitted in any form, electronic or mechanical, including photocopying, recording or by means of any information storage or retrieval system without prior permission in writing from the publishers; or ii) used or reproduced in any way for the training, development or operation of artificial intelligence (AI) technologies, including generative AI technologies. The rights holders expressly reserve this publication from the text and data mining exception as per Article 4(3) of the Digital Single Market Directive (EU) 2019/790.

Bloomsbury Publishing Plc does not have any control over, or responsibility for, any third-party websites referred to or in this book. All internet addresses given in this book were correct at the time of going to press. The author and publisher regret any inconvenience caused if addresses have changed or sites have ceased to exist, but can accept no responsibility for any such changes.

A catalogue record for this book is available from the British Library.

A catalog record for this book is available from the Library of Congress.

ISBN: HB: 978-1-3501-7911-0
       PB: 978-1-3504-2275-9
       ePDF: 978-1-3501-7912-7
       eBook: 978-1-3501-7913-4

Series: Histories of Internationalism

Typeset by Integra Software Services Pvt. Ltd.

For product safety related questions contact productsafety@bloomsbury.com.

To find out more about our authors and books visit www.bloomsbury.com and sign up for our newsletters.

Contents

List of figures	viii
List of contributors	ix
Acknowledgements	xi
List of abbreviations	xii

	Introduction: Beyond relief and rehabilitation: UNRRA in historical perspective *Samantha K. Knapton and Katherine Rossy*	1
1	'UNRRA: You never really rehabilitate anyone': Problems of rehabilitation in definition and practice *Samantha K. Knapton*	17
2	'Low in health and spirits': The hygiene and health campaign in UNRRA camps in Germany and Austria as a form of rehabilitation *Katarzyna Nowak*	37
3	Paving the way for a new democracy? UNRRA in Italy *Silvia Salvatici*	57
4	The muse of rural assistance in Greece for relief and rehabilitation: The Near East Foundation and United Nations Relief and Rehabilitation Administration, 1944–7 *Joshua Thew*	73
5	Looking at refugees: Relief and rehabilitation in UNRRA/CNRRA photographic representations of refugees in post-war China *Caroline Reeves*	103
6	The forgotten 'R': UNRRA's Central Tracing Bureau and the recovery of missing persons in post-war Germany, 1945–7 *Katherine Rossy*	133
7	The Pate Reports and UNRRA: The beginning of UNICEF, 1946 *Lisa Payne Ossian*	151
8	The UNRRA: The ambiguity of 'rehabilitation', suppressed discourses, and unlearned lessons from FDR's post-war assistance operation *Dan Plesch and Grace Schneider*	175
	Afterword UNRRA: An overview *Peter Gatrell*	194
	Select bibliography	210
	Index	214

Figures

4.1	Greece: Relief and Rehabilitation Propaganda, 1942	85
4.2	Tents at Nuseirat, Southern Palestine. UNRRA's Biggest Camp for Greek Refugees	89
5.1	Trucks are unloaded from a river barge at Changsha	111
5.2	UNRRA-sponsored food processing training school in Shanghai	112
5.3	CNRRA home food preservation specialist working with local	113
5.4	Refugees dusted with DDT on arrival at the refugee camp in Wuchang	114
5.5	Mrs Wang Koo Shee given food and tea at Nantao refugee camp in Shanghai supplied by UNRRA and operated by CNRRA	115
5.6	Henan Province (China), elderly refugee woman waiting in the crowd	116
5.7	Refugees from the famine-stricken parts of Henan Province	117
5.8	'Cannibalism' woodcut	120
5.9	The Beijing Buddhist Relief Society working with a Shanghai Merchants Organization to deliver relief to the stricken mountainous region of west Zhili by the Shanxi border	122
5.10	The Chongqing Chapter of the Chinese Red Cross	123
5.11	The Tianjin Red Chapter of the Chinese Red Cross, Longting Refuge	124
5.12	The Medical Ship of the General Office of the Chinese Red Cross arriving in Shanghai from Henan Province	124
8.1	Number of publications in JSTOR containing the phrase 'UNRRA' (in title, body and/or citations) from 1940 through 2020	179

Contributors

Peter Gatrell taught at the University of Manchester from 1976 until his retirement in 2021. His publications include *A Whole Empire Walking: Refugees in Russia during World War 1* (1999); *Free World? The Campaign to Save the World's Refugees, 1956–1963* (2011); and *The Making of the Modern Refugee* (2013). His latest book, *The Unsettling of Europe: The Great Migration, 1945 to the Present*, appeared in 2019. He is Fellow of the British Academy.

Samantha K. Knapton is Assistant Professor of History at the University of Nottingham, UK. Her research interests focus on twentieth-century central and east-central Europe, displacement and international humanitarianism. She has published on Anglo-Polish relations in post-1945 Germany and generated a network of scholars focusing on the United Nations Relief and Rehabilitation Administration (UNRRA). Her first book *Occupiers, Humanitarian Workers, and Polish Displaced Persons in British-occupied Germany* was published with Bloomsbury Academic in 2023.

Katarzyna Nowak is Research Fellow at the Vienna Wiesenthal Institute for Holocaust Studies, Austria. Her research interests centre around cultural and social history of Eastern Europe, refugees and humanitarianism. Her first monograph, *Kingdom of Barracks. A Cultural History of Polish Displaced Persons in Allied-occupied Germany and Austria, 1945–1952*, was published with McGill-Queen's University Press in 2023.

Lisa Payne Ossian is Emeritus Professor of Des Moines Community College. She has a number of works, including: *The Forgotten Generation: American Children and World War II* (2011) and *The Home Fronts of Iowa, 1939–1945* (2009). With funding from the Truman library, she is currently working on her latest book, *'The Grimmest Spectre': The World Famine Emergency, Herbert Hoover's Mission, and the Invisible Year, 1946*.

Dan Plesch is Professor of Diplomacy and Strategy at SOAS, University of London. His publications include *Verification in the Age of Google* (2022); *Human Rights after Hitler* (2017); and *America, Hitler and the UN* (2012). His research engages with global strategies for peace and security. He is a member of the barrister's chambers of Stephen Kay QC in recognition of his contribution to origins and future of international criminal law.

Caroline Reeves is Associate in Research at the Harvard University Fairbank Centre. Her research focuses on the history and development of Chinese traditions of charity and humanitarianism through the present day. She has published widely on the history of the Chinese Red Cross Society, the treatment of the dead in early-twentieth-century China, China as a model for the Global South, and on the intersection of photography and charitable activity. She is currently working on a comprehensive history of Chinese charity.

Katherine Rossy is Assistant Professor of International History at the Royal Military College of Canada. Her research interests include human rights, humanitarian systems and international organizations. The recipient of two grants from the Social Sciences and Humanities Research Council of Canada as well as the Alice Wilson Award from the Royal Society of Canada, Rossy has published widely on military occupation and humanitarian intervention in the aftermath of the Second World War. She is currently working on a monograph on emergency humanitarianism towards children from the Second World War to the Universal Declaration of Human Rights (1939–48).

Silvia Salvatici is Professor of Modern History at the University of Florence, Italy. Her research interests focus on the refugees, gender and humanitarianism. She has published on UNRRA and the relief of Europe in the aftermath of the Second World War. Her most recent book is *A History of Humanitarianism, 1755–1989: In the Name of Others* (2019).

Grace Schneider studies Development Economics with the Department of Economics at SOAS, University of London. Her research interests include historicizing Development Economics, with a specific focus on the pluralistic nature of 'development' in the twentieth century.

Joshua U. Thew is PhD Researcher at The Graduate Institute Geneva. His research focuses on how American attitudes and ideas about race, ethnicity and religion influenced and determined rural education and development practices in the Middle East across the twentieth century. His broader research interests reside in the fields of community organization, agriculture – and particularly agrarian outreach – health and recreation as vehicles for knowledge exchange.

Acknowledgements

The idea for this edited volume blossomed during the first-ever workshop on the United Nations Relief and Rehabilitation Administration at Newcastle University, UK, in June 2018. Organized by Samantha K. Knapton and Katherine Rossy, the workshop was funded by Newcastle University's Humanities Research Institute, Cultural Significance of Place, and Forced Migration Group. While the Covid-19 pandemic caused significant delays for many of our contributors who were unable to access archival material and sources, the resulting collection of chapters reveals that the long wait has been worth it. We, as the editors of this volume, extend our heartfelt thanks to each contributor for their willingness and persistence throughout the process. Without them, this volume would not have been possible.

We are also grateful to the three anonymous reviewers as well as the Histories of Internationalism series board members, particularly Jessica Reinisch and David Brydan, for their constructive criticism and encouragement which made this volume shine. Their willingness to house this volume within their series is testament to their confidence in what lies herein, and we are thankful for their keen reception. We are also indebted to Maddie Holder and Megan Harris at Bloomsbury Academic. Their professionalism and attention to detail have made them a pleasure to work with. Finally, we would like to thank our families for their encouragement and support throughout this process.

While by no means an exhaustive account of UNRRA's history and legacy, we hope that this edited collection will pave the way towards further work on this unique and foundational international humanitarian organization.

Abbreviations

AAI	*Amministrazione per gli Aiuti Internazionali* (Administration for International Aid, Italy)
AWH	American Women's Hospital
CCP	Chinese Communist Party
CNRRA	Chinese National Relief and Rehabilitation Administration
COBSRA	Council of British Societies for Relief Abroad
CSB	Child Search Bureau
CTB	Central Tracing Bureau
DP	displaced person
FAO	Food and Agricultural Organization
FAU	Friends Ambulance Unit
FDR	Franklin Delano Roosevelt
FSA	Farm Security Administration
IGCR	Intergovernmental Committee on Refugees
ILO	International Labour Organization
IRO	International Refugee Organization
ITS	International Tracing Service
MERRA	Middle East Relief and Refugee Administration
MESC	Middle East Supply Centre
NEF	Near East Foundation
NGO	non-governmental organization
NPA	National Planning Association (United States)

OFRRO	Office of Foreign Relief and Rehabilitation Operations
RSC	Refugee Settlement Commission
SHAEF	Supreme Headquarters Allied Expeditionary Forces
UNDP	United Nations Development Programme
UNESCO	United Nations Educational, Scientific, and Cultural Organization
UNHCR	United Nations High Commissioner for Refugees
UNICEF	United Nations Children's Fund
UNIO	United Nations Information Organization
UNRRA	United Nations Relief and Rehabilitation Administration
UNRWA	United Nations Relief and Works Agency
WHO	World Health Organization

Introduction

Beyond relief and rehabilitation: UNRRA in historical perspective

Samantha K. Knapton and Katherine Rossy

In her 1995 Turin speech on the challenges of 'rehabilitation', United Nations High Commissioner for Refugees Sadako Ogata addressed the complex issues that the UN faced in a mid-1990s world.[1] Rehabilitation, the speech revealed, still remained undefined in relation to humanitarian aid over fifty years after the creation of the United Nations Relief and Rehabilitation Administration (UNRRA), the United Nations' first state-driven organization and specialized humanitarian agency. Created in 1943 to rid the world of illness, starvation and destitution caused by the Second World War, UNRRA functioned as a blueprint for future efforts to relieve those who suffered from the horrors of war and forced displacement. Contrary to the opinion of UNRRA contemporaries and subsequent experts, both of whom are quick to credit the organization as a failure, this edited volume argues that UNRRA was the start of something new – an ambitious, international experiment that gave way to the creation of contemporary UN specialized agencies, such as UNICEF, UNESCO, WHO and UNHCR. This collection also posits that it is impossible to understand successive UN humanitarian cultures and practices without first studying UNRRA's second 'R' as well as its practical and theoretical successes and failures.

UNRRA was central to the social, political and economic reconstruction of Europe after the end of the Second World War. While it predates the formal creation of the United Nations in October 1945, its role in mediating the realms of public health, agriculture, infrastructure, education and culture established the very foundations that continue to shape international frameworks and institutions in the world today. Ongoing humanitarian crises in Syria, South Sudan, Yemen, Venezuela and Ukraine have generated unprecedented levels of upheaval and displacement that have long surpassed that of the Second World War and its immediate aftermath. This volume is thus a timely and topical contribution to understanding the interaction between forced migration and humanitarian responses, socio-economic advancement, and peace and security.

Part of the reason UNRRA continues to be perceived as a failure is due to the confusion that surrounds the concept of 'rehabilitation' and the inability to understand it as a distinct entity from 'relief'. This collection of case studies builds on theoretical understandings of 'rehabilitation', both by UNRRA contemporaries and scholarly experts, to emphasize the disparity between planning and reality. Although certain contributions in this volume interpret rehabilitation as the provision of immediate needs for people, others view it as the establishment of long-term systems and structures that aim to promote peace and international security.

Relief, as this volume argues, is often understood as the provision of food, medicine, shelter and clothing while rehabilitation, which is seemingly harder to define, ranges from the rehabilitation of the perceived 'status quo' through the repatriation and resettlement of people, the psychological, physical and spiritual rehabilitation of the person, or the agricultural, economic and structural rehabilitation of an area. There could be no rehabilitation without immediate relief, making it impossible to understand one concept without linking it to the other. By foregrounding how UNRRA implemented 'relief' and 'rehabilitation' policies in the post-war world alongside international case studies of their varied application, this study will trace the arc of UNRRA's successes and failures that have since established the blueprint for modern-day international humanitarianism.

UNRRA's creation and inclusion of the second 'R'

UNRRA's first opening session in Atlantic City in November 1943 was framed by its member nations as an organization that was created to 'help the people help themselves'.[2] This mantra, often repeated throughout UNRRA informational and promotional materials, became the bedrock upon which 'rehabilitation' was to be implemented. During his first speech as UNRRA's director general, Herbert H. Lehman stated, 'we have been called upon twice within the span of a life-time to devise a peace in which all men can live in freedom from want. We failed once. We dare not fail again.'[3] UNRRA served as the principal humanitarian organization of the post-military period and was tasked with coordinating the health, welfare, registration, administration and repatriation of all United Nations refugees and displaced persons (DPs) found in enemy or ex-enemy territory.[4] Aside from its director general, UNRRA consisted of a General Council composed of all forty-four UN nations that met biannually as well as a smaller Policy Committee consisting of the 'Four Great Powers': China, the Soviet Union, the United Kingdom and the United States. This smaller committee ultimately made most decisions that directed the distribution of relief and guided the implementation of policy.[5]

The agency faced a colossal task. One of UNRRA's chief concerns was that of forced migration and displacement. Anywhere between thirty and sixty million people had been displaced by war in Europe alone, both within and outside of their countries.[6] As Lehman pointed out in 1944, 'One of the most serious and difficult problems developing out of the war is the problem of displaced persons […] Germany, in the pursuit of her military, political, economic and racial objectives, has shifted the populations of Europe at will'.[7] In light of such unprecedented displacement, it was clear that a new kind of professionalized humanitarianism was needed. UNRRA's mission was debated during its second meeting in Montreal in September 1944, where it was decided 'to avoid the now acknowledged errors committed in 1919':

> Then, assistance was confined to relief; now relief is to be extended to include rehabilitation. Then, relief consisted in the main of foodstuffs drawn from the United States and distributed chiefly in France and Belgium, which were more accessible than Eastern Europe, whose distress was in fact greater; now the range of relief is to be wider, clothing in particular being included.[8]

This shift from 'relief' to 'relief and rehabilitation' had a profound impact upon millions of displaced men, women and children. In many ways, as UNRRA historian Jessica Reinisch argues, UNRRA was an 'agent of internationalism', defined as a 'broad umbrella term for the complex social, cultural, political and economic connections between individuals from different states, regions and locales' that can be applied to 'the domain of international relations, as formal diplomatic contacts between nations, as much as the movement (both linear and circular) of people and their ideas, networks and imaginations across borders'.[9] As a specialized UN agency, UNRRA's work on the international stage radically altered the humanitarian blueprint for decades to come.

One marker in this shift from short-term relief practices to long-term rehabilitation strategies was the introduction of agricultural reform, mass tracing operations and vocational training for DPs, all of which transformed humanitarian ideology and practice. By 1943, it was no longer enough to temporarily stop a problem; rather, the goal was to identify its source and adopt a preventative strategy. In post-war China, mired by years of Japanese occupation, famine and disease, the solution was not simply to provide food and medicine but to carry out dramatic agricultural reform to proactively prevent famine outbreaks. In Allied-occupied Germany, where mass tracing operations were implemented to physically locate the missing and set them on the path towards rehabilitation, refugees and forcibly displaced persons were now seen as able-bodied and capable drivers of the economy rather than a burden on countries who took them in.

While there was certainly much to celebrate about the post-war humanitarian experiments of the 1940s, not everyone was entitled to enjoy the benefits of international protection. UNRRA aid was markedly political and only certain categories of people fell under its care. It was mandated to help 'United Nations Nationals' who had been internally or externally displaced by war from 1 September 1939 and onwards, including stateless persons and displaced Italian nationals.[10] Excluded from assistance were those who did not belong to a UN member state, such as 'enemy or ex-enemy nationals' from Austria, Bulgaria, Germany, Hungary, Japan, Romania and Siam; nationals of neutral countries; ex-Wehrmacht personnel; 'war criminals, collaborators, quislings or traitors of whatever race, nationality or religion'; and, finally, '*Volksdeutsche*' (ethnic Germans) and 'German Balts' from Latvia, Estonia and Lithuania.[11] UNRRA's stringent eligibility criteria would have dire ramifications upon the millions of DPs who found themselves on the move after the Second World War as the Iron Curtain made its swift descent across Eastern Europe. One of the categories excluded from UNRRA care were Germans from the East, differentiated by the word *Vertriebene*, or expellees.[12] The political origins of UNRRA and its humanitarian practices caused many to characterize it as a failure by the time it closed its doors in 1947.[13] Many states east of the Iron Curtain and under Soviet control were not able to tap into its vast aid and resources while others, such as the Soviet Union itself, viewed it as the archetype of American exceptionalism and as an obnoxious bastion of Western imperialism.

This edited volume has two objectives. It will provide the first, comprehensive analysis of what 'rehabilitation' means within the context of post-war humanitarianism. Then, it will emphasize the impact UNRRA had on the creation of contemporary agencies through its work in multiple areas around the globe, ranging from refugees and forced migration, emergency and disaster response, and mass recovery and conflict resolution. Experts, humanitarians and practitioners alike struggled to reach a clear consensus on the meaning and definition of 'rehabilitation', a challenge that caused continuous problems throughout its mandate. This absence of clarity and consensus has likewise translated into historiographical misconceptions, some of which this volume seeks to rectify. Scholars who work on the history of humanitarianism, international development, and war and forced migration often attribute UNRRA's short mandate as a failure or, worse, as an organization that made no real impact on the humanitarian practices of the twentieth and twenty-first centuries. This study also engages with the creation of other contemporary international organizations, such as the United Nations International Children's Emergency Fund (UNICEF), founded in 1946 to provide emergency clothing, food and medical supplies for children, and the World Health Organization (WHO), which resumed UNRRA's work on public health, emergency medical supplies and international sanitary conventions.[14] The creation of these agencies marked the 'internationalization' of UN humanitarianism and effectively set a precedent for the emergence of the modern-day United Nations Refugee Agency (known as, UNHCR), formed 'as a compromise' after UNRRA and its successor agency, the International Refugee Organization (IRO), both shut their doors. David Kennedy argues, the creation of the UNHCR made it clear that 'the post-war refugee problem had not been resolved'.[15]

By analysing the many tasks that UNRRA attempted to carry out, often simultaneously and in stunning succession, this volume reveals that UNRRA was overwhelmingly responsible for the brunt of post-war relief work carried out on the international stage between 1943 and 1947. Although UNRRA worked with several established non-governmental organizations (NGOs), such as the International Red Cross and Quakers Friend's Relief Service, the Allies had designed UNRRA in such a way to ensure that NGOs were subordinate to UNRRA control, especially in Germany and Austria. Tasked with public health, refugee work, emergency supplies and reform, its dizzying array of responsibilities were eventually resumed by successor agencies that were mandated to tackle specific problems. Studying the relief and rehabilitative work of UNRRA, while challenging historiographical misconceptions about its inefficiencies, reveals that it was the first modern international project of its kind. One that not only revolutionized mid-twentieth-century migration policies, conflict resolution processes and universal human rights but also the way in which states would interact with one another in the spirit of multilateralism. In exploring UNRRA's centrality to international humanitarian systems and the power it exerted on a socio-economic level, this volume contributes to the history of internationalism by illuminating how its administrative policies clashed and conflicted with practical implications in the field, often at a very sizeable human cost.

UNRRA and post-war humanitarianism in the historiography

As suggested in the introduction to this volume and throughout its chapters, UNRRA has occupied the place of little more than a footnote in works on the post-war period throughout the past several decades. Histories of 1945, and of Germany and Europe in particular, only mention UNRRA in passing despite their efforts to 're-place' or resettle populations, re-determine borders and trace the development of Cold-War tensions. Most of these endeavours would have had a different outcome without the intervention of UNRRA and its successors, as these organizations played a key role in all post-war processes. After an initial burst of histories on population movement alongside official and semi-official histories of UNRRA and its successor organizations, scholars paid little attention to UNRRA or DPs.[16] In the decades that ensued, a number of personal memoirs and diaries were published that have since thus become indispensable sources, all of which recount experiences working with or alongside UNRRA. Yet, it was not until the historical turn of the 1980s that a small, qualitative repository of post-war histories was published with the aim of working from the bottom up.[17] Over the next forty years, histories on the post-war period expanded significantly to include histories of individual DP groups, particular areas or camps, UNRRA teams, splinter organizations, personal histories, occupational studies and sweeping histories of both the structures of international humanitarianism and 'refugeedom' alongside the voices of refugees themselves. This volume is a valuable contribution to the ever-growing literature on the history of post-war international humanitarianism, in that it revisits the organization that started it all. Although there were attempts to create and sustain state-driven international humanitarian organizations before UNRRA, none of these had as vast a scope, a multilingual and multifunctional workforce, or, perhaps most crucially, a wealth of finances at their disposal.[18] Since UNRRA's inception, successor and splinter organizations have continued to apply 'rehabilitation' to specific humanitarian contexts, often with excellent results. Yet for UNRRA, the problem was that it attempted to apply the notion to every aspect of its work while expecting those on the ground who were tasked with enforcing it to know what it meant.

In the last twenty years, studies on internationalism, displacement and humanitarianism have grown rapidly. This expansion is commented upon in the introductions to articles and edited volumes[19] where authors have sought to place the histories of these disparate, yet intrinsically linked histories into context using case studies, often bound by area, nationality or ethnicity.[20] More recently, historians have attempted to situate organizations like UNRRA within a grander narrative. Many of these have turned to the thorny issue of 'rehabilitation', which indicate the successive organizations and policies that emanated from UNRRA. Yielding considerable space to refugee voices, Peter Gatrell's seminal work *The Unsettling of Europe* (2019) provides insight into how various migrants experienced daily negotiations within DP camps. Under UNRRA care, and confronted with issues of nationality, citizenship and border changes, Gatrell elicits questions regarding 'rehabilitation'. Although he states that 'no one was very certain what this term meant', he analyses how ideas of rehabilitating the mind were linked to producing acceptable world citizens.[21] Paul Betts' *Ruin and Renewal* (2020) focuses on efforts to 'recivilize' Europe after the Second World War. Although Betts never problematizes 'rehabilitation', the idea of creating an acceptable world citizen is again posited, as he sees UNRRA's second R as 'an updated colonial-era idea of rehabilitation through labour'.[22] David Nasaw's work focusing on *The Last Million* (2020), the term given to those left in DP camps after initial repatriation drives in 1946, does not address issues of rehabilitation but instead makes it inseparable from discussions about relief.[23] These works have made an excellent contribution to understanding the wider legacies of the post-Second World War era with Gatrell and Betts in particular considering the ongoing impact of relief and rehabilitation work as it extended into the breakdown of empires. Yet, this volume argues that UNRRA's disjointed and multifaceted understanding, and thereby application, of the second R is also the product of earlier humanitarian endeavours.

Placing UNRRA and immediate post-war efforts to 'rehabilitate' into the wider lens allows us to see the connections between colonial rule outside of Europe and the process of decolonization. Works on the breakdown of Empire and creation of 'human rights' in the aftermath of the First World War provide a backdrop for those seeking to 'rehabilitate' victims of war in the post-1945 world. Bruno Cabanes' *The Great War and the Origins of Humanitarianism* (2011) emphasizes the impact of transnational activism through a case study of five individuals. From Fridtjof Nansen to Eglantyne Jebb, Cabanes shows how the First World War brought with it a new humanitarian impetus hinged on the concept of 'human dignity' and concludes that rehabilitation, in its many iterations, was on the minds of those seeking to create a better world and humanize the former enemy as 'the nationalisation of bodies ... gradually gave way to a transnational conception of rehabilitation of wounded bodies'.[24] Histories of humanitarianism are then developed and complicated when the longer-arc of humanitarianism is considered. Davide Rodogno's *Night on Earth* (2021), focusing on Central and East-central Europe, the Balkans, and the Near East between 1918 and 1930, charts the intervention of Western humanitarianism, often influenced by colonialism, to provide both relief and rehabilitation. His work emphasizes the complexity of such missions when the 'rehabilitation' aspect often becomes a synonym for 'development'.[25] Emily Baughan's *Saving the Children* (2020), then traces the 'rehabilitation' of the child from the foundations of the Save the Children fund in the post-1918 era through to the post-1945 era and beyond while highlighting the ties between paternalism, humanitarianism and colonialism.[26] These histories provide an illuminating insight into how these often transnational organizations viewed the task of humanitarianism and providing rehabilitation before UNRRA's creation. Together they show links between colonial and imperial practices and UNRRA's later attempts to reconstruct nations.[27] Yet, as the first state-driven international humanitarian organization, UNRRA's makeup was still unique. Through tracing and recognizing the influence of early-twentieth-century practices onto UNRRA's structures and processes, these works help to highlight continuities but also developments in what was even considered 'rehabilitation' by 1943.

Moving away from grand narratives, numerous works have contributed to a nuanced and developed understanding of the experiences of displaced persons (DPs). While most of these often cast DP experiences in conjunction with ruling authorities in particular occupation zones, some have also enriched the historiography on UNRRA and its successor organizations by providing analysis of staff, functions and materials as supplementary to particular group experiences.[28] Others, furthermore, have made the machinery governing the DPs their primary focus.[29] Of note is Laure Humbert's *Reinventing French Aid* (2021), which offers a detailed, three-chapter analysis about how 'rehabilitation' was conceived through mind and body, work, and assimilation. As Humbert states, the chapters 'reveal that the French often understood the work of rehabilitation in paternalistic terms and adopted a genuinely civilizational posture; the relationship between relief workers and DPs was informed by ideas about "French" superiority'.[30] Humbert's work then poses the question of how zonally dependent understandings of 'rehabilitation' were.

Although UNRRA and its legacy are often present in the literature, especially in works that seek to place it within a larger narrative, the organization often remains a mere footnote within the vast historiography. Writing in 2000, one-time UNRRA worker, popular writer, and journalist Gitta Sereny lamented that UNRRA suffered from the 'goodie goodie' problem, as the 'modern world' is transfixed by the depraved and not the altruistic, claiming that 'evil is sexy, goodness is dull and organised goodness the dullest of all'.[31] This is no longer the case as scores of works on internationalism, humanitarianism and charity have come to fruition in the last few decades. Yet, UNRRA's contributions to the development of the post-war world are often obscured. Aside from sweeping histories like Mark Mazower's *Dark Continent* (1999), Tony Judt's *Post-war* (2005) or Michael Barnett's *Empire of Humanity* (2011), many institutional works relegate UNRRA to the margins.[32] Such is the case with Amy L. Sawyward's *The United Nations in International History* (2017), which focuses on the creation of the UN while only mentioning UNRRA a handful of times. Jennifer Morris' *Origins of UNICEF* (2015) is a notable exception that emphasizes the direct link between UNICEF and UNRRA, as UNICEF was born from a need to continue UN-sponsored child welfare work as UNRRA's mandate came to a close.[33] Whereas, Jessica L. Pearson in *The Colonial Politics of Global Health* (2018) shows how UNRRA, and in particular the creation of the World Health Organization (WHO), prompted the French to re-conceptualize their colonial project abroad in a shift from 'civilizing mission' to 'international development'.[34]

Rising Cold-War tensions further aggravated the challenges associated with defining UNRRA's second 'R'. A rapidly changing world order engendered assertions of national sovereignty and border changes, while potential immigrants learned to script their pleas for resettlement in tune with Anglo-American buzzwords of the day. To be considered eligible for resettlement, numerous receiving countries were looking at displaced persons in dichotomous terms: a DP was either good or bad, a hero or a villain, victim or perpetrator, innocent or guilty, and this was measured through haphazard screening procedures that borrowed heavily from the Allies' denazification programme. DPs thus needed to prove their worth by striking the 'right' chord with resettlement officers. For American resettlement officers, for instance, this could mean displaying strong anti-communist sentiment, being part of a wholesome family unit, and being fair skinned, where dubious wartime records were often overlooked in favour of anti-communist fervour. This volume, therefore, also seeks to understand how 'rehabilitation' was understood in these immediate post-war and Cold-War contexts.

Chapter overviews / Aims of the volume

In addition to its primary focus on rehabilitation, this volume also explores UNRRA's legacies. Although each of the chapters in this collection addresses the cumbersome conception and implementation of 'rehabilitation', many likewise engage with the policies and organizations that materialized during and after UNRRA's mandate. Each of these was inextricably linked to UNRRA, including the setting-in-motion of long-term welfare reform and agricultural development policies as well as the emergence of new organizations that stemmed from UNRRA's inability to deal with its colossal mandate. UNRRA was no stranger in attempts to effectively interpret what 'rehabilitation' meant. Part of the organization's significance is that it actively grappled with the nature of rehabilitation and its balance in relation to relief, a challenge that has beset other humanitarian organizations since.

The opening chapter by Samantha K. Knapton assesses the organization's inability to define 'rehabilitation' from its inception. As planners sought to avoid more loaded terminology, such as 'reconstruction', Knapton shows continuity in Anglo-American planning from predecessor organizations and emphasizes the ramifications of this undefined policy for post-UNRRA agencies. In the DP camps of Austria and Germany, Katarzyna Nowak looks at how health and hygiene campaigns were used as a form of rehabilitation that sought to 'recivilize' DPs in the aftermath of war. In assessing the efforts of UNRRA teams to teach DPs about health and hygiene, Nowak shows how these rehabilitative efforts were a step towards creating new citizens that ushered in a new era in international humanitarianism. Silvia Salvatici shows how UNRRA's Welfare Division in Italy developed its own objectives and pursued them through programmes implemented during the organization's existence in a bid to democratize in the wake of fascism. UNRRA sparked a new professionalization of welfare in Italy not by taking the American New Deal model as wholesale but instead by intertwining it with local resources and new institutional aims that influenced the first few years of the Italian Republic's life.

Furthering the idea that attempts at 'rehabilitation' were often guided by a considerable overlap of individuals and ideas passing through multiple organizations, Joshua Thew studies the Near East Foundation (NEF)'s impact on UNRRA as they worked alongside one another in Greece. Thew shows how rehabilitative policies were only briefly started before a return to relief measures became necessary, often as a precursor to the 'uplift' programmes designed to aid 'reconstruction'. Focusing on education, the chapter shows how legacies of interwar assistance developed into post-war attempts at rehabilitation and formed the structure of the United States' educational ladder. Using visual sources to understand rehabilitation within UNRRA's mandate in China, Caroline Reeves analyses UNRRA's and CNRRA's (Chinese National Refugee and Rehabilitation Administration) representations of refugees through attempts to communicate rehabilitation through photography. By comparing efforts to convey refugee struggles through Chinese disaster relief photography, Reeves highlights the tensions that developed in the post-1945 era between relief and rehabilitation as well as between Europe and Asia. Katherine Rossy's chapter on UNRRA's Central Tracing Bureau (CTB) in post-war Germany demonstrates that the recovery of missing persons was a central, yet separate, process within UNRRA's broader humanitarian programme. Offering in-depth analysis of the Bureau's mass tracing operations and the way in which they interacted with UNRRA's zonal, national and international partners, Rossy makes the case that the CTB's work set a new post-war precedent in mass international tracing processes.

The chapter by Lisa Payne Ossian combines former President Herbert Hoover's private papers with post-war famine relief surveys to trace the genesis of UNICEF. Ossian explores how UNRRA's inability to define rehabilitation and recognize the severe impact of war on children led to UNICEF's creation – all the while emphasizing the longer arc of the organization's inception in American planning. Dan Plesch and Grace Schneider seek to locate UNRRA's position within the current literature on foreign aid and post-conflict reconstruction by arguing that UNRRA has since been eclipsed by the legacy of the Marshall Plan but nevertheless has valuable lessons to teach. Focusing on UNRRA's mantra of 'help the people to help themselves', Plesch and Schneider show that although UNRRA has mostly been neglected in the historiography on post-conflict resolution, the organization played a vital role in rehabilitation through self-sufficiency and self-administrative encouragement in the camps. This volume concludes with an afterword by Peter Gatrell on UNRRA's place in the post-UNRRA world, the lessons it has taught, and those that can still be gleaned through a closer look at this foundational organization's intentions, practices and legacies.

The contributions to this volume emphasize the importance of this short-lived and fleeting international organization that impacted humanitarian policies and interventions in the latter half of the twentieth century. As stated in UNRRA promotional material, 'UNRRA's job was immediate. When the task is completed, other organizations of the United Nations must continue to build the peace in the field of long-range reconstruction. Meanwhile, UNRRA represents first things first.'³⁵ In assessing the organization's attempts to define and implement rehabilitation, one can hope to better understand UNRRA's contributions to post-war, state-driven international humanitarianism. While it is certainly clear that UNRRA sought to 'rehabilitate' in every way imaginable, the feasibility of such an endeavour will no doubt strike the reader as this volume's chapters reveal the multifaceted nature of such loaded terminology, the haphazard implementation of policy, and the will – or lack thereof – to 'help the people to help themselves'.

Notes

1. Accessible here: UNHCR – 'Helping Refugees to Reintegrate: The Challenges of Rehabilitation' – Address by Mrs Sadako Ogata, United Nations High Commissioner for Refugees, at the 14th Workshop on Management of Field Coordination for Senior United Nations System Representatives, Turin, 4 April 1995 – last accessed, 12 July 2022.
2. Francis. B. Sayre cited in The National Planning Association, 'UNRRA: Gateway to Recovery', *Planning Pamphlets* (1944), 16.
3. NPA, 'Gateway', 3–4.
4. *Archives Nationales*, Paris, France (hereafter, AN), AJ/43/14, 'U.N.R.R.A., Aug. 1944–Jan. 1947'. Agreement between UNRRA and SHAEF, 14 October 1944.
5. Expansion to seven Great Powers was a topic of considerable debate during UNRRA's creation, with other major suppliers such as Canada lobbying to join the Great Powers, however the decision to remain at four eventually triumphed. See The National Archives, Kew, London (hereafter TNA), Foreign Office (hereafter FO) 370/1716, 'Paper on the origins of UNRRA. Code 402 file 541', UNRRA Background and Formation, 1–55. Rosemary Miller, 27 January 1948.
6. Estimates about DPs range considerably and there is no scholarly consensus on how many people were displaced in the immediate aftermath of war. Contemporary estimates by Russian demographer Eugene Kulischer put the number around thirty million by 1943, while SHAEF geographer Malcolm J. Proudfoot thought it to be as high as sixty million, both during and after the war. Recent estimates by historians like Mark Mazower cite forty-six million displaced people while Peter Gatrell estimates that the number is roughly forty million. Eugene M. Kulischer, *The Displacement of Population in Europe* (Montreal: International Labour Office, 1943), 160–3; Malcolm J. Proudfoot, *European Refugees, 1939–1952: A Study in Forced Population Movements* (Evanston: Northwestern University Press, 1956), 21; Mark Mazower, *Dark Continent: Europe's Twentieth Century* (New York: Vintage Books, 1998), 214; Peter Gatrell, *The Making of the Modern Refugee* (New York: Oxford University Press, 2013), 89.

7   Herbert H. Lehman, 'Half a Billion Hungry People', *New York Times Magazine*, 30 January 1944.
8   'UNRRA and Its Tasks', *The Times*, 9 September 1944.
9   Jessica Reinisch, 'Introduction: Agents of Internationalism', *Contemporary European History* 25:2 (May 2016), 200.
10 AN, AJ/43/16, Statement on Displaced Persons, 24 January 1946.
11 AN, AJ/43/18, Order No. 52: Eligibility for UNRRA Assistance, 24 June 1946.
12 See R. M. Douglas, *Orderly and Humane: The Expulsion of Germans after the Second World War* (New York: Yale University Press, 2012).
13 Although UNRRA ceased most operations in 1947, the entire organization was not fully wound up across the world until 1948. See George Woodbridge (ed.), *U.N.R.R.A. The History of the United Nations Relief and Rehabilitation Administration*, vol. I–III (New York: Columbia University Press, 1950).
14 Jennifer M. Morris, *The Origins of UNICEF, 1946–1953* (Maryland: Lexington Books, 2015), 1; Iris Borowy, *Coming to Terms with World Health: The League of Nations Health Organisation 1921–1946* (Frankfurt: Peter Lang, 2009), 437.
15 David Kennedy, *The Dark Side of Virtue: Reassessing International Humanitarianism* (Princeton: Princeton University Press, 2004), 201.
16 For UNRRA and successors, see Woodbridge (ed.), *U.N.R.R.A*; Grace Fox, 'The Origins of UNRRA', *Political Science Quarterly*, 65:4 (December, 1950), 561–84; Louise Holborn, *The International Refugee Organization: A Specialized Agency of the United Nations: Its History and Work, 1946–1952* (Oxford: Oxford University Press, 1952); Arnold Toynbee and Veronica M. Toynbee (eds.), *Survey of International Affairs, 1939–1946: The Realignment of Europe* (Oxford: Oxford University Press, 1955). For histories of population displacement, see Kenneth G. Brooks, 'The Re-establishment of Displaced Peoples', in *When Hostilities Cease: Papers of Relief and Reconstruction Prepared for the Fabian Society* (London: Victor Gollancz, 1943); Jacques Vernant, *The Refugee in the Post-war World* (London: George Allen & Unwin Ltd, 1953); Joseph B. Schechtman, *European Population Transfers 1939–1945* (New York: Oxford University Press, 1946); Proudfoot, *European Refugees*; Kulischer, *Europe on the Move*.
17 Michael Marrus, *The Unwanted: European Refugees in the Twentieth Century* (Oxford: Oxford University Press, 1985); Mark Wyman, *DPs: Europe's Displaced Persons, 1945–1951* (New York: Cornell University Press, 1989); Wolfgang Jacobmeyer, *Vom Zwangsarbeiter zum Heimatlosen Ausländer. Die Displaced Persons in Westdeutschland, 1945–1951* (Göttingen: Vandenhoeck & Ruprecht, 1985).
18 For works on organizations prior to UNRRA attempting to carry out international humanitarianism, see: Tommie Sjöberg, *The Powers and the Persecuted: The Refugee Problem and the Intergovernmental Committee on Refugees* (Lund: Lund University Press, 1991); Silvia Salvatici, *A History of Humanitarianism, 1755–1989: In the*

Name of Others (Manchester: Manchester University Press, 2019); Bruno Cabanes, *The Great War and the Origins of Humanitarianism, 1918–1924* (Cambridge: Cambridge University Press, 2014); Keith David Watenpaugh, 'The League of Nations' Rescue of Armenian Genocide Survivors and the Making of Modern Humanitarianism, 1920–1927', *The American Historical Review*, 115:5 (December, 2010), 1315–39.

19 Many works comment on the expansion of this literature, for example: Matthew Frank and Jessica Reinisch (eds.), *Refugees in Europe, 1919–1959: A Forty Year Crisis?* (London: Bloomsbury Academic, 2017). Pamela Ballinger, 'Impossible Returns, Enduring Legacies: Recent Historiography of Displacement and the Reconstruction of Europe after World War II', *Contemporary European History*, 22 (2013), 127–38; Johannes Paulmann (ed.), *Dilemmas of Humanitarian Aid in the Twentieth Century* (Oxford: Oxford University Press, 2016).

20 For example: Adam Seipp, *Strangers in a Wild Place: Refugees, Americans, and a German Town, 1945–1952* (Indiana: Indiana University Press, 2013); Atina Grossmann, *Jews, Germans and Allies: Close Encounters in Occupied Germany* (New Jersey: Princeton University Press, 2007); Stefan Schröder, *Displaced Persons im Landkreis und in der Stadt Münster 1945–1951* (Münster: Aschendorff, 2005); Czesław Łuczak, *Polacy w Okupowanych Niemczech 1945–1949* (Poznań: Pracownia Serwisu Oprogramowania, 1993); Anna D. Jaroszyńska-Kirchmann, *The Exile Mission: The Polish Political Diaspora and Polish Americans, 1939–1956* (Ohio: Ohio University Press, 2004).

21 Peter Gatrell, *The Unsettling of Europe: How Migration Reshaped a Continent* (New York: Basic Books, 2019), 42–4.

22 Paul Betts, *Ruin and Renewal: Civilising Europe after the Second World War* (London: Profile Books, 2020), 59–61.

23 David Nasaw, *The Last Million: Europe's Displaced Persons from World War to Cold War* (New York: Penguin Press, 2020).

24 Cabanes, *The Great War*, 309. See also, Tehila Sasson, 'From Empire to Humanity: The Russian Famine and the Imperial Origins of International Humanitarianism', *Journal of British Studies*, 55:3 (2016), 519–37.

25 Davide Rodogno, *Night on Earth: A History of International Humanitarianism in the Near East, 1918–1930* (Cambridge: Cambridge University Press, 2021). See also, Davide Rodogno, 'Beyond Relief: A Sketch of the Near East Relief's Humanitarian Operations, 1918–1929', *Monde(s)*, 2:6 (2014), 45–64.

26 Emily Baughan, *Saving the Children: Humanitarianism, Internationalism, and the British Empire* (Berkeley: University of California Press, 2020).

27 See also, Michelle Tusan, *The British Empire and the Armenian Genocide: Humanitarianism and Imperial Politics from Gladstone to Churchill* (London: I.B. Tauris, 2019); Alan Lester, 'Humanitarian Governance and the Circumvention of Revolutionary Human Rights in the British Empire', in Michael Barnett (ed.),

Humanitarianism and Human Rights: A World of Differences? (Cambridge: Cambridge University Press, 2020), 107–26.

28 Ruth Balint, *Destination Elsewhere: Displaced Persons and Their Quest to Leave Post-war Europe* (New York: Cornell University Press, 2021); Katarzyna Nowak, *Kingdom of Barracks: Polish Displaced Persons in Allied-Occupied Germany and Austria, 1945–1952* (Montreal, Canada: McGill–Queen's University Press, 2023); Sherif Gemie et al., *Outcast Europe: Refugees and Relief Workers in an Era of Total War, 1936–48* (London: Continuum International Publishing, 2012); Anna Holian, *Between National Socialism and Soviet Communism: Displaced Persons in Post-war Germany* (Ann Arbor: University of Michigan Press, 2011).

29 Ben Shephard, *The Long Road Home: The Aftermath of the Second World War* (London: Bodley Head, 2010); Gerard D. Cohen, *In War's Wake: Europe's Displaced Persons in the Post-war Order* (New York: Oxford University Press, 2012); Tara Zahra, *The Lost Children: Reconstructing Europe's Families after World War II* (New York: Harvard University Press, 2011); Jessica Reinisch, *Perils of Peace: The Public Health Crisis in Occupied Germany* (Oxford: Oxford University Press, 2013); Susan Armstrong-Reid and David M. Murray, *Armies of Peace: Canada and the UNRRA Years* (Toronto: University of Toronto Press, 2008); Jessica Reinisch, '"We Shall Build Anew a Powerful Nation": UNRRA, Internationalism and National Reconstruction in Poland', *Journal of Contemporary History*, 43:3 (July, 2008), 451–76, https://doi.org/10.1177/0022009408091835; Jessica Reinisch, '"Auntie UNRRA" at the Crossroads', *Past & Present*, 218, Supplement 8 (2013), 70–97, https://doi.org/10.1093/pastj/gts035.

30 Laure Humbert, *Reinventing French Aid: The Politics of Humanitarian Relief in French-Occupied Germany, 1945–1952* (Cambridge: Cambridge University Press, 2021), 33–4.

31 Gitta Sereny, *The German Trauma: Experiences and Reflections, 1938–2000* (London: Penguin, 2000), 25.

32 Mark Mazower, *Dark Continent: Europe's Twentieth Century* (London: Penguin Books, 1999); Tony Judt, *Post-war: A History of Europe since 1945* (New York: Penguin, 2005); Michael Barnett, *Empire of Humanity: A History of Humanitarianism* (New York: Cornell University Press, 2011).

33 Morris, *The Origins of UNICEF*.

34 Jessica L. Pearson, *The Colonial Politics of Global Health: France and the United Nations in Post-war Africa* (Cambridge, MA: Harvard University Press, 2018).

35 Office of Public Information for UNRRA, '50 Facts about UNRRA', 15 February 1947, 1. https://www.cvce.eu/obj/brochure_on_the_tasks_and_activities_of_unrra_washington_15_february_1947-en-99178db2-e7f0-4298-88b2-38a4dd1ecb25.html. Accessed 7 January 2022 – last accessed 11 January 2022.

1

'UNRRA: You never really rehabilitate anyone': Problems of rehabilitation in definition and practice*

Samantha K. Knapton

Introduction

In Europe alone, it has been estimated that up to sixty million people were on the move by May 1945, while millions more across the globe were displaced from their homes by reasons of war. The ultimate goal of the United Nations Relief and Rehabilitation Administration (UNRRA) was to provide these peoples with 'relief and rehabilitation'. How that was to be implemented, however, remained to be seen as the organization struggled to define what it meant by 'rehabilitation' throughout its lifetime and thereafter.

UNRRA has not occupied a prominent place among the histories of other state-driven international humanitarian organizations or histories dealing with the impacts of 1945.[1] When UNRRA is mentioned, however, it is often framed within works based on particular displaced persons (DP) groups, events, the formation of agencies, or in an analysis on post-war aid. Although its creation marked a new watershed in international cooperation, the events of the Second World War and the Cold War tower over it, thus obscuring the impact of this foundational organization. To understand how and why current organizations have constructed and enforced policies relating to 'rehabilitation', such as other UN agencies like UNICEF, the UNHCR and WHO, it is imperative to recognize UNRRA's own construction as an organization.

---

* Special thanks go to Eliza Hartrich, the volume's anonymous reviewers, and *Histories of Internationalism* series editors (David Brydan and Jessica Reinisch) for their comments on this chapter.

The success of implementing UNRRA's first R (relief) is not contested here. Although UNRRA's contemporary critics lambasted the organization for its ineffectual administration, UNRRA did, in fact, provide relief. It also prevented widespread starvation and an epidemic similar to influenza following the First World War.[2] Through mapping the different modes of thought regarding UNRRA's second 'R', from its creators to those on the ground who implemented UNRRA policies, this chapter provides a sweeping overview of the knotty issue of 'rehabilitation' and considers the reasons why the organization insisted on using two R's instead of three, given that reconstruction was also a major component of UNRRA's mandate. The bigger question this chapter attempts to answer, however, is whether UNRRA was able to 'rehabilitate' anyone (or any area) at all due to an ill-conceived definition of 'rehabilitation' from the very outset – a question that is often confronted in later chapters within this volume using specific case studies.

The confusion over the meaning of UNRRA's second R plagued the organization from the beginning. Even those who founded the organization, such as Dean Acheson, believed that the second 'R' held no firm connotation. In his autobiography, Acheson asserted that 'UNRRA would have done its work and passed away before we were to know what "rehabilitation" really required from us'.[3] Thus the popular acronym of UNRRA's name, 'You Never Really Rehabilitate Anyone', became a well-known substitute.[4] In a 1944 pamphlet detailing UNRRA's objectives, the National Planning Association (NPA) stated that it was not a matter of relief followed by rehabilitation but 'rather a single process in which relief and rehabilitation become interdependent forces'.[5] The term 'help the people to help themselves' was often cited as UNRRA's mantra denoting that as the relief was dispensed, the means to carry on self-sustained production was also made available. Within the same text, however, the problem arises of separating rehabilitation from long-term plans of reconstruction. According to Hiram Motherwell, writing in *Harper's Magazine* in 1943, UNRRA's two R's should either have been reduced to one R or expanded to three as 'the three R's of post-war Europe will often be indistinguishable'.[6] Similarly, the problem of defining what came under the term 'rehabilitation' was in dispute throughout UNRRA's existence. Some viewed it as solely the rehabilitation of institutions in war-torn countries, primarily the resolve of the military, while others viewed it as the rehabilitation of Europe's people, the individuals who had been displaced, and therefore for whom repatriation, under the guise of rehabilitation, would be necessary. The line seemingly did not delineate based on political affiliation, nationality or past experience. Ordinarily, when referring to rehabilitation policies within historical works on UNRRA, all of the above are included in its meaning since no defining parameters were set during UNRRA's inception.

This chapter discusses the lasting implications of UNRRA's inability to define its second 'R'. Starting with UNRRA's foundation in Anglo-American conceptions of post-war relief, this chapter will then discuss how the lack of definition for 'rehabilitation' also impeded efforts to plan the cessation of hostilities. It will then analyse how the make-up of UNRRA, and specifically those tasked with looking after DPs, effected how the so-called 'rehabilitative' measures were carried out which will lay the basis for understanding the implications on post-UNRRA organizations. By analysing the confusion over the meaning of rehabilitation, its intentions and implementation this chapter will illustrate the wider implications of administrative uncertainty over definitions on the organization's achievement of its overall goals and it place in post-war historiography.

The birth of UNRRA: Faute de Mieux

The creation of UNRRA, as covered in the Introduction to this volume, was from the need to care for those devastated by war. As early as 1940, British Prime Minister Winston Churchill declared in the House of Commons that the peoples of Europe would experience 'food and freedom'. It was in this spirit that the Inter-Allied Committee on Post-War Requirements was set up with Sir Frederick Leith-Ross, the UK's Chief Economic Advisor, as chairman.[7] Leith-Ross was given the formidable task of ensuring that food and medical supplies would reach Europe at the end of the war.[8] The impetus behind the creation of this committee and the Allied Post-War Requirements Bureau which spawned from it, eventually led to the creation of UNRRA, and the exclusion of Germans from its remit. In the United States, President Franklin DeLano Roosevelt claimed it was the first real test of international cooperation, and declared at a small ceremony marking the signing of the UNRRA agreement, that 'the sufferings of the little men and women who have been ground under the Axis heel can be relieved only if we utilize the production of ALL the world'.[9] Although consisting of forty-four member nations, UNRRA's 'real parents' were the United States and Britain: accounting for 72 per cent and 13 per cent of UNRRA's income, respectively.[10] The notion of Anglo-American relations spearheading UNRRA operations became a constant theme throughout UNRRA's existence before merging into the International Refugee Organization (IRO) in 1947 and ultimately evolving into the perennial United Nations Refugee Agency (UNHCR) in 1952. UNRRA established its headquarters in Washington and its European Regional Office in London under the direction of Sir Frederick Leith-Ross as a replacement for the Inter-War Committee on Post-War Requirements.

Britain, eager to retain its position as a global superpower, realized the necessity of ensuring they were at the forefront of international cooperative organizations, and UNRRA was the pinnacle. Although the United States had little issue with contributing such vast sums of money to UNRRA's coffers, Britain was struggling to come to terms with the post-war situation. Plagued by economic instability, Britain would eventually step out of the international spotlight as the United States took centre stage. Indeed, one of the United States' stipulations for joining UNRRA was the reassurance that UNRRA's director generals were always American.[11] This was partly to avoid splitting primacy, as with the League of Nations, but also to ensure the United States was at the forefront of cooperative internationalism that would dominate the post-war world.

In Britain, the perception of UNRRA even before the war's end was lukewarm at best. Although the initial declaration of the organization was greeted with admiration by many, opinion in Whitehall thought it a poor decision to allow prominent American control. Writing at the time, US Army officer and geographer Malcolm J. Proudfoot asserted that the major cause for lack of appropriate staff was because 'it proved a well-nigh insuperable difficulty to check the reliability of individual work records'.[12] The necessity for 'top-men' to work in UNRRA's administration was hindered from the outset by the requirements of the war effort; other nations were also unwilling to contribute their finest as they were intent on keeping them for their own governmental agencies. On top of administrative chaos, the military made it particularly difficult for UNRRA to prepare supplies for liberated territories as they felt disclosing information could potentially weaken any advantage they held over the enemy at the time.[13] Due to administrative chaos, a lack of sufficient personnel and the ongoing war, UNRRA had achieved very little in its first fifteen months. By February 1945, a high-achieving young Australian Naval Officer, Commander Robert Jackson, was drafted in to revamp the administration before the war's end to ensure it could work alongside the military, rather than in place of it. This was a seemingly mammoth and potentially impossible task, as it was thought 'there is a real danger that U.N.R.R.A. may be frustrated by jealousy and prejudice' created by a civilian organization working alongside the military.[14] Indeed, as Lieutenant General Sir Frederick Morgan was being asked to fill the position of chief of operations for the UNRRA Mission in Germany, he lamented in his private papers when presented with his role: 'reading this document helped confirm my impression that we have got the whole thing wrong somewhere. The whole machine seems too vast and cumbersome for the task it is to perform.'[15] In Morgan's reading of the situation, the task was merely repatriation and anything else was considered 'extra'. Given the chaotic start to UNRRA's operations before the first teams had even been dispatched to Europe, it is not particularly shocking that communications about UNRRA's second 'R' were scant.

Planning and definition

The two principal discussions between the four powers in UNRRA's Policy Committee revolved around the basic need for relief, in an effort to prevent any epidemic that may sweep across Europe, and the need to rehabilitate those devastated by war and their economies. The question of relief was readily addressed due to similar organizations existing throughout the nineteenth and twentieth centuries that dealt with relief during war time, the most prominent being the Red Cross. Questions of rehabilitation were not as easily understood, however, particularly as a revival of industrial and agricultural sectors pertaining to war-torn countries had only been attempted on a limited scale by past humanitarian organizations and often without great success.[16] Thus, when the issue of rehabilitation, as well as relief, was raised within a Soviet Memorandum of 10 January 1942 discussing the potential of post-war cooperation, it also posed serious complications regarding its implementation.[17] The Allies were unaware of the scale of such a task at this time, yet the inclusion of rehabilitation seemed to some, such as Leith-Ross, to be inseparable from the purposes of relief. As a result, in order to make the international machinery of UNRRA effective, the two principles had to become synonymous.[18]

Heralding the advent of UNRRA's official creation, numerous press clippings from those involved commented on UNRRA's task. On 12 November 1943, only three days after it was signed into existence, Dean Acheson was quoted declaring: 'It will be something between soup-kitchen relief and a reconstruction of the whole world.'[19] Although, perhaps at this early juncture, the term 'rehabilitation' was intentionally left vague due to the many 'imponderables' the term could imply.[20] On 26 November 1943, *The Times* had picked up on UNRRA's ambiguity and stated, 'where relief and rehabilitation as such end and where long-term recovery and reconstruction begin cannot be accurately defined'.[21]

In the pamphlet, *Helping the People to Help Themselves: UNRRA – The Story of the United Nations Relief and Rehabilitation Administration* published in 1944, the declaration on the inside cover begins by proclaiming they will provide aid and relief to those liberated, alongside:

> [A]id in the prevention of pestilence and in the recovery of the health of the people, and the preparation and arrangements shall be made for the return of prisoners and exiles to their homes and for assistance in the resumption of urgently needed agricultural and industrial production and the restoration of essential services.[22]

In this iteration, the psychological element of rehabilitation is missing, and instead rehabilitation has been posited as a cross between repatriation and reconstruction.[23] Furthering this, the pamphlet goes on to detail the make-up of the organization and states there were four main committees, and five sub-committees created under the leadership of Dean Acheson. One of which, Committee IV on Relief and Rehabilitation Policies, was said to be divided into six sub-committees:

> [E]ngaged in discussing the technical aspects of relief distribution, health and medical care, welfare services and voluntary relief agencies, assistance to displaced persons, agricultural rehabilitation and rehabilitation of industries, transport and other services essential to relief.[24]

Again, as we can see here, even the committee focusing on elements of relief and rehabilitation has not provided simple parameters. Indeed, 'rehabilitation' is only mentioned in connection with agriculture, industry, transport and other 'services' essential to relief, but what of 'assistance to displaced persons', should that include their own rehabilitation? If so, does that mean psychologically, spiritually, economically, or perhaps assisting displaced persons with repatriation. When Ernest Bevin became foreign secretary of the United Kingdom, he pledged support to UNRRA even though in August 1945, he viewed the organization as a 'kind of dole' which should stimulate the efforts of other nations.[25] Yet, shortly after UNRRA entered Europe in April 1945 and the DP operations were underway with the help of the Allied military, the connotations of 'rehabilitation' became more readily linked to rebuilding a person in every way. UNRRA proclaimed in June 1945:

> The United Nations Administration is concerned not only with relief – that is with the provision of material needs – but also with rehabilitation – that is with the amelioration of psychological suffering and dislocation. For men do not live by bread alone.[26]

Indeed, this sentiment came from the *Inter-Allied Psychological Study Group* who, in 1944, drafted reports on DPs' 'psychological issues' which resulted in a welfare worker's guide to assist DPs in their 'mental rehabilitation'. According to Stella Maria Frei, what this also encompassed, however, was 'ideas of the ideal "democratic self", meaning what kind of psychosocial constitution would best serve a democratic future of post-war Europe'.[27] There is a significant difference, however, between psychological and psychosocial rehabilitation of a DP or DP community, and UNRRA was effectively tying the two together. It is perhaps unsurprising that the term 'rehabilitation' was never given a specific definition during UNRRA's formation. In UNRRA's official history published in 1950, George Woodbridge noted that one of the particular peculiarities of the organization from the outset was 'the vagueness of the financial aspects and the definition of the scope of work to be done'.[28] What it meant on a practical level, however, caused significant dislocation for those charged with UNRRA's remit of providing 'relief' **and** 'rehabilitation'.

The debate over the meaning of UNRRA's second 'R' during its lifetime was continuous. Between those who created UNRRA and signed it into existence, the trainers at UNRRA centres in France, and the welfare workers on the ground in the DP camps there was no single definition to be found. Firstly, the confusion lay in whether the second R really meant reconstruction as a form of 'rehabilitation'. 'Reconstruction' implied the building up of new industries and the creation of agricultural sectors, whereas 'rehabilitation' implied supplying the necessary equipment to enable people to help themselves by building the aforementioned machinery in order to create a stable economy, leading to self-sufficiency. Yet, for ordinary welfare workers, sometimes 'relief' was the only word of significance. In Francesca Wilson's book *Aftermath*, wherein the first half is based upon her time in Germany, the words 'rehabilitation', or in fact 'reconstruction', do not appear once.[29] Although Wilson is a Quaker, she worked alongside UNRRA personnel to institute policies on the ground.

'Rehabilitation' was also considered to be the psychological rehabilitation of individuals, and collective communities aided through 'building up' the person.[30] This was the understanding often favoured by American-trained welfare workers, many of whom were accustomed to the New Deal welfare model which sought to be 'active' rather than 'passive'.[31] Yet, it was still linked to networks of pre-existing charities. UNRRA realized it would need the cooperation of voluntary organizations, many of whom already had experience of caring for those affected by war in its aftermath. The voluntary organizations of Britain had, by 1943, already coordinated with one another in order to create the Council of British Societies for Relief Abroad (COBSRA), an indispensable agency that immediately absorbed itself into the larger operations conducted by UNRRA.[32] Similarly, voluntary societies in the United States had also pooled together their knowledge and resources in 1942 to create the Office of Foreign Relief and Rehabilitation Operations (OFRRO).[33] These two conglomerate organizations joined together to work under the auspices of UNRRA's Director General Lehman upon UNRRA's creation in 1943. As well as British and American volunteers, a vast amount of welfare workers came from European charitable organizations (for instance, various sections of the Red Cross, former French Resistance workers and International Volunteers for Peace).[34] These voluntary organizations, although there to provide immediate relief for the DPs, were also focused on the 'rehabilitative' aspect of their work similar to how they carried out their tasks in the past. For those associated with religious organizations and charities, this would be the spiritual 'rehabilitation' of a person, which often went hand-in-hand with 'rehabilitation' of the community.

How 'rehabilitation' was to be carried out also affected planning. One of the main reasons planning was skewed from the outset was the Allies' inability to accurately predict when the war would end. The Anglo-American committees had sourced their own reports on post-war requirements and paying attention to numerous academic works, including those of Louise Holborn and Eugene Kulischer, the projected aftermath of the Second World War with an estimate of forty million displaced, were taken into consideration.[35] Yet, in 1943, as UNRRA was created, planners predicted numbers of those displaced and areas devastated based on another year of warfare. If the war had ended in 1944 (as predicted), the funds available may have stretched further. In reality, due to the increased devastation, UNRRA's initial funds were barely enough to ensure that primary relief measures were met. Increasing issues concerning national sovereignty, although UNRRA could only operate in areas where they were invited, further increased tensions between the Allies as the geographical delineations of countries were hardly definite by the war's end.[36]

Implementing 'rehabilitation' in the camps

How UNRRA was to implement 'rehabilitation' in the DP camps when the connotation was unclear was exacerbated by constant conflict between UNRRA and the Allied Military. The Allied Military were to carry out repatriation of all DPs as set out in a revised version of *The SHAEF Guide to Displaced Persons* in Germany in May 1945.³⁷ This guide emphasized that the military were also to ensure that 'welfare' of DPs was the highest priority, mainly through solving logistical complications with housing, separating nationalities, and eventual transportation.³⁸ UNRRA, on the other hand, was tasked with the care of all United Nations DPs.³⁹ This covered immediate relief, but also the creation of recreational activities to dissuade idleness. Although the duties of UNRRA and the Allied military towards DPs were meticulously detailed on paper, the reality was much different as neither the military nor UNRRA had sufficient personnel to carry out these tasks separately. Reluctantly, the Allied Military realized a working relationship with UNRRA was required to organize and repatriate the vast number of DPs under their care, although they clearly longed to work with more familiar organizations, such as the Red Cross.⁴⁰ Simultaneously, UNRRA had overpromised the number of personnel and teams that could be sent to work in DP camps, and it was realized early on that the military would be needed to maintain control of the vast numbers.⁴¹

The UNRRA welfare workers, therefore, became the 'carers' and the military personnel the 'protectors'. The relationship between UNRRA and the military was one of constant tension. UNRRA, unable to run the DP camps alone had become reliant on the military and its personnel to carry out essential tasks such as security and transport. Most military officials, on the other hand, were disinterested in UNRRA's daily tasks of caring for the DPs and were eager to return home. Additionally, the Allied military often regarded UNRRA staff as ill-trained and incompetent; UNRRA staff were, however, equally disparaging of the Allied military. Inflaming the relationship further, UNRRA's staff were often paid significantly more than their counterparts. In one of the only modern works focusing on UNRRA, Susan Armstrong-Reid and David R. Murray show the average wages of Canadian UNRRA staff operating in Europe. A Matron, for instance, would be on $1600 annual Civilian pay, but could earn $2400 upon entering UNRRA, which would increase further before leaving the organization to over double the Civilian amount.⁴² As Michael Marrus succinctly asserted in his seminal work on DPs, the ultimate downfall of UNRRA's rehabilitation efforts were mainly due to the 'perpetual subordination of UNRRA to the Allied armies'.⁴³ These tensions are apparent in UNRRA welfare worker, Allied military, and sometimes voluntary worker's diaries and memoirs. The appointment of Lieutenant General Sir Frederick Morgan as the Chief of Operations for the UNRRA Mission in Germany was intended to fuse the two sides together. Morgan, however, was a military man above all else and frequently made disparaging remarks about UNRRA personnel, labelling them as 'do-gooders, crooks and crackpots'.⁴⁴

Within the camps themselves, ultimately the make-up of UNRRA's teams was one of the primary reasons for the haphazard and disjointed implementation of policy. UNRRA's welfare workers were an assortment of peoples; some were professional social workers, some inexperienced but driven towards helping one's fellow man in the old humanitarian tradition, whilst others were merely looking for a job. As Laure Humbert posits in her work on UNRRA in the French occupation zone, 'the evidence suggests that, in some case, enrolment with UNRRA was driven by escapism'.[45] Their job was to help the displaced, an altruistic and worthy cause, but for many UNRRA welfare workers the opportunity also presented numerous positives: travel, food, meeting new people, and for some an escape from old situations such as Susan Pettiss who left an abusive, alcoholic husband in Mobile, Alabama. A case of, if not now, then when. She goes on to describe in her memoir-cum-history that those she trained with in Maryland were similarly excited, commenting that 'I realised that I had been bored most of my life'.[46] Many, like Susan Pettiss, did not actually realize the scale of the task they were about to undertake, but were instead lured by the promise of new and exciting opportunities.

The variety of those working for UNRRA led Morgan to describe them not so much as a 'mixed bag' but a 'receptacle of "all sorts"' which ensured conflicting views over policy implementation were rife.[47] Silvia Salvatici argued that due to the absent nature of guidelines for hiring UNRRA welfare workers, a clear concept of how to provide for the DPs was never organized, thereby allowing rehabilitative programmes to be 'inspired by specific models of society and socialization' and not by a common internationalist perspective.[48] Consequently, rehabilitation policies and care for DPs was indirectly dictated by individual nationalisms amongst the welfare workers on the ground. Jessica Reinisch also argues that the construction of an international organization, such as UNRRA, brought with it a shift from the concern over universal rights of individuals to 'ideas concerning the rights of sovereign nations, particularly in matters of repatriation and reconstruction'; two of the other R's often bound-up with UNRRA's supposed 'rehabilitation' policies.[49] Other historians, such as Gerard D. Cohen, have referred to UNRRA's rehabilitation work as having succeeded by separating problems concerning DPs from those concerning other areas of rehabilitation, such as the 're-organization of public health'.[50] Arguably necessary for the rehabilitation of a community, but indistinguishable from ideas of reconstruction.

DP policies were not only determined by the UNRRA offices in Washington and London, or indeed by zone-specific administrations, but, as Laure Humbert asserts, they were 'also heavily dependent upon how local agents interpreted and implemented official instructions in the field'.[51] Throughout her memoir-cum-history of UNRRA entitled *The Stagnant Pool*, Rhoda Dawson alludes to various activities welfare staff were undertaking to help 'people to forget their troubles'.[52] She details the litany of tasks from helping Polish DPs put on church services, including finding a 'funny little doctor ... [and] a still funnier little chaplain from the hospital' as well as an altar, cloth, flowers, candles and repurposed crockery,[53] to running miles 'in that beastly great camp with a reel of cotton for one woman and some needles for another'.[54] For Rhoda, the element of rehabilitation UNRRA was expecting to be performed was focused on the individual. Susan Pettiss similarly experienced 100 jobs in one upon arriving in Munich. After a stint with the Child Search teams, Pettiss was assigned to a transit centre set up at the *Deutsches Museum* where DPs were sent to be repatriated. By May 1946, however, it was clear that many, including Poles, Balts, Ukrainians, Yugoslavs, and Jews, were unwilling to 'return' anywhere. For UNRRA workers like Pettiss, 'repatriation' became synonymous with 'rehabilitation' and, as she comments, 'the fact that repatriation efforts were not meeting with eager response in the DP population was somewhat of a surprise to many in UNRRA'.[55] Similarly, for Kathryn Hulme, working at *Wildflecken* in the US zone of occupation, 'rehabilitation' was the immediate care of DPs coupled with fast and fierce repatriation drives. She questioned whether the higher-ups giving orders had ever seen a DP, and lamented 'our repatriation statistics sent weekly to HQ were regarded as a sort of scoreboard to be compared with the records of other repatriating camps'.[56] Among the UNRRA workers, however, were those working on behalf of voluntary organizations often attempting to provide 'relief and rehabilitation' for DPs while influencing the much more inexperienced UNRRA workers. Margaret McNeill, Bertha Bracey and Kanty Cooper, all Quaker relief workers working within UNRRA structures, interpreted UNRRA's second R as the rehabilitation of an individual; primarily, the physical followed by the psychological.[57]

Yet, a commonality among welfare workers, military officials, and those working on behalf of voluntary organizations cited the perpetual subordination of UNRRA to the Allied military and confusion over who was in charge of what as a limiting factor when it came to 'rehabilitation' of the DPs. Although UNRRA did not officially take full control of the camps, the lack of clarity concerning

UNRRA operations in the camps was debilitating. As Marvin Klemmé, an American UNRRA worker who was highly critical of the organization in his memoirs, asserted:

> [T]he line of responsibility between UNRRA and the military government officials was not always too clear … the UNRRA official who was in charge of the actual work in the field, especially the Team Director, was often in a quandary as from whom he was to take orders.[58]

Welfare workers such as Susan Pettiss, Francesca Wilson, Kathryn Hulme and Marvin Klemmé were all in agreement that the chaotic coordination between policy and implementation was the source of much anxiety amongst both the workers as well as the DPs within the camps.[59] This nervous tension became increasingly apparent as the policies were often wholly unsuited towards 'rehabilitating' DPs due to the lack of personnel with adequate experience, and instead had to rely on the military who were little interested in anything other than repatriation.

As UNRRA began to shut its doors in 1947, the Preparatory Commission for the IRO acted as a 'stop gap' measure for DP operations until UNRRA's official successor organization, the IRO, could fully take over in 1948.[60] The shift in rhetoric between UNRRA and the creation of the IRO, showed a departure from certain ideas concerning 'rehabilitation' and a move firmly towards 'resettlement'. Between 1947 and 1948, 'Rehabilitation' came to mean unburdening the camps of DPs and restoring the Allied-friendly status quo. Those who remained, particularly in Germany under IRO care, were faced with new tasks, but the state-driven international humanitarian structure had been erected and an 'alphabet soup' of humanitarian organizations were created.[61]

Conclusion

There was no shortage of criticism for UNRRA in the years after its dissolution. Writing for *The Daily Mail* in 1947 on UNRRA's closure, David M. Cole surmised that the 'First point to be made abundantly clear has been that, though UNRRA's name proclaims that it is concerned with relief and rehabilitation, almost the whole of its work has been devoted to emergency relief measures.'[62] As this chapter has demonstrated, the confusion over the second R weighed the organization down from its inception. Pre-UNRRA planning through the American-led OFRRO and the British-led Inter-Allied Committee on Post-War Requirements set the scene for a post-war Anglo-American-led organization.[63]

The term 'rehabilitation', it seems, was carried over from OFRRO. Indeed, after 'rehabilitation' was added to what was meant to be a relief organization's policy, the US ambassador in London, John G. Winant, requested a definition of rehabilitation within the context of post-war planning. Acheson surmised, 'A good question it was, but never answered'.[64] He then further dwells on the incongruous use of 'rehabilitation' that could never be defined, lamenting in his memoirs that 'the word had no definition: rather it was propitiation by the unknown'.[65]

Within the UNRRA agreement, signed on 9 November 1943, the term 'rehabilitation' is mentioned no less than eleven times, yet not once does the term have a definition attached to it. In contradiction to this, the term 'relief' is also mentioned numerous times, yet by Article One (a) it had already been given definition.[66] Without a clear definition of what the term 'rehabilitation' was meant to imply, it is difficult to discern to what extent rehabilitation had, or had not, been completed. Furthermore, had the term explicitly applied to any one of areas concerning rehabilitation (industry, agriculture, the individual DPs – physically and psychologically – or repatriation), it would be difficult to confirm any degree of success as none of the aims were completed to the extent required of them within UNRRA's lifetime.

UNRRA's creation was the first step in state-driven international humanitarianism. Its intended purpose to provide relief and 'help the people help themselves' has gone a long way to setting up other state-driven international humanitarian organizations. Yet, UNRRA's goals were unfinished due to the splintering of international relations as national concerns took priority; even with the termination of UNRRA's successor organization, the IRO in 1952, methods and relations were still in need of improvement.[67] Jessica Reinisch has stated that once the Cold War rift between East and West began to appear, 'the political compromise upon which UNRRA's structure rested proved no longer viable'.[68] UNRRA was created in line with the principles of the Atlantic Charter; to enshrine universality, equality of nations and national sovereignty. Ultimately, UNRRA was cut short by rivalry and protectionism as the United States' dominating presence centralized power by the fifth Council session in 1946.[69]

Towards its closure, UNRRA's shift away from internationalism due to the Great Powers' control can be regarded as similar to UNRRA's lack of definition towards policies in the first instance. Arguably, the term 'internationalism' to describe UNRRA's outlook was employed to satisfy its member nations. Due to the League of Nations debacle in the interwar period, it was imperative that any attempt at recovery on a grand scale would be international in character to set the precedent for future operations. Similarly, the promise of rehabilitation was used as a means of advancing previous efforts of post-war relief and humanitarian projects in line with the pace of progression throughout the twentieth century.

Yet, as Peter Gatrell has succinctly questioned, 'what is meant by "refugee rehabilitation"?'[70] In the post-war era this amounted to fitting DPs into categories in which they could be classified as eligible for work programmes or resettlement based on repetitive and intrusive examination of an individual's background, their health and the increasingly important issue of political affiliation. UNRRA's realization as an organization of what 'rehabilitation' was and how it was to be carried out was ultimately obscured by the chaotic postwar situation greeting teams on the ground. This then fed into the structures of future state-driven international organizations splintering from UNRRA's make-up, often with a much narrower scope. The United Nation's Children Fund (UNICEF), which was created in 1946 for the explicit purpose of providing 'relief aid for children and mothers throughout the world', found its origins in UNRRA.[71] Created as an emergency relief service, UNICEF came to encompass some of the aspects of 'rehabilitation' that welfare workers were striving for in the DP camps, with a particular focus on health and education. Maurice Pate, UNICEF's first Executive Director, had reused the UNRRA mantra of helping the people to help themselves and applied it specifically to children and mothers, citing 'there are no enemy children'.[72] The IRO, which took over DPs operations and became the United Nations Refugee Agency (UNHCR), also found inspiration in UNRRA. Varied understandings of 'rehabilitation' have since fed into current and ongoing UNHCR programmes across the globe, each seeking to be defined within a particular context, which is arguably the only way 'rehabilitation' could be carried out. UNRRA was intended to be temporary from the outset. As British diplomat, and contemporary observer of UNRRA, Frank Ashton-Gwatkin stated, UNRRA 'was distinguished among its kind by being temporary without being ephemeral; for the very idea of bringing such an organization into existence was a new departure in history'.[73] This is an astute observation, as UNRRA's legacy continues into the twenty-first century.

Notes

1   In each of the following titles, UNRRA is only mentioned concerning immediate post-war relief and/or repatriation, or sometimes not mentioned at all: Amy

L. Sayward, *The United Nations in International History* (New York: Bloomsbury, 2017); Alexander Betts, Gil Loescher and James Milner, *UNHCR: The Politics and Practice of Refugee Protection*, 2nd ed. (London: Routledge, 2008); Nitsan Chorev, *The World Health Organization between North and South* (New York: Cornell University Press, 2012); Mark Mazower, *Governing the World: The History of an Idea* (London: Allen Lane, 2012); Tony Judt, *Post-war: A History of Europe since 1945* (New York: Penguin, 2005); Richard Bessel, *Germany 1945: From War to Peace* (London: Simon & Schuster, 2009); Keith David Watenpaugh, *Bread from Stones: The Middle East and the Making of Modern Humanitarianism* (California: University of California Press, 2015). As an exception, the following work contains an insight into the legacy of UNRRA and its bearing on the creation of UNICEF but does not problematize the concept of 'rehabilitation', Jennifer M. Morris, *The Origins of UNICEF, 1946–53* (Lexington Books: Maryland, 2015).

2   See Jessica Reinisch, *Perils of Peace: The Public Health Crisis in Occupied Germany* (Oxford: Oxford University Press, 2013).

3   Dean Acheson, *Present at the Creation: My Years in the State Department* (New York: W. W. Norton, 1969), 69.

4   The acronym of UNRRA's name has been mentioned in the majority of texts concerning the early works of UNRRA as an organization in Europe, however for specific use of the phrase by a Red Cross worker, see B. Shephard, *The Long Road Home: The Aftermath of the Second World War* (London: The Bodley Head, 2010), 14 & 143.

5   The National Planning Association, 'UNRRA: Gateway to Recovery', *Planning Pamphlets* (1944), 16.

6   Hiram Motherwell cited in NPA, 'Gateway', 16.

7   UK, *House of Commons Debate*, 20 August 1940, vol. 364, cc1161-3 – 'War Situation' – Prime Minister (Mr Churchill) to the House.

8   Dan Plesch, *America, Hitler and the UN: How the Allies Won World War II and Forged a Peace* (London: I.B. Tauris, 2011), 121.

9   FDR cited in Grace Fox, 'The Origins of UNRRA', *Political Science Quarterly*, 65:4 (December, 1950), 561–84; 584.

10 See UNRRA, *The Story of U.N.R.R.A.* (Washington DC: UNRRA, Office of Public Information, 1948); Daniel S. Cheever and H. Field Haviland, Jr., *Organizing for Peace: International Organization in World Affairs* (London: Steven & Sons Limited, 1957), 227; Shephard, *Long Road Home*, 151.

11 Herbert H. Lehman (January 1944–March 1946); Fiorella LaGuardia (April 1946–December 1946); Major General Lowell Howard Rooks (January 1947–September 1948), UNRRA operations in Europe ceased 30 June 1947, however operations in the Far East continued till September 1948, see Anon., 'Farewell to U.N.R.R.A', *Social Service Review*, 21:3 (September, 1947), 398–401.

12 Malcolm J. Proudfoot, 'The Anglo-American Displaced Persons Program for Germany and Austria', *American Journal of Economics and Sociology*, 6:1 (October, 1946), 41.
13 The National Archives, London (hereafter TNA), Foreign Office (FO) 371/62823 – 'Final Report on the Work of UNRRA. Code 50 File 4934' – Commander Jackson's 'Life and Death of UNRRA' – Robert Jackson, 15 September 1947.
14 'Letters to the Editor: U.N.R.R.A, and Europe', *The Manchester Guardian*, 22 July 1944, 4.
15 Imperial War Museum, London, UK (hereafter IWM), 02/49/01, Lt. Gen. Sir F. Morgan, *'Diary as Director of Operations for UNRRA Mission in Germany 01.09.1945–27.08.1946'*, Diary entry Wed. 10 September, 1945, 6.
16 See Davide Rodogno, *Night on Earth: A History of International Humanitarianism in the Near East, 1918–1930* (Cambridge: Cambridge University Press, 2021); Bertrand M. Patenaude, *The Big Show in Bololand: The American Relief Expedition to Soviet Russia in the Famine of 1921* (Stanford, CA: Stanford University Press, 2002).
17 TNA, FO 370/1716, Miller, 12.
18 Ibid., 25. This was also later echoed, with hindsight, in official UNRRA histories, see UNRRA, *The Story of UNRRA*, 4–6.
19 'World "Soup Kitchen". UNRRA Has Chief', *The Daily Mail*, 12 November 1943.
20 TNA, FO 370/1716. Miller, 30.
21 'U.N.R.R.A. Makes Ready', *The Times*, 26 November 1943, 5.
22 United Nations Information Organization (Great Britain), 'Helping the People to Help Themselves: UNRRA – The Story of the United Nations Relief and Rehabilitation Administration' (London: His Majesty's Stationary Office, 1944), inside front cover.
23 It is, of course, an unfortunate coincidence that numerous words that seem to become synonymous with UNRRA's second 'R' also begin with 'R'. Repatriation, in particular, was a primary focus of the Allies once it was realized just how many had been displaced.
24 United Nations Information Organization (Great Britain), 'Helping the People to Help Themselves', 7–8.
25 'Labour's Foreign Policy Defined: "Continuity First" is Bevin's Pledge', *The Daily Mail*, 21 August 1945, 2.
26 UNRRA, 'Psychological Problems of Displaced Persons', June 1945, Jewish Relief Unit Cooperation with other relief organizations, Wiener Library (WL), London, UK, 1.
27 Stella Maria Frei, '"For Men Do Not Live by Bread Alone": Conceptualizing UNRRA's Psychosocial Rehabilitation Approach for Displaced Persons in the Immediate Post-war Months', in Nikolaus Hagen, Markus Nesselrodt, Philip Strobl and Marcus Velke-Schmidt (eds.), *Displaced Persons-Forschung in Deutschland und*

Österreich: Eine Bestandsaufnahme zu Beginn des 21. Jahrhunderts (Berlin: Frank & Timme, 2022), 199–224, 200–202.

28 George Woodbridge (ed.), *U.N.R.R.A. The History of the United Nations Relief and Rehabilitation Administration*, vol. I-III (New York: Columbia University Press, 1950), vol. I, 7.

29 Francesca Wilson, *Aftermath: France, Germany, Austria, Yugoslavia, 1945 and 1946* (London: Penguin Books, 1947), 1–155.

30 See also, Audrey Duchesne-Cripps, *The Mental Outlook of the Displaced Persons as Seen through Welfare Work in Displaced Persons Camps* (Cambridge, 1955).

31 Gerard D. Cohen, 'Between Relief and Politics: Refugee Humanitarianism in Occupied Germany 1945–1946', *Journal of Contemporary History*, 43:3, Relief in the Aftermath of War (July, 2008), 437–49, 438.

32 COBSRA consisted of forty British organizations, eleven of which sent teams to Europe: The British Red Cross Society and Order of St. John of Jerusalem; The Friends Relief Service; The Friends Ambulance Unit; The Young Women's Christian Association; The Save the Children Fund; The Salvation Army; The Catholic Committee for Relief Abroad; The Jewish Committee for Relief Abroad; The International Voluntary Service for Peace; The Boy Scouts Association; The Guide International Service – see TNA, FO 936/698 – Council for British Societies of Relief Abroad – Yearly Report (1947).

33 Jessica Reinisch, 'Introduction: Relief in the Aftermath of War', *Journal of Contemporary History*, 43:3, Relief in the Aftermath of War (July, 2008), 378.

34 Silvia Salvatici, '"Help the People to Help Themselves": UNRRA Relief Workers and European Displaced Persons', *Journal of Refugee Studies*, 25:3 (June, 2012), 434.

35 Eugene M. Kulischer, *The Displacement of Population in Europe* (Montreal: The International Labour Office, 1943); Louise W. Holborn, 'The League of Nations and the Refugee Problem', *Annals of the American Academy of Political and Social Science*, 203 (May, 1939), 124–35.

36 Jessica Reinisch, 'Old Wine in New Bottles?', in Matthew Frank and Jessica Reinisch (eds.), *Refugees in Europe, 1919–1959: A Forty Years' Crisis?* (London: Bloomsbury, 2017), 150–8.

37 SHAEF – The Supreme Headquarters Allied Expeditionary Force – was dissolved in July 1945 and replaced by respective military commands in each zone of occupation.

38 United Nations DPs were the only ones eligible for UNRRA care. Initially, there was confusion over who was a 'DP' and who was a 'refugee'. Therefore, sometimes, the contemporary literature refers to those in the camps as specifically 'United Nations DPs'. See Samantha K. Knapton, *Occupiers, Humanitarian Workers, and Polish Displaced Persons in British-Occupied Germany* (London: Bloomsbury Academic, 2023).

39 For information on the genesis of who was classified as a United Nations DP, see Reinisch 'Old Wine in New Bottles', 150–8.
40 *Archives Nationales*, Paris, France (hereafter, AN), AJ-43-1162, 'Education of Polish Refugees in West Germany' – *SHAEF Guide to the Care of Displaced Persons in Germany*, G5 Division, revised ed. May 1945; TNA, War Office 219/580. 'UNRRA: relations with the military and assumption of responsibility for relief and rehabilitation'. 3 March 1945.
41 UNRRA had promised the military 450 complete teams in February 1945, however due to lack of sufficient personnel the actual numbers were much fewer. IWM, Morgan, *'Diary as Director'*, letter from Hansi Pollak to Morgan, 5 November 1947.
42 Susan Armstrong-Reid and David M. Murray, *Armies of Peace: Canada and the UNRRA Years* (Toronto: University of Toronto Press, 2008), Appendix C. Using the example of Frances Ward, 379.
43 Michael Marrus, *The Unwanted: European Refugees in the Twentieth Century* (Oxford: Oxford University Press, 1985), 321.
44 Lieutenant General Sir Frederick Morgan, *Peace and War: A Soldier's Life* (London: Hodder & Stoughton, 1961), 222–9.
45 Laure Humbert, *Reinventing French Aid: The Politics of Humanitarian Relief in French-Occupied Germany, 1945–1952* (Cambridge: Cambridge University Press, 2021), 113.
46 Susan Pettiss and Lynne Taylor, *After the Shooting Stopped: The Story of an UNRRA Welfare Worker in Germany, 1945–47* (Indiana: Trafford Publishing, 2004), 8.
47 Morgan, *Peace and War*, 256–62.
48 Salvatici, "Help the People to Help Themselves", 446.
49 Jessica Reinisch, '"We Shall Rebuild Anew a Powerful Nation": UNRRA, Internationalism and National Reconstruction in Poland', *Journal of Contemporary History*, 43:3, Relief in the Aftermath of War (July, 2008), 475–6.
50 Cohen, 'Between Relief and Politics', 440.
51 Humbert, *Reinventing French Aid*, 79.
52 IWM, 95/26/1, Rhoda Dawson, Typescript, *'The Stagnant Pool: Work among Displaced Persons in Germany, 1945–1947' [c. 1992]*, quoting Biddulph, 35.
53 Dawson, *The Stagnant Pool*, 43.
54 Ibid., 54.
55 Pettiss, *After the Shooting Stopped*, 172–3.
56 Kathryn Hulme, *The Wild Place* (London: Pan Books, 1959), 39.
57 Margaret McNeill, *By the Rivers of Babylon* (London: The Bannisdale Press, 1950); Kanty Cooper, *The Uprooted: Agony and Triumph among the Debris of War* (London: Quartet Books, 1979), Bertha L. Bracey, 'Practical Problems of Repatriation and Relocation', *International Affairs*, 21:3 (July, 1945), 295–305.

58 Marvin Klemmé, *The Inside Story of UNRRA: An Experience in Internationalism; A First-Hand Report on the Displaced People of Europe* (New York: Lifetime Editions, 1949), 215. See also, Reinisch, 'Old Wine in New Bottles', 161.
59 Pettiss, *After the Shooting*; Wilson, *Aftermath*; Hulme, *The Wild Place*; Klemmé, *The Inside Story*.
60 For more information on Preparatory Commission for the International Refugee Organization (PCIRO), see Louise Holborn, *The International Refugee Organization: A Specialized Agency of the United Nations: Its History and Work, 1946–1952* (Oxford: Oxford University Press, 1952).
61 As many organizations became acronyms, the immediate post-war period has been dubbed a veritable alphabet soup of Allied organizations, see Patricia Clavin, *Securing the World Economy: The Reinvention of the League of Nations, 1920–1946* (Oxford: Oxford University Press, 2013), 298.
62 Their emphasis, *The Daily Mail*, 29 May 1947, 4.
63 OFRRO was led by Herbert H. Lehman, who became UNRRA's first Director General, and the Inter-Allied Committee on Post-war Requirements was led by Sir Frederick Leith-Ross, who headed UNRRA's European regional office in London.
64 Acheson, *Present at the Creation*, 69.
65 Dean Acheson cited in Cohen, 'Between Relief and Politics', 442.
66 TNA, T 188/335 – 'United Nations Relief and Rehabilitation Administration (UNRRA): Articles and Correspondence' – *Agreement for the United Nations Relief and Rehabilitation Administration* – 1943.
67 See J. Donald Kingsley cited in Pettiss, *After the Shooting*, 234.
68 J. Reinisch, 'Internationalism in Relief: The Birth (and Death) of UNRRA', *Past and Present*, 210, Supplement 6 (2011), 258–89, 285.
69 For the increasing control of 'Anglo-Saxon' & American orientation, see Reinisch, 'Internationalism', 288–9; TNA, FO 1049/468 – 5th UNRRA Council; Cheever & Haviland, Jr., *Organizing for Peace*, 227.
70 Peter Gatrell, 'Trajectories of Population Displacement in the Aftermaths of Two World Wars', in Jessica Reinisch and Elizabeth White (eds.), *The Disentanglement of Populations: Migration, Expulsion and Displacement in Post-War Europe, 1944–1949* (London: Palgrave Macmillan, 2011), 3–26, 17.
71 Morris, *The Origins of UNICEF*, 1.1.
72 This popular phrase is recounted across all of UNICEFs modern social media – see: www.unicef.org or Twitter: @UNGeneva, 11 December 2020.
73 Frank Ashton-Gwatkin in Arnold Toynbee and Veronica M. Toynbee (eds.), *Survey of International Affairs, 1939–1946: The Realignment of Europe* (Oxford: Oxford University Press, 1955), 51.

2

'Low in health and spirits': The hygiene and health campaign in UNRRA camps in Germany and Austria as a form of rehabilitation

Katarzyna Nowak

Introduction

The members of an UNRRA team assigned to the Rhine Barrack Camps in Allied-occupied Germany in September 1945 could not hide their shock at the living conditions of Displaced Persons (DPs). There was no central heating due to the Allied bombing. The floors were covered in dirt, and the barracks littered with refuse. There were not enough latrines, so people relieved themselves around the camp. Swarms of flies and mosquitoes buzzed over the human faeces. As Dr Hendrickx noted, the team dedicated the first weeks to 'directing and assisting in a general clean-up of the premises and making them less revolting as a place of residence'.[1] It was, by no means, an isolated case. Two years later, DPs from the Hannover region complained that they did not receive enough soap, combs, brooms and cloths to maintain a good level of hygiene. They considered the conditions as 'an affront to the most primitive requirements of humanitarianism'.[2] The path from filthy camps to well-organized living centres became a part of the narrative for social workers, indicating how they organized and, to some extent, civilized, the space of the post-war chaos and dirt. For DPs, it was a grim daily reality. Yet, it was also a trump card to convince the authorities and the international community that they were being victimized again.

DPs liberated at the end of the Second World War by Allied armies were considered a logistical and moral problem, as well as a threat to public health.[3] Providing for and then repatriating 11 million individuals – mainly forced labourers, inmates of concentration camps and prisons, children kidnapped for Germanization, and escapees from the East – was a gargantuan task.[4] Those from the Western countries came back relatively quickly, while Soviet citizens were subject to forced repatriation.[5] Other Eastern Europeans, including Poles, Balts and Jews, could choose to refuse to return to their homelands where the Soviets had established power. The camps, hastily organized by the armies, were taken over by UNRRA and later on by the International Refugee Organization (IRO).[6] The programmes of relief and rehabilitation, including the psychological needs of the displaced, drafted during the war became difficult to implement in the field.[7] Public health was a key problem for the occupiers.[8] Dr Neville Goodman, Director of UNRRA's European Division of Health emphasized that 'restoration of health is a major step in rehabilitating war victims'.[9] Health and hygiene campaigns in the camps aimed to combat 'two of war's worst by-products – filth and disease'.[10] UNRRA posters promised 'food, health and hope'.[11] Complaints about poor sanitation in the camps went hand in hand with anxieties about the psychological and moral decay of DPs, particularly in relation to the spread of venereal diseases.[12] Through small steps, their rehabilitation was to contribute to the rebuilding of civilization by preparing them to live as honest and valuable citizens, participating in the work of post-war reconstruction.[13] UNRRA aid workers joined forces with the national social elites to target the linguistic and cultural sensitivities of the DPs. Polish, Ukrainian, Jewish, Baltic, Belarussian, and other national leaders also had at heart the physical, mental and moral uplifting of the communities after the disastrous war, but with a different aim: strengthening the nations in exile.[14]

This chapter analyses the health and hygiene campaigns in the DP camps in Allied-occupied Germany and Austria. It considers them as a form of rehabilitation and examines practices directed at DPs. Firstly, it explains how the discussion of the decline of civilization caused by the war informed a series of interventions in the camps. Secondly, it shows how observations of the on-ground conditions influenced the organization of healthcare, and health and hygiene propaganda campaigns implemented by the relief workers along with staff and activists recruited from the national social elites and DPs. It shows how concerns about health and morale grew into a series of practices of controlling, recording and intervening, employed in the space of refugee camp as it was easier to control than population scattered through the countryside and towns of the destroyed country. Thirdly, this chapter focuses on the examples of health propaganda posters and guidebooks, discussing how East European medical personnel and activists cooperated with UNRRA to improve the health and morale of the DPs. This chapter will therefore show how these health and hygiene campaigns in the camps contributed to the splintering of opinion when it came to UNRRA's second R, as rehabilitation became linked with notions of (re)civilization.

Civilizational decline and interventions in the DP camps

'The sanitary condition of the [Brauweiler] camp was appalling' – reported Medical Officer M. W. Rabl from DP Area Junkersdorf in Germany – 'Latrines were shallow trenches, the camp area littered with refuse and faeces. The existing WC system was choked and brim-full with excrement. The quarters unhygienic, overcrowded, soiled with old refuse and garbage. The water was not potable, although the running system was intact. The Sick Bays were extremely dirty and neglected.'[15] In the first post-war months such reports were plentiful and often evoked the images of civilization in ruin, justifying radical action.

The debate over the decline of civilization in Europe translated into a series of interventions in the DP camps. Amid the landscape of destruction throughout Europe, as Paul Betts asserts, 'civilization shifted from its traditional status as a lexicon of elites to a call to alms for the victims of war'.[16] UNRRA and social elites envisaged DPs as future citizens of democratic societies. Regaining health meant more than just strengthening the body: it was seen as a prerequisite to 're-civilize' and re-educate victims of war.[17] William van Ark, UNRRA camp director and later IRO employee, depicted the work of 'physical and moral rehabilitation' carried out by international organizations in the following way:

> The DPs were in a pitiful condition when they were gathered in the Assembly Centers, their stomachs could be filled, clothes and temporary shelters provided, but it was horrible to see how Hitler's hordes had succeeded in kicking them in the gutter and making slaves out of them. Thanks to the United Nation's efforts, UNRRA was able to rehabilitate these masses and an excellent job was done to recover decency and make them feel and enjoy the privileges of civilized people again. The response was a pleasure to behold. Their first act was to plan regular church services, their domestic life was put in order and under leadership of UNRRA officers, a form of self-government established.

Doctor Neville Goodman, Director of UNRRA European Division of Health, considered the welfare programme as a part of repatriation drive: 'We have found that good treatment creates no desire to stay in the camps indefinitely. On the contrary, in proportion as we restore health and mental stability, these war victims become eager to face the problems of life again in their home countries and help restore what has been damaged or destroyed by the war.'[18] In another speech, he insisted that eradication of disease in DP camps would increase productivity and therefore speed up the economic and social reconstruction.[19]

Anxieties around health and hygiene drove UNRRA officials and fieldworkers in their mission. The enemy to fight, according to aid workers, was not only dirt and squalor but also DPs' mental disposition. Many social workers worried that the mission of rehabilitation and restoring civilization was challenging because of the DPs' attitudes. They complained about 'the ignorance of the most elementary rules of sanitation which exists amongst certain elements of the DP population'.[20] UNRRA officials often viewed DPs as backwards and dredged up stereotypes of ethnic groups when describing them. William C. Rees, Acting Director of UNRRA Team 335 in Jundenburg camp, complained about problems with 'common cleanliness' in the camp caused by Jewish DPs. 'Practically without exception they are dirty and lazy and destructive' – he wrote in a narrative report in November 1945 – 'They seem incapable of helping themselves and each considers himself entirely transitory, hence entirely disinterested in the Camp for the Camp's sake'.[21] In one of the subsequent reports he insisted that the Jewish population made health control checks more difficult: 'Every effort is being made to check them. Again, while they are dirtiest and least hygienic of our people, they give the greatest trouble in carrying out our "disinfestation" programmes'.[22] Driven by such convictions, UNRRA staff tried to influence and teach camps inhabitants about proper hygiene and stop them from carrying out behaviours destructive to the camp communities.

Other officials and fieldworkers showed more understanding, realizing it took immense effort to take care of communal space and hygiene under such difficult conditions. Donald Morton, Team Director of UNRRA Team 25 in Etzel observed:

> When you consider that these people are living in conditions below the slum level with a complete lack of privacy their present efforts loom considerably larger. … [T]hey are living 7 people in a room 10 × 12 feet in 2 single beds and sharing it with a lot of luggage or in the case of the larger rooms, where they do not appear so congested one finds 8 families – about 23 people – in a room originally intended for 10 soldiers. There are no toilet or washing facilities attached to these rooms, such facilities as exist are at the ends of the corridors; are necessarily communal and are shared by anything from two to three hundred people. There are three seats at either end and about eight feet of washing space.[23]

It became increasingly obvious that improving material conditions and the camp space was a necessary first step of rehabilitation, and that it could be done only with the cooperation of DPs.

Thus, UNRRA social workers along with the social elites among DPs tried to teach camp inhabitants how to clean their rooms, wash themselves, do laundry and avoid disease. The aid delivered by American, British, Canadian and other foreign social workers had a distinctively Western character. Rehabilitation, never ultimately defined, described as 'the amelioration of psychological and social suffering and dislocation', was backed up by the new, mostly American, expertise in nutrition, medicine, sociology and psychology.[24] Civilization in fact often denoted Western civilization, juxtaposed with Soviet and Eastern barbarity.

In spring 1946, the UNRRA Team 199 planned 'Great Camp Festivities', or 'The First of May – Spring Holiday' in Kufstein DP camp in Austria. The design of this event brought together the ideals of the nation: Americanization, health, self-improvement and bodily strength. The programme of festivities ran from 1 to 12 May and tried to channel the usual energies of traditional spring holidays in Eastern European nations into one American-style spring-festival. It was supposed to be free from the burden of class struggle and national hatred: 'As opposed to the customary May Holidays of the past in different countries of our continent, where this holiday was always coloured by the struggle of classes and mutual party hatred, we experienced for the first time the May Holiday as a Spring Holiday.' Within the programme there were so-called 'national days' where Polish, Latvian, Russian, Yugoslav, Lithuanian, Estonian and Czechoslovakian DPs could celebrate and display their national cultures. Special emphasis was placed on arts and crafts, folk traditions, gardening, vocational training and theatre. In other words, the focus was on non-militaristic and future-oriented skills that would help them to find jobs and contribute to their new, possibly multi-ethnic, communities. The celebration of the May queen and planting trees together was seen as 'a justified hope that future generations would live in peace and concord'. School children took part in hygiene contests: 'hands and teeth were inspected, and a prize awarded to the best class'. Social aid workers and DP medical staff taught DPs first aid and organized an exhibition of health posters. The festivities finished with a mass and Polish folksongs.[25]

Such activities were not limited to festivities but unfolded in the camps on a fairly regular basis. Doctors and nurses gave talks and lectures, as well as practical demonstrations, on various topics related to health and hygiene. In Lexenfeld camp, housing Ukrainian DPs, hygiene lectures were given weekly and health propaganda was delivered through newspapers and posters.[26] To improve hygiene, the camp authorities decided to establish a brush and broom factory in the camp, as well as manufacturing soap for general cleaning.[27] A bulletin board was set up in the camp with information about health and hygiene practices. Camp news, delivered in national languages, reminded DPs to 'clean the floor and the windowsills every day' and 'use baths once a week on designated days'.

They cautioned them not to 'do laundry in the room to avoid mould' and stop 'throwing rubbish from the windows'.[28]

Health education was carried out in most of the camps. Medical, welfare and DP personnel, as well as group leaders, taught the camp population about health laws. This included general cleanliness and personal hygiene, the handling of the water supply and sewage, as well as garbage disposal. Those working in the kitchen were instructed to wash their hands after using the toilet, keep nails clean and report any skin infections.[29] In Itzling camp in the US zone of Austria, DP doctors opened up a clinic to offer mothers and pregnant women advice on nursing and prenatal hygiene.[30] Nurses distributed leaflets on TB, baby feeding and the bad effects of using a pacifier.[31]

Film screenings also became an effective means of health propaganda. In 1944, UNRRA together with the Overseas Branch of Office of War Information, a US government propaganda and information agency, prepared a project producing a series of medical films to educate DPs about diseases and prevention entitled "To your health!"[32] The outlines were written before seeing the reality of the DP situation, based on the American experience in healthcare and emergency planning.[33] Three main aims of the film series were: first, to promote 'good-will for the United States by performing an essential service in time of need'; second, 'to increase the prestige of the United States along scientific and cultural lines, a field in which the enemy has consistently proclaimed his superiority'; third, to 'simplify the problems of military stabilization, of morale and of rehabilitation where ignorance and local custom interferes with effective medical relief'.[34]

Short films on health, disease and nutrition aimed to teach the displaced victims of war about public health dangers and instruct them how to behave in daily life to mitigate them. *The Miracles of Milk* talked about the importance of breastfeeding and fresh milk alimentation. *Murder Skin Deep* was on immunization and personal hygiene for typhus prevention, while familiarizing the audience with DDT powder. *The Fly and the Vulture* sought to alert people to the role the fly plays in the transmission of typhoid, dysentery, cholera and other diseases and to teach them practical ways of killing flies and preventing further breeding. *We Who Are About to Live* focused on adolescents and the role of proper nutrition. While other films had a strongly militaristic rhetoric – showing the contaminated food as enemy to fight or talking about the 'war against the louse' – this one showed how young people were the ones who would build world peace through physical and moral reconstruction. The outline stated: 'it is today's teen-agers who must carry the real burden of rebuilding and revitalizing the war-torn world, their health and spirit may well determine the nature of post war civilization'.³⁵ Public health was seen as a cornerstone of rebuilding civilization and it started with 'mass education' that included explaining 'modern mass control measures'.³⁶ Detailed planning preceded the mission of rehabilitating war victims by rebuilding their health and spirits. Yet, it was only when the first military and UNRRA personnel started their work in liberated territories in early spring 1945 that the action started to take shape.

Observation of the on-ground conditions, transformation of the camp space, and the organization of healthcare

Marta Korwin, a Polish welfare officer working for UNRRA, observed the devastation of Germany in summer 1945: 'The town had just been taken, of course no light and water. A dead town, no inhabitants, ruins, stench of burned things and dead. In front of the building bombed trains and bombed railway station. The trees were dead, there were not even birds to make nests in that dead place.'³⁷ The facilities provided for DPs were no exception. In Bocholt camp, where she was assigned, DPs were housed on a block floor of a former factory, while the rest of the factory was bombed out and reduced to a 'heap of debris'. Russians, Poles, Estonians, Yugoslavs, Italians and people of other nationalities were crowded there, trying to survive from day to day. Korwin wrote with alarm: 'The situation was critical and nearly out of control. More than three thousand people of different nationalities all mixed together. No lavatories, too little food.'³⁸ Her report fits into the familiar tale UNRRA, as a humanitarian organization, wished to promote. The path from chaotic, dirty and 'out of control' camps, with an unruly population prone to disease, to well-organized and clean settlements, guided by social workers, became a familiar narrative of UNRRA workers and was used in their publicity campaigns. In this narrative, UNRRA was a carrier of civilization, whose values were often expressed through simplified statistics: a number of cans of milk provided, a number of lectures given, a decline in the number of DPs ill with typhus. Korwin's report, unsurprisingly, was used for a press release.

The transformation of the camp space and its inhabitants, in Korwin's account and in many others, started with a big clean-up while establishing hygiene rules made part of the daily routine. Korwin asked the commanding officer to involve DPs with organizing a children's centre in a devastated building. 'People responded to the appeal' – she noted – 'Parties of men and women came to first floor of a nearby factory. All windows were gone and masses of debris and other rubbish were strewn on the floor. The work was difficult because we had no tools. But on Sunday the 8th the place was ready to receive the children.'[39] In Judenburg camp, after forcing DPs to clean the camp, aid workers tried to ensure they were not only sprayed with DDT but also thoroughly washed. William C. Rees, preoccupied with a lack of any bathing facilities at Kaserne camp, organized a team of DPs to install and fit a spacious bathhouse and laundry for the camp. Still, he complained that some of the DPs, especially Jewish ones, did not want to take part in improving the camp, he wrote down under 'unsolved problems' in his report: 'Jewish DPs. No progress may be reported in bringing these people to a realisation that community effort and Camp pride are worthwhile essentials to decent living.'[40] Relief workers often considered encouraging or forcing DPs to do the cleaning and tiding up as the only practical choice. They also followed the UNRRA directives of teaching them about communal spirit and bolstering self-organization.

Practices of controlling and recording were vital for planning these interventions. L. Hahn, Medical Officer from UNRRA Team 13, reported that he started to take measurements of the height and weight of all inhabitants at the centre and estimate of the state of malnutrition, and promised to deliver the compiled results in due time. Also, he introduced periodical examinations of all the children in the camp, taking place every Saturday at the same time.[41] Korwin, reporting from Bocholt, wrote: 'All children were weighted and measured and medically inspected.' They found that only five out of twenty-six children were within the norm.[42] These observations were quickly translated into intervention: children were to be fed with food high in calories to gain weight. At 11am and 4pm they were given milk with sugar and biscuits or bread. Once a day they got a piece of chocolate. With time, controlling and recording became more organized. Nurses and doctors weighed DPs periodically and wrote down the numbers to track the change. When they noticed a drop in their weight, they prepared new ration scales based on 'reports of weighting teams'.[43] In Bocholt, the majority of children had scabies and some had lice, as Korwin pointed out. To alleviate this situation, a stove to warm the water was installed so mothers could bathe their babies three times a week. These first experiences in the field helped aid workers to assess the needs of DPs. Observing them and the conditions in which they lived, usually described in reports, helped to prepare more effective measures of care and control. It also made it clear UNRRA needed to rely on doctors, nurses and other skilled individuals from the DP community itself if they wanted to reach the wider masses.

The barracks and other living quarters were often infested with vermin. Inspecting the rooms and the kitchens, UNRRA staff complained about cockroaches and rats.[44] Sanitation squads were organized in some camps to control the space, report back on the encountered problems and the achieved progress, and force the DPs to comply with the rules. Filth bore the epidemics, UNRRA and military authorities feared. This motivated them to supervise and transform the conditions in the camps with the help, voluntary or forced, of their inhabitants. In December 1945, General Smith described filthy conditions in Landsberg camp and complained DPs did not want to work to clean it up: 'There is … danger of epidemics of typhoid and dysentery due to complete disregards of elementary sanitary precautions in some parts of the camp.'[45] As cleaning and improved nutrition was not enough, the authorities tried to vaccinate as many DPs as possible.

The immunization campaign was one of the top priorities of the military government and UNRRA.[46] In Austria, by the end of February 1946, UNRRA had managed to vaccinate over 75 per cent of DPs in the American, British and French zones across thirty-six big camps against typhoid fever, typhus, diphtheria and smallpox.[47] Vaccinations were entrusted to eight teams composed for this purpose, each team consisting of three doctors, three nurses and three secretaries. They worked under the control of the doctors and received detailed instructions on how to proceed: 'Before they left they were assembled at Rastatt on the 10th of January 1946 and given special instructions and a detailed programme of vaccinations to be carried out.'[48] As the medical director noticed, due to supply problems the campaign was patchy, with many camps with 100 per cent immunization rate and others near to zero.[49] Camp leaders recruited from DPs assisted the campaign, in some cases threatening those opposing the vaccination with eviction from the camp.[50]

Throughout different zones, regions and camps of occupied Germany and Austria epidemic control did not have a uniform character, which was also the case for other public health policies and measures.[51] Medical teams in the field took advice from the top but also introduced their own measures to prevent the spread of diseases. When acute poliomyelitis endangered the population of Lower Saxony, the medical officer advised the doctors and health authorities at Pyrmont 'to start a vigorous campaign against flies and [instruct] the population … by leaflets to obey strictly sanitary regulations re. disinfection and personal hygiene'.[52] Often medical officers saw the gathering of people in bigger camps from scattered small camps where DPs lived 'under the most unhealthy and filthy conditions' as a way to improve hygiene and prevent epidemics: 'There is no need to emphasize the fact that scattering the DPs over a large area makes control of health and sanitation almost impossible and in view of the present epidemic of poliomyelitis in this town the danger of communicable diseases would be increased not only for the troops and the civilian population.'[53] DPs living by themselves were not trusted to follow the sanitary rules and thus institutionalization in the camps was seen as the right response to the health crises.

The reports of the increasing levels of venereal diseases caused alarm, too. Fighting promiscuity, thought to be common in the camps, was not enough. Education and prohibitive measures – such as VD talks and posters or curfews – did not bring the expected results. The officials and fieldworkers determined the procedure of screening and reporting, leading to forced treatment. As treatment was often coerced, it caused frustration and incited protest among DPs. M. W. Rabl, an UNRRA Medical Officer reported how this looked in the Junkersdorf area: 'To check [VD] as best as possible, your M.O has given instructions to round up all suspect women in and around the camps. These are apprehended and examined in the General Hospital in Brauweiler. If found diseased German women are handed to P.H. in Cologne, others than German retained for treatment in Brauweiler.'[54] The spread of venereal disease, noted in reports to the top authorities, justified mass, and often coerced, screening. Other mass medical screening included radiography to check for tuberculosis, which was only possible thanks to mobile X-ray units.[55]

Organizing the healthcare provision in DP camps according to American, British and French standards was not only in hands of military authorities but also of UNRRA employees: 'UNRRA health officers completed an expanded program of medical care last winter for the remaining DPs in assembly centres in occupied Germany with full scale hospital and dispensary services, and extensive schedule of preventative medicine used on standard American public health procedures.'[56] As will be shown in the next part of this chapter, national elites who worked for UNRRA or as activists among the DPs, contributed with their varied expertise and ideas to public health work.

Health propaganda, national elites, and relief workers

Brochures, posters and leaflets flooded the camps. They aimed to educate DPs, who often came from rural sections of the society, about disease prevention, nutrition and health. To ensure that this form of health promotion was successful, UNRRA capitalized on Central-Eastern European doctors and activists' knowledge and enthusiasm to provide material and organize events in national languages. This material was often richly illustrated. While it was helpful to convey the message quickly to the masses of the displaced, it was also a necessary step to reach those who were illiterate or barely literate. Step-by-step photo guides taught how to wrap a baby in the nappy following the 'Anglo-American style'.[57] Posters in Polish and Ukrainian warned them against flies and used pictures to show how to ensure a child's healthy development. The 'Hygienic ABC' in Belarusian explained basic sanitary rules. Physicians in the camps in Germany were often foreigners, sometimes Jewish, as UNRRA employee Cynthia Nash reported, and at times provided care not only for the camp population but also for Germans in the vicinity.[58] While UNRRA aimed to recruit British and American personnel, the reality was much different. 'There have been various indications of a good many medical personnel of non-German nationality in Germany' – Nash noted.[59] Dr Goodman admitted this to the public: 'In many of the camps displaced physicians and nurses were found who have given considerable assistance to the UNRRA medical teams.'[60] In order to extend key medical work on the ground, DP doctors and nurses were sorely needed.

In some regions, officials and fieldworkers provided more comprehensive health education. In April and May 1947, Dr Mikołaj Minkiewicz acting as an UNRRA Medical Officer offered lessons for men, women and pupils in fourteen camps. The topics included child feeding and care, venereal disease, tuberculosis, rickets, dental care, anatomy and infectious diseases.[61] Lectures on alcoholism, scabies and rachitis were complemented by hygiene lessons at schools. Dr Minkiewicz designed a series of illustrated posters, also displayed during the lectures. Those on more academic subjects included 'The human body in diagrams', 'Nervous system' and 'Bacteriology', while those on practical matters explained issues such as 'How to preserve the child from rachitis?', 'First help in need' (with 17 pictures), and 'Sound teeth – sound man'. Many posters were printed in colour on quality paper to the merit of Dr Minkiewicz whose resourcefulness and enthusiasm led him to personally locate paper and secure access to German printing presses. The materials were printed in the highest number the amount of paper allowed. A booklet on VD was reproduced in 1,000 copies, a pamphlet on alcoholism in 1,000 as well, a poster 'The fly as carrier of infectious diseases' had a circulation of 2,000 copies. All of which were in Polish or Polish and Belarusian. Three thousand booklets 'Inyhygienical [sic] customs' were printed in Polish and 'White-Ruthenian', while 'Hygiene ABC' was printed in 'White-Ruthenian', presumably to reach the peasant population.[62] UNRRA endorsed the material and hoped to print a number of posters and booklets in each of the major languages of the DP groups.[63]

Women and children were at the core of efforts to educate and civilize displaced victims of war. The Polish-language guidebook entitled *My child: hygiene, nutrition, upbringing: instructions for pregnant women and young mothers* published in Hanover in 1946 is an example of coordinated efforts to reach women with a message on how to improve health and hygiene.[64] Polish doctor Michał Lechimski and Danish nurse Ellen Krusell co-authored the booklet, drawing on their experiences in DP camps and based on a series of talks in Bothfeld DP camp in 1946. As they stated in the introduction, it grew out of the practice of working with children in Poland and in Denmark as well as in DP camps, including in a DP hospital in Hanover. Additionally, the authors drew on Polish and Western medical literature. It was published in cooperation with two specialists, as well as two organizations – UNRRA and the grassroots Polish Association of the Forcibly Displaced in Hanover (*Polski Związek Wychodźctwa* [sic] *Przymusowego w Hanowerze*). As the publisher states in the introduction, the book was to be distributed widely and for free in the camps' doctors' offices. This parenting guidebook is an example of cooperation between the UNRRA staff and national social elites in educating DPs, however, UNRRA did not provide the paper as they promised, thus fewer copies were printed.

The booklet was directed at expectant and new mothers. In plain language, it instructed them how to take care of their babies and how to behave while pregnant to have a strong and healthy child. Nationalist and patriarchal rhetoric was interwoven with the medical discourse:

> In the post-war period, in which we currently live, the duty of every Polish family is to have healthy and strong children to at least in part compensate the losses we incurred in combat, on battlegrounds, in prisons and concentration camps. That's why now we must take care of every child, that's why we must attend to the pregnant woman with care. Mother Poles must remember millions of noble Mothers – Poles who run through the whole history of our nation and take example from them. The Polish Woman must be morally and physically healthy, and she must continue to lead the way, educate and guide the Polish family closely connected with brotherly love. This is her duty, here in the exile and there in our beloved country. We must remember that and always protect and care for every woman – present or future mother – and every child.[65]

Fear of venereal disease, common in the post-war period, prompted advice on intimate matters. The authors were abhorred at the 'horrifying' moral and physical consequences of camp life. Alarmed at the early sexual initiation among the DP youth, they called for stricter measures. Also, they urged women to make sure their partners were not infected. To minimize the risk of infection and maintain proper hygiene, pregnant women were advised to immediately urinate and wash genitalia with warm water and soap after sexual intercourse. 'The intimate life of a woman, especially in this period [of pregnancy] must be particularly regulated' – the doctor and the nurse insisted.[66] Women in particular were to be on guard against venereal contagions, and careful it does not enter their bodies; and through them, the body of the nation.

My child favoured professional medical advice over traditional knowledge. The authors reviled quackery and denounced 'charlatanish practices'. Women who feel unwell should never listen to 'advice of so-called experienced friends or older "babkas"', they cautioned.[67] There is no detailed information on children's diseases because, as they said, that could prevent mothers from consulting a doctor: 'some of our [female] readers after a cursory reading of these notes would think that they are physicians and can treat their children themselves. I warn you against it and I don't recommend it – it would be a pity to waste your child's life this way!'[68] Respecting medical authority was shown as the only way of safeguarding the safety and the correct upbringing of children: 'Only a doctor must decide about feeding the baby and a nursing mother must diligently follow all the orders and recommendations of the doctor.'[69] Adding vodka to the baby's dummy was condemned in the strongest terms. While the world 'father' does not crop up even once in the thirty-eight pages of the publication, the mother is treated as the one solely responsible for her baby.

The physicians construed feeding the children as rehabilitating not just individuals but the nation. Fighting for the future of the nation through nutrition, especially of mothers and children, meant educating and disciplining women.[70] The booklet provided detailed nutritional advice instructing mothers to feed their children with milk and rye bread, as well as plenty of fresh fruit and vegetable to provide vitamin C. Margarine, 'especially the one from the USA', was recommended, too. The publication included a section with recipes for baby food and a table with weight and height of a healthy child. The authors recommended monthly check-ups with a doctor who should instruct the mother what she can and cannot do. At the same time, they assured that doctors would keep everything they shared confidential. As they insisted, women had to follow this advice as their patriotic duty: 'The mother feeds two persons – herself and the child – and we cannot forget that during the whole six years of enslavement we were fed badly on purpose.' Breastfeeding, strengthening the baby with mother's milk, was also deemed necessary and played an important role in reckoning with war and building a new order.

Regulating family life, disrupted by war and displacement, was seen as the first step in rebuilding the national life. *My child* enlisted four main rules to be followed with new-born babies: it must be calm and quiet in the flat, punctuality in feeding and bathing must be observed, cleanliness of all the bottles and clothes, as well as of space and personal hygiene must be maintained, and washing hands and nails before handling a baby was necessary. Among other advice, given in quite a paternalistic tone, it also forbade playing with a child 'like it was doll'.[71] Emphasizing that through cleanliness people can prevent illness, it also explained what bacteria were – 'tiny creatures – organisms which cause diseases' and how they could cause illness.[72] Dr Lechimski and nurse Krussel called upon women to maintain high hygienic standards: 'Even under the conditions of the camp, we must care about cleanliness of the flat. "It is not that hard to do!"' As the reports and testimonies show, it was very hard to do in the shared accommodation with shortages of even the most basic cleaning equipment and soap.

This booklet serves also as an illustration of knowledge transfer between the West and the East, with the ideological centre of power located in the former. The publication drew on Western medical literature, available in Allied-occupied countries, as well as on personal and professional observations and contact between medical personnel from various countries, as well as fieldwork among the displaced. Personal contacts between medical practitioners from various countries left its mark as well. The effects of that are easily traceable in new publications. Dr Lechimski in *My child* mentioned that some Danish doctors asserted that a new-born should be put to the mother's breast right after waking up from the nap after labour.[73] Exposure to Western practices and norms also came through the training and lectures organized by UNRRA, for example nurses refresher courses.[74] International refugee aid in the post-war period rapidly professionalized, modernized and Westernized, and the encounters of the medical professionals and DPs in the camps bore witness to these changes.

Conclusion

Discussing difficult conditions in the first post-war months, including the lack of adequate water supply, Director of Health Andrew Topping wrote to Medical Officer Dr M. Rabl from UNRRA Team 25: 'I heartily congratulate on having, in spite of all the difficulties, been able to bring order out of such chaos.'[75]

Transforming 'out of control' camps into safe and clean centres supporting the project of rehabilitation became a part of the UNRRA narrative of aiding and civilizing displaced victims of war in the 'barbaric' lands of the former Third Reich.

The health and hygiene campaign was a cornerstone of establishing peace as well as the effort to rehabilitate the masses of DPs. The physical and the mental aspects were seen as connected: curing the body cured the mind, while curing the mind cured the body. 'The influence of the mind on the body was most significantly emphasized in these camps. If the camp was well organized and a welfare program set in action to keep everyone well occupied, the sickness rate was always much lower' – Dr Goodman emphasized – 'We quickly recognized, however, that to combat the diseases was not in itself enough. The morale of a large percentage of our patients had utterly crumbled. … We had to recognize on the health side of the extreme importance of a simultaneous welfare program.'[76] UNRRA leaders saw combatting illness and dirt coupled with health education as an intrinsic part of rehabilitation.

To show that these efforts never achieved a high level of coordination and travelled a bumpy road, the plural – campaigns – would be probably more apt. It helps to notice not only that there were a vaccination campaign, a campaign against venereal disease, a health propaganda campaign, and others but also to emphasize that even though there was usually a common idea and reasoning behind the intervention, it frequently unfolded in the field in a piecemeal fashion. While there were procedures and templates, although different for various zones and regions, it was individual army officials, UNRRA employees, camp commandants, and activists who often took final decisions and shaped the interventions on the ground. The initiative of individual medical professionals and activists – as was the case of Dr Minkiewicz and his prints, or Dr Lechimski and nurse Kursell and their talks among DP mothers which resulted in a publication – played a huge role in how the health campaign played out among the DPs.

Constantly fearing an epidemic, officials and relief workers declared war on filth and disease. Through education and coercion, they tried to teach DPs how to live a healthy life in a modern society. Using the toilet, cleaning their nails and abandoning village habits were necessary to prepare them to face the dangers lurking in the modern world, and learning to recognize the modern threats – lice, flies and bacteria. Infectious diseases, especially venereal ones, were seen as a threat to rebuilding European peace, as well as to the nations reviving after the hecatomb of war. Nationalist and patriarchal rhetoric interwove with the medical discourse in construing pathogens as a contaminant that can enter the national body through the bodies of women and their babies. Fighting for the health of DPs meant fighting for the new order, constructed after the Western fashion, and for the strong nations.

Notes

1. UNRRA Collection, United Nations Archives, New York (hereafter UNA), S-0414-0001-16. J. Balfour Kirk, British Zone, Report on Trip, 13 September 1945.
2. Piłsudski Institute of America Archives, New York (hereafter PIA), f.471/024. *Biuletyn Prasowy Zjednoczenia Polskiego*, Hannover, 5 January 1949.
3. Jessica Reinisch, *The Perils of Peace : The Public Health Crisis in Occupied Germany* (Oxford: Oxford University Press, 2013).
4. Mark Wyman, *DPs: Europe's Displaced Persons, 1945–51* (Ithaca-London: Cornell University Press, 2014). Anna Holian, *Between National Socialism and Soviet Communism: Displaced Persons in Post-war Germany*, (Michigan: University of Michigan Press, 2011). Gerard D. Cohen, *In War's Wake: Europe's Displaced Persons in the Post-war Order* (New York: Oxford University Press, 201).
5. Nikolai Tolstoy, *Victims of Yalta* (London: Hodder and Stoughton, 1977); Sheila Fitzpatrick, 'The Motherland Calls: "Soft" Repatriation of Soviet Citizens from Europe, 1945–1953', *The Journal of Modern History*, 90:2 (2018), 323–50.
6. Louise Holborn, *The International Refugee Organization: A Specialized Agency of the United Nations: Its History and Work, 1946–1952* (London, 1956); Jessica Reinisch, 'Internationalism in Relief: the Birth (and Death) of UNRRA', Past & Present, 6 (2011), 258–89; Jessica Reinisch, '"Auntie UNRRA" at the Crossroads', Past & Present, Supplement 8 (2013), 70–97; Silvia Salvatici, '"Help the People to Help Themselves": UNRRA Relief Workers and European Displaced Persons', *Journal of Refugee Studies* 25:3 (2012), 428–51.
7. UNRRA, *Psychological Problems of Displaced Persons*, London, June 1945; Tara Zahra, '"The Psychological Marshall Plan": Displacement, Gender, and Human Rights after World War II', *Central European History* 44:1 (2011), 37–62.
8. Reinisch, *Perils of Peace*, 2.
9. UNA, S-1301-0000-2366-00001. Dr Neville Goodman, Director of UNRRA's European Division of Health, Salisbury from Bryan, Incoming Telegram, 25 October 1945, p. 2.
10. UNA, Photography, item: S-0800-0003-0004-00012.
11. UNA, Photography, item: S-0800-0003-0007-00013.
12. Lisa Haushofer, 'The "Contaminating Agent" UNRRA, Displaced Persons, and Venereal Disease in Germany, 1945–1947', *American Journal of Public Health* 100:6 (2010), 993–1003.

13 On wider discourse on civilizing Europe after the Second World War, see Paul Betts, *Ruin and Renewal: Civilizing Europe after the Second World War* (London: Profile Books, 2020).
14 Jan-Hinnerk Antons, 'The Nation in a Nutshell? Ukrainian Displaced Persons Camps in Post-war Germany', *Harvard Ukrainian Studies* 37 (2020), 177–211; Katarzyna Nowak, *Kingdom of Barracks. Polish Displaced Persons in Allied-Occupied Germany and Austria, 1945–1952* (Montreal, Canada: McGill–Queen's University Press, 2022).
15 UNA, S-1448-0000-0169-00001. M.W. Rabl, MD, UNRRA Medical Officer, DP Area Junkersdorf, Germany to UNRRA Health Division, Director of Health, Andrew Topping, London, 13 May 1945.
16 Betts, *Ruin and Renewal*, 39.
17 UNRRA, *Psychological Problems of Displaced Persons*, London, June 1945, 1.
18 UNA, S-1253-0000-0450-00001. "More than 1,000 UNRRA Health Specialists in Europe", UNRRA Weekly Bulletin no 64, 27 October 1945.
19 UNA, S-1301-0000-2366-00001. Salisbury from Bryan, Incoming Telegram, 25 October 1945, p. 2.
20 *Archives Nationales*, Paris, France (hereafter AN), AJ/43/328, E. Meyers, Health Monthly Narrative Report – November, December 1948, January 1949, 22 February 1949, p. 10.
21 UNA, S-1494-0000-0114-00001. William C. Rees, Acting Director, UNRRA, British Zone, Area Steiemark, Jundenburg camp, Austria, UNRRA Team 335, Narrative Report, November 1945.
22 UNA, S-1494-0000-0114-00001. William C. Rees, Acting Director, UNRRA, British Zone, Area Steiemark, Jundenburg camp, Austria, UNRRRA Group 335, Narrative Report, December 1945.
23 UNA, S-1253-0000-0460-00001. Donald Morton [Team Director], UNRRA Team 25, Etzel, Cologne, to S.L. Sommer, UNRRA, Washington, DC, 10 August 1945.
24 UNRRA, *Psychological Problems*, 1.
25 UNA, S-1253-0000-0039-00001. The First of May – Spring Holiday, Weekly Camp Kufstein, UNRRA Team 199, vol. 2, no 36, 7 May 1946, Austria: DP in Camps, Deskbook & Other Analyses.
26 UNA, S-1494-0000-0334-00001. T.C. Lockard, Narrative Report, August 1946, Camp Lexenfeld 4, UNRRA Team 323, Salzburg-Austria.
27 UNA, S-1494-0000-0334-00001. T.C. Lockard, Director of UNRRA Team 323, Camp Lexenfeld 4, Salzburg-Austria, Narrative Report, Month of July 1946.
28 PIA, 598/155. Biuletyn Obozowy, *Świt Wolności*, 23 March 1947 and 23–25 December 1945.
29 UNA, S-1494-0000-0334-00001. Walter Lee Shephard, Narrative Report, UNRRA Team 323 [November/December 1945].

30 UNA, S-1494-0000-0296-00001. Monthly Health Report from Camp Itzling, Zone Salzburg, March 1946.
31 UNA, S-1494-0000-0141-00001. Miss Brydone, Public Health Nursing Officer, Narrative Report for Month of December 1946 of Camp Landeck, 30 December 1946.
32 UNA, S-1271-0000-0112-00001. As Irving Jacoby from the Office of War Information explained the contribution of UNRRA was bigger than officially admitted: "I am afraid that not enough credit has been given to you and your staff, particularly Drs. Reckie and Foy, for all the assistance we received, but it is still official policy to stress the OWI rather than the UNRRA sponsorship of these films". Irving Jacoby, Chief, Non-Theatrical Division Motion Picture Bureau Overseas Branch to Dr James C. Crabtree, Medical Division UNRRA, Washington, DC, 16 May 1944.
33 Marja Roholl, 'Preparing for Victory. The U.S. Office of War Information Overseas Branch's illustrated magazines in the Netherlands and the foundations for the American Century, 1944–1945', *European Journal of American Studies*, Special Issue: Wars and New Beginnings in American History, 7-2 | 2012 (online).
34 UNA, S-1271-0000-0112-00001. "To Your Health!" Production Outline for a New Series of Short Films, Non-Theatrical Division, Motion Picture Bureau, Overseas Branch Office of War Information.
35 UNA, S-1271-0000-0112-00001. "To Your Health!" Production Outline for a New Series of Short Films, Non-Theatrical Division, Motion Picture Bureau, Overseas Branch Office of War Information, p. 5.
36 UNA, S-1271-0000-0112-00001. "To Your Health!" Production Outline for a New Series of Short Films, Non-Theatrical Division, Motion Picture Bureau, Overseas Branch Office of War Information, p. 2, 4.
37 UNA, – S-1253-0000-0460-00001. Marta Korwin's Report Fragments, Information for the Press, no 143, 25 July 1945. Information for the Press, no 143, 25 July 1945, Germany – Assembly Centres – UNRRA Administration.
38 UNA, S-1253-0000-0460-00001. Marta Korwin's Report Fragments, Information for the Press, no 143, 25 July 1945. Information for the Press, no 143, 25 July 1945, Germany – Assembly Centres – UNRRA Administration.
39 Ibid.
40 UNA, S-1494-0000-0114-00001. William C. Rees, Acting Director, UNRRA, British Zone, Area Steiemark, Jundenburg camp, Austria, UNRRRA Group 335, Narrative Report, December 1945.
41 UNA, S-1448-0000-0169-00001. Abstracts from Weekly Medical Reports, UNRRA Team 13, Medical Officer L. Hahn, received 3 August 1945.
42 UNA, S-1253-0000-0460-00001. Marta Korwin's Report Fragments, Information for the Press, no 143, 25 July 1945. Information for the Press, no 143, 25 July 1945, Germany – Assembly Centres – UNRRA Administration.

43 UNA, S-1253-0000-0450-00001. Germany, July 1946, Nutrition, British zone.
44 UNA, S-1494-0000-0094-00001. Monthly Health Reports, French Zone, UNRRA Austrian Mission.
45 UNA, S-1174-0000-0059-00001. Incoming Telegram, Communications Section Division of Administrative Services, from Margolin Frankfurt, 9 December 1945.
46 UNA, S-1253-0000-0450-00001. Health Services for DPs, Draft, 4 January 1947.
47 UNA, S-1448-0000-0158-00001. Achieved Immunization Percentages as of 28 February 1946.
48 UNA, S-1448-0000-0158-00001. Gen. des Cilleuls to Dr Goodman. Translated from French, 19 February 1946.
49 UNA, S-1448-0000-0158-00001. Principal Medical Officer, Relief Services to Director of Health, ERO, Immunisation in DP Camps, Austria, 28 February 1946.
50 UNA, S-1510-0000-0012-00001. Hellbrunn – Team 316 – Medical Reports.
51 Reinisch, *Perils of Peace*, 5–6.
52 UNA, S-1448-0000-0169-00001. Abstracts from Weekly Medical Reports, UNRRA Team 13, Medical Officer L. Hahn, received 3 August 1945, no 8, 22 June 1945, p. 13.
53 UNA, S-1448-0000-0169-00001. Abstracts from Weekly Medical Reports, UNRRA Team 13, Medical Officer L. Hahn, received 3 August 1945, no 10, 5 July 1945.
54 UNA, S-1448-0000-0169-00001. M.W. Rabl, UNRRA Medical Officer, Junkersdorf, 31 July 1945, Medical Officer's Report, DP Sub-Area Junkersdorf, Germany to UNRRA Health Division, London.
55 UNA, S-1253-0000-0450-00001. Health Services for DPs, Draft, 4 January 1947.
56 Ibid.
57 UNA, 0406-0034-0001. Mikołaj Minkiewicz, *Pielęgnowanie niemowląt w obrazkach*, Lippstadt, 1946.
58 UNA, S-1253-0000-0450-00001. Cynthia Nash to Mr. Stauffer, Doctors in Germany, 21 February 1945, Germany, Health for DPs.
59 Ibid.
60 UNA, S-1301-0000-2366-00001. Dr Goodman, Salisbury from Bryan, Incoming Telegram, 25 October 1945, p. 2.
61 UNA, 0406-0034-0001. Dr Mikolaj Minkiewicz, Medical Officer UNRRA Team 6, Paderborn, Lippstad, to Zone Medical Officer, 400 UNRRA HQ Lemgo, DP Health Education, 22 May 1947.
62 UNA, 0406-0034-0001. Dr Mikolaj Minkiewicz, Medical Officer UNRRA Team 6 (formerly 248), Lippstadt, to Zone Medical Officer, 400 UNRRA HQ Lemgo, DP Health Education, 8 April 1947.
63 UNA, 0406-0034-0001. Assistant Director Field Operation for Zone Director, Procurement of printing type, 29 January 1947.
64 1.463.643-A, National Library, Warsaw, *Moje dziecko. Higiena, dietetyka, wychowanie. Wskazówki dla kobiet ciężarnych i młodych matek*, Zebrali materiał i

przygotowali do druku: Dr J. Michel-Lechimski, wraz z p. Ellen Krusell, oficer lekarz i siostra UNRRA, Wanito Polskiego Związku Wychodźctwa Przymusowego w Hanowerze, 1946.
65 *Moje dziecko*, 7–8.
66 Ibid., 7.
67 Ibid., 7.
68 Ibid., 27.
69 Ibid., 13.
70 Atina Grossmann shows how the language of grams and vitamins came to indicate the level of entitlement and victimization: Atina Grossmann, 'Grams, Calories, and Food: Languages of Victimization, Entitlement, and Human Rights in Occupied Germany, 1945–1949', *Central European History* 44:1 (2011), 118–48.
71 *Moje dziecko*, 8.
72 Ibid., 5.
73 Ibid., 10.
74 UNA, S-1940-0001-0012-00001. 10 Polish Nurses Graduate From Little Drutte Refresher Course, UNRRA Team News, vol. 1, no 24, 1 December 1946.
75 UNA, S-1448-0000-0169-00001. Andrew Topping, MD, Director of Health to Dr M.W. Rabl, Medical Officer, UNRRA Team 25, US Army, 29 May 1945.
76 UNA, S-1301-0000-2366-00001. Dr Goodman, p. 2–3, Salisbury from Bryan, Incoming Telegram, 25 October 1945.

3

Paving the way for a new democracy? UNRRA in Italy

Silvia Salvatici

The missing history of the UNRRA Italian mission

In 1952, when Italy was dreaming of at last leaving behind the heavy burden of the war's effects, the head of the *Amministrazione per gli Aiuti Internazionali* [Administration for International Aid, AAI], Lodovico Montini, stated: 'We have set out to have a book written on UNRRA in Italy. It will be a document as useful as perhaps unexpected in the history of the great age that spans from the collapse of our country to its supremacy in European rehabilitation.'[1] Yet, he continued, this book had not yet seen the light of day, though the work had been started. Montini had played a key role in the history of the United Nations Relief and Rehabilitation Administration (UNRRA) in Italy. He was a prominent representative of the Christian Democratic Party, brother of the future pope Paul VI and personal friend of the Minister for Foreign Affairs (and later Prime Minister) Alcide De Gasperi, who in 1945 appointed him as the head of the governmental body in charge of official relations with UNRRA.[2] Seven years later Montini was still the key man for the international aid programmes in Italy, but he saw the immediate post-war period as a chaotic and miserable one that many people wished to forget: he did not regret that the book on UNRRA had not yet seen the light.

Scholars didn't fill in the gap left by this unfinished and unpublished official history of UNRRA in Italy in the following decades. Historians studying the post-war years have given short shrift to the UNRRA programmes and have approached them mainly as the prehistory of the Marshall Plan. As has been successfully argued, until the 1990s the historiography on European reconstruction was 'intimately bound up with the Cold War' and research on Italy was no exception.[3] The UNRRA mission has been seen as the embodiment of the American presence on the peninsula, and its relief programme as the attempt of the United States to lead the country's economic reconstruction.[4] This is why most of the work has been devoted to the plan promoting industrial and agricultural rehabilitation,[5] which covers all the measures taken by the Administration to re-start national production (for instance supplying Italy with fertilizers, pesticides, coal, rubber and raw materials).[6] The branch of the country programme dealing with the assistance of civilians has received less academic attention, though it absorbed 70 per cent of the total budget for Italy.[7] While a new generation of scholars has shed some light on these UNRRA welfare activities, they have usually looked at them as part of a different story (e.g. the history of international organizations in Italy, childhood in post-war Italy, the history of the Italian social services), rather than scrutinizing them in their own right.[8]

This chapter cannot, of course, wholly fill these gaps in the historiography; it just seeks to offer some new insights into the history of UNRRA in Italy. It focuses on the welfare programme and analyses both the Administration's objectives and the methods it used to achieve them. I will show how Italy's political class and institutions received, recast and manipulated relief programmes. The entanglement of local objectives with international aid was crucial for (re)shaping welfare policies and practices in the context of post-war reconstruction and the transition to democracy. The analysis of national cases such as Italy is essential not only for a comprehensive reconstruction of UNRRA's transnational history, but also for opening up new approaches to the history of international humanitarianism.

'There is not enough food to feed the people': UNRRA's arrival in Italy

In July 1944, UNRRA's Observers' Mission officially landed in Italy, more precisely in Naples. Eight months earlier, when UNRRA was born, in his inaugural speech Franklin Delano Roosevelt had included Italy among the countries where 'many ruthlessly shattered cities and villages' offered tragic evidence of the Nazis' destructive fury.[9] Yet, Italy's peculiar and ambiguous status as a 'co-belligerent' and an 'ex-enemy' country could not be ignored. Great Britain and the United States had initially considered the possible intervention of UNRRA on Italian territory under the Allies' control only for the relief of displaced persons (DP), that is, non-Italian refugees entitled to international care.[10] The official task of the UNRRA experts was thus to report on the situation of DPs.[11] Nevertheless, the American government did put pressure on other member states of UNRRA to allow local civilians to be included among the recipients of the Administration's aid in Italy. The American Director General of UNRRA, Herbert H. Lehman, had instructed the 'observers' to gather information and to draw up a possible programme of activities that was not restricted to foreign refugees.[12] 'There is not enough food to feed the people', was the first sentence of the report that the Observers' Mission submitted to the UNRRA Council after two months in Italy.[13] In twenty pages, the chief of the Observers' Mission – Spurgeon M. Keeny Sr – summarized the enormous damage caused by the ongoing war to Italy's communications system, public and private buildings, industrial plants and agricultural production. Keeny, of course, was aware that UNRRA could not fully remedy such devastation, since 'expenditure on this scale in an ex-enemy country seems to be out of the question'.[14] He, therefore, suggested that medical services be provided together with a food programme aimed at particular groups, such as children. Food was at the very basis of the need pyramid and children were the quintessential innocent victims of the war: Keeny's proposal seemed suitable for an 'ex-enemy' country.[15]

The Council approved the resolution ratifying the intervention in Italy after a tense debate and only thanks to pressure from the United States. The budget for the operations in the ex-enemy country was 50 million dollars: merely a tenth of the 500 million dollars needed for a one-year 'minimum import programme' according to the Allied Control Commission and the Italian authorities.[16] The Council accepted the recommendations of the Observers' Mission and the only relief for Italian civilians was to be a supplementary food programme for children, expectant and nursing mothers; there would also be a scheme for the care of internally displaced persons.[17]

By as early as August 1945, however, the UNRRA Council had removed the limitations on its operations in Italy (which had now been given equal status in the UN to full members, though it would not officially become a member until 1955)[18] and greatly increased the funding.[19] Of UNRRA's country missions in Europe, that in Italy ranked second in terms of the monetary value of the supplies shipped (first was Poland and third was Yugoslavia).[20] The plan of action included the rehabilitation of agriculture and industrial plants, and an expanded welfare programme, in terms of both resources and objectives. The feeding of children, expectant and nursing mothers remained the core of the welfare activities, but on a wider scale and with more ambitious aims. The implementation of the new scheme – which started at the beginning of 1946 – was meant to be the turning point from mere relief to true rehabilitation.

Rehabilitation as modernization of social welfare

Phoebe Bannister, head of UNRRA's Welfare Division in Rome, firmly believed that in her field of work the term 'rehabilitation' had only one meaning: moving beyond first aid and 'offering help to the Italian Government on the organization and reorganization of its services to all the persons who could not to help themselves'.[21] Bannister was an American social worker, with a very good knowledge of social services in the United States.[22] She perfectly embodied the spirit of the Welfare Division, which aimed to implement in the recipient countries 'constructive program[s] which would stimulate and bring about "self-help"'.[23] In the case of Italy, the goal was not just to treat the country's war wounds, but to support the development of a modern welfare system so that local institutions could provide for people in need.

According to several UNRRA surveys, in Italy the lack of proper structures and policies to take care of those who 'could not to help themselves' was not just a consequence of the war, it was evidence of the country's failure to construct a fully developed democracy. In the Liberal Age (1861–1922), the state had proved to be unable to build a centralized national welfare system, and religious charities had continued to play a large role. Under Fascism, welfare had been mainly a means of propaganda and a way of exercising social control. The Italian welfare system went on to suffer almost complete collapse as a result of the war.[24] Bannister pointed out the outcomes of this recent history: a large number of unevenly distributed charitable foundations, poor coordination between private and public agencies, the lack of any real standards of operations and the fact that there was no department of the central government directly responsible for any welfare service.[25] Against this background, supporting Italy in the construction of a modern welfare system meant providing its most disadvantaged citizens with better living conditions but also with democratic institutions and a new democratic spirit.

Although Bannister did not mention the issue in her reports, Italian authorities were well aware of the importance of welfare for the country's reconstruction. Within the anti-Fascist coalition that governed Italy during the period when UNRRA was operating in the country, every political party recognized the urgency of a reform that would tailor welfare services to the needs of the population.[26] But there were differing views regarding the principles and objectives that should inspire this reform. At the risk of oversimplification, these views can be categorized as tradition versus modernity, or charity versus social rights. The latter view was held mainly by the secular social democratic parties. They believed that social rights should be enshrined as an indispensable element of citizenship in a new democratic Italy. It was therefore the state's job to guarantee social security and to take the leading role in providing welfare services to citizens; charitable associations would be relegated to the sidelines. The Christian Democrat camp saw things differently, especially in relation to the incompatibility between public assistance and private charity. That camp considered it inevitable and perhaps even essential that the state would be involved in welfare, but that this should not be to the detriment of private charity, which was held to be an expression of pluralism, whereby various social agents would be free to take initiatives. The goal should not be to have the state take over welfare services but instead to have the state rationalize and coordinate private initiatives, which would complement public efforts; moreover, such initiatives would embody a long tradition within Italian culture and society.[27] One of the staunchest defenders of this approach was Lodovico Montini, the head of the AAI and therefore UNRRA's most important contact figure.

Montini and the AAI could not accept unreservedly the call from UNRRA to modernize the national social services and to place them under the leadership of the central government, in order to address 'the intermingling of the Governmental and the voluntary agencies' which – according to Bannister – had 'made the Italian welfare picture extremely patchy'.[28] Thus, as Italian and international (mainly American) partners negotiated and sought for points of mediation, UNRRA's goals and methods were recast in the particular context of Italy.[29] The entanglement between local and international programmes is epitomised by the resolutions taken in the field of social work education.

Professional education was one pillar of the Welfare Division's programme.[30] The Division, based in New York, framed the issue in two ways. UNRRA was seeking to promote the professionalization of relief work by selecting personnel to run its international missions who had appropriate qualifications; to this end, it had set up special training courses.[31] In turn, those personnel were expected to promote the professionalization of local welfare officers working in the recipient countries. Modernization was thus seen as the abandonment of the amateur provision of non-specialist bodies such as religious charities in favour of dedicated professional provision. The modernization of international relief and the modernization of local welfare provision in a given recipient country were closely connected. Professional training of social workers was a crucial issue because it was intended to provide a counter-impetus to the charitable impulse of the philanthropic tradition. For instance, only the use of appropriate professional instruments could give an accurate, objective assessment of an individual's needs. Thus, a professionally trained cadre and standardized practices were prerequisites for fair and efficient social services.

In Italy the lack of skilled welfare workers was particularly evident.[32] UNRRA's first provision in this field was a small programme of scholarships so that young Italians could study social work abroad, mainly in the United States but also in Great Britain. This was certainly nothing new in terms of professional training programmes in the area of international aid.[33] But the overseas scholarship scheme was also accompanied (and this is the most innovative aspect) by the creation of local social work schools. Unlike the United States and many European countries,[34] Italy did not have yet a network of schools for social workers, though the need for professional training was a prominent (and contested) issue in the post-war debate on welfare reform.[35] UNRRA's impulse was decisive for the flourishing of the so-called 'new schools': ten of these were created between 1946 and 1947, distributed mainly between Rome and Milan.[36] Phoebe Bannister fought a personal battle to have the Italian government invest in them a small portion of the 'Lira fund', a fund that had resulted from the sale of some of the supplies that UNRRA had shipped to Italy. This would guarantee the survival of the schools beyond their limited period of direct support from Administration.[37]

All the schools were in receipt of some public money, but they were largely funded and wholly run by a variety of private agencies, in a mirror image of the multiplicity of social work providers in the immediate post-war period. Some of these agencies had roots in Catholic philanthropy or in the solidarity practices of the socialist tradition, while others were born out of anti-Fascist movements and the commitment to restoring democracy to Italy. Different orientations impacted the curricula of the schools. All of them had the same required courses, according to a national scheme that UNRRA helped to shape, but the offer of elective courses varied from school to school, following the view of social work that inspired each of them.[38] The educational track for social workers, which was seen as a cornerstone of the modernization of welfare, was effectively an amalgam of an American, already standardized model and the widely differing views and priorities of the various local agencies running the schools. Thus, in Italy, social work did not begin simply as a profession imported from abroad in the frame of post-war humanitarianism. Rather, it stemmed from the interplay between an external impulse from UNRRA and the endogenous efforts of state and non-state actors. It marked a step forward in the modernization of Italy's social services more generally, but at the same time it was rooted in Italy's long tradition of charitable provision.

'Hungry people must be fed. But this is not enough'

Feeding children, expectant and nursing mothers was the core welfare activity while UNRRA remained in Italy, and thereafter it continued through the 'Lira fund'. Food aid, of course, was at the centre of the humanitarian response to the post-war emergency, but for Phoebe Bannister it was also crucial for reorganizing the Italian welfare system.[39] UNRRA staff saw food distribution as having two objectives: feeding malnourished children and improving social services. From the beginning, it was clear that the available resources were enough to reach only a small proportion of the 'target population': approximately the 20 per cent, according to the preliminary assessment drafted by the Welfare Division.[40] The geography of distribution was therefore designed in accordance with the available data on people's access to food and per capita calorie intakes across the country's different areas. In July 1945, after the Allied Army had handed the administration of the liberated Tuscany to the Italian government, Lodovico Montini and Phoebe Bannister agreed that all the provinces of the region required less assistance than Italy's southern provinces. They also decided to prioritize urban centres rather than the rural population, though Montini asked for a larger allocation of sugar and milk, desperately lacking in Tuscany as everywhere.

According to the plans, local institutions for children ('*convivenze infantili*', i.e. orphanages, houses for disabled children, but also schools) were to be the main points within the distribution network.[41] When the first food programme started in spring 1945, however, many of the buildings in liberated regions were still badly damaged and schooling had consequently been suspended. In Naples – one of the most heavily bombed Italian towns – many schools had broken windows and lacked any sort of heating,[42] while in Tuscany and Emilia 'there were no buildings in which to collect the children'.[43] The plans were therefore revised to allow for a larger proportion of the food supplies to be distributed directly to individuals. Accordingly, a series of provincial (sometimes known as communal) committees were appointed to be the main actors in the food programme at local level. These committees were made up of UNRRA officers, representatives of local institutions (prefects, health officials, school authorities) and the local bishop, but they could also include the representatives of private agencies engaged in helping the needy.[44] Each provincial committee cooperated with many such agencies, from the *Pontificia Commissione di Assistenza* (the most important Catholic organization and ancestor of Caritas Italiana) to the *Unione Donne Italiane* (the national association of women, born out of the Resistance and monopolized by parties of the left). In many cases, the distribution of food parcels drew on 'countless smaller welfare groups', such as 'home and schools for the blind, convent and religious bodies, private schools and kindergarten, children's homes etc'.[45] Reporting on the food programme in Tuscany and Emilia, UNRRA welfare officers emphasized the variety – from the standpoint of political, cultural and religious affiliation – of the private agencies to which they by and large entrusted the task of implementing the relief and rehabilitation project. This variety resulted in many visions and practices of welfare, as well as in different social networks through which recipients were selected and food supplies distributed. Thus, UNRRA's plan for the modernization of welfare driven by central government ambiguously relied on the particularism of a plethora of Italian charities.

Frequent complaints about the iniquity of such a distribution system arrived on Spurgeon M. Keeny's table: dozens of letters from different provinces lamented the unfairness of recipient selection, the disappearance of foodstuffs, the lack of transparency in distribution.[46] UNRRA welfare officers admitted that 'in a number of localities only a frequent and careful observation prevented political or religious discriminations',[47] while UNRRA's headquarters in Rome concluded that 'the selection left to the Communal Committees gives bad results and is often influenced by dishonesty and favouritism'.[48] But this was not the only worry for the Administration.

During the first phase of the food programme, problems seemed to arise from the delivery of supplies to individuals rather than to children's institutions. According to UNRRA officers, this solution led to a significant misallocation of food. For instance, entire families often benefitted of the rations meant to be only for children; this undermined the spirit of the food programme and favoured the persistence of child malnourishment.[49] Moreover, most Italians proved to be unable to cook or unwilling to consume much of the food distributed by UNRRA. Many reports stated that Italians generally disliked condensed milk, oatmeal and dried soup, all of which were components of the UNRRA food supplies. In the Latina province, people fed the pigs with the powdered milk because they did not know how to dissolve it, and the prefect was asked to take action to prevent this.[50] In the view of Bannister and other UNRRA officers, the waste of food aid was just the tip of the iceberg. Italians did not have any knowledge of the principles of nutrition, and this was one of the causes of their malnourishment. Thus, it was not sufficient to feed them: they had also to be taught how and what to eat.

A switch from the distribution of raw food to the delivery of cooked meals aimed to achieve this goal. At the end of 1945, when a number of schools re-opened and collective distribution on a wider scale became feasible, school lunch was selected as one of the main channels for food aid.[51] The aim was not only to limit the misuse of UNRRA food. At the third UNRRA Nutrition Conference, held in August 1946, the American nutritionist Sue Sadow looked at the US experience[52] and explained that the school lunch programme there had not only provided children with good food, but also afforded an opportunity to educate them to eat well.[53] Sadow's speech was part of a programme which included three main meetings aimed at Italian public health and welfare officers (held in Rome, Naples and Florence), as well as a number of lectures on nutrition given in different places (Padua, Torino, Bologna). These initiatives generated many publications: a collection of 150 recipes to use the food distributed by UNRRA,[54] the proceedings of the conferences on nutrition, and a practical guide on how to set up a school lunch programme.[55] In the view of the Welfare Division in Rome, the training of local personnel went hand in hand with the preparation of materials that could be used after the end of the UNRRA mission.

The short-term objective was to encourage Italians to consume UNRRA supplies in spite of their cultural resistance to oatmeal and powdered milk. But the ultimate aim was to promote nutritional education in the country and develop a 'dietetic conscience, which will reform in various ways [Italians'] nutrition'.[56] In their conferences addressed to local welfare officers, UNRRA nutritionists not only provided the audience with practical advice (how to store cereals, cook soya and rehydrate dried food), they also aimed to eradicate 'prejudices and incorrect food beliefs', for example that the consumption of meat would reinforce aggressive temperaments.[57] This approach did not take into consideration the inadequate levels of consumption across the country, that even in the pre-war years had resulted in only 'slighter higher than the minimum requirements and far below optimal standards'.[58] The consumption of meat, for example, was extremely low and provided Italians with only 2.8 per cent of their calorie intake (in the United Kingdom the percentage was 16.7 and in the United States 12.8).[59] UNRRA experts sought to promote a rational model of 'adequate nutrition', based on scientific principles and freed from any influence of culture and tradition.[60] In their view, welfare officers were responsible for the circulation of this model among the people, while Italian institutions were supposed to base their food policies on that same model.

Congratulating the chief of the mission in Rome, the acting director of the Welfare Division at UNRRA headquarters stressed 'the important part which the nutrition specialists have played in the feeding program in Italy', and optimistically concluded: 'there is every reason to believe that the good work thus started will continue long after UNRRA operations in Italy cease'.[61] Undoubtedly, the same principles of nutrition continued to guide the food programme when it was supported through the Lira fund, after UNRRA had left the country in spring 1947. At the end of the same year, the AAI signed with UNICEF a new agreement for food aid aimed at children as well as expecting and nursing mothers.[62] The combination of the distribution of 'nutrients' needed for a healthy diet with food education inspired in particular the section of the programme aimed at increasing the consumption of milk. According to the AAI, milk not only was hardly available for Italian children, it was also 'scarcely appreciated, particularly in the poor classes, and it [was] consumed almost reluctantly in certain areas'.[63] In the first phase of this new programme, UNICEF shipped to Italy 27,000 tons of powdered milk; then it supported the establishment of modern dairies in several towns. In the early 1950s state-of-the-art milk factories contributed to both the development of Italian industry and agriculture, and the changing nutrition habits of a country that was striving to join the ranks of modern, industrialized nations. It is hard to say whether it was indeed UNRRA that paved the way for this complex process, but undoubtedly its food programme, started in 1945, had an impact on the long-term social, economic and cultural changes that took place in the first decade of the Italian Republic.

Conclusion

In October 1946 the UNRRA regional director for Tuscany and Emilia forwarded to the chief of the mission a confidential document he had drafted after a conversation with the welfare officer based in Florence. She had reported to him the comments on the Administration shared with her by Dr Filo della Torre, one of the members of the local provincial committee. Filo della Torre had been working with UNRRA for almost two years, but during a recent field trip he became very critical about UNRRA in general (in his opinion it was 'making propaganda for the USA') and about the Italian mission in particular. In his view, the welfare programme was nothing other than a crowd of women 'who don't understand anything about Italian life but they think themselves very clever'. 'What right do they have' – he wondered – 'to come and teach us our own business?'. Filo della Torre also said he was waiting anxiously for 31 December, when the departure of all UNRRA representatives would bring 'real "relief" to the country'.⁶⁴ Such harsh criticism disappointed the regional director, who however admitted that 'nobody is so naive as to feel that the Italian people feel exactly as we do about UNRRA and its significance'.⁶⁵

Undoubtedly the UNRRA mission was significant in many different ways and for many different parties – humanitarians and recipients, institutions and citizens, locals, and international officers. This is a crucial consideration when looking at the history of post-war humanitarianism in Italy. We can safely say that the impact of UNRRA's welfare activities went beyond the immediate relief of the two million children it claimed to have fed. The call for the modernization of welfare provision did not fall into a void; on the contrary, it gave impetus to the professionalization of welfare officers, promoted the nutritional sciences and their relevance for welfare policies, and helped to open up the debate on the reform of social services. In other words, UNRRA contributed to the 'rehabilitation' of Italy, meant as the 'organization and reorganization' of the public assistance 'to all the persons who could not to help themselves'. At the same time, the case of Italy convincingly shows that the impact of UNRRA cannot be seen exclusively as the internationalization of the 'New Deal-style problem solving', i.e. as the expansion of the American model which shaped the restoration of European democracies.⁶⁶ UNRRA's methods, practices and objectives intertwined with Italian local resources, institutional aims and the legacy of the past welfare system.

The entanglements between international aid and local impulses were marked by tensions and ambiguities, but they had a key role in reframing the approach to social welfare in the Italian Republic's first years of life. On the one hand, the case of Italy sheds light not only on the multi-scale dimension (international, national and local) of UNRRA's actions, plans and policies, but also on the reception and manipulation of them in the different areas of operations. On the other hand, it offers fruitful insights into both the interplay between donors and recipients, and the interaction of their ideas on 'rehabilitation', which collided, competed and conflated.

Notes

1   Lodovico Montini, 'Prefazione', in *L'Amministrazione per gli Aiuti Internazionali. Origini, ordinamento, funzioni, attività* (Roma: ABETE, 1952), v.
2   The Delegazione del Governo Italiano per i Rapporti con l'UNRRA, renamed Amministrazione per gli Aiuti Internazionali in 1947.

3   Mark Mazower, 'Reconstruction: The Historiographical Issues', *Past & Present*, 210, supplement 6 (2011), 17.
4   John Lamberton Harper, *America and the Reconstruction of Italy, 1945–1948* (Cambridge: Cambridge University Press, 1986).
5   Andrea Ciampani (a cura di), *L'Amministrazione per Aiuti Internazionali. La ricostruzione dell'Italia tra dinamiche internazionali e attività assistenziali* (Milano: Franco Angeli, 2002); Andrew Martin Karmarck, *Politica finanziaria degli alleati in Italia: luglio 1943–febbraio 1947* (Roma: Carecas, 1977).
6   George Woodbridge, *UNRRA. The History of the International Relief and Rehabilitation Administration*, vol. II (New York: Columbia University Press, 1950), 278–80, 282–6.
7   Ibid.
8   Angela Villani, *Dalla parte dei bambini. Italia e UNICEF tra ricostruzione e sviluppo* (Milano: Cedam, 2016); Silvia Inaudi, 'Assistenza e povertà infantile negli anni dell'inchiesta sulla miseria', in Clara Allasia, Bruno Maida and Franco Prono (eds.), *Infanzia e povertà. Storie e narrazioni nell'Italia del dopoguerra (1945–1950)* (Avellino: Edizioni Sinestesie, 2019); Domenica La Banca, *Welfare in transizione. L'Esperienza dell'ONMI (1943–1950)* (Napoli: Edizioni Scientifiche Italiane, 2019); Rita Cutini, *Promuovere la democrazia. Storia degli assistenti sociali nell'Italia del secondo dopoguerra* (Roma: Viella, 2018).
9   'Address of the President of the United States', *United Nations Relief and Rehabilitation Organization Journal*, I (10 November–2 December 1943), 2.
10 Silvia Salvatici, 'Between National and International Mandates: Displaced Persons and Refugees in Post-war Italy', *Journal of Contemporary History*, 49:3 (2014).
11 The National Archives, Kew, UK (TNA), FO, 371/42741, Displaced Persons Sub-Commission in Italy, 'UNRRA Observers on Displaced Persons in Italy', 2 June 1944.
12 Woodbridge, *UNRRA*, vol. II, 258. On the debate about the inclusion of Italy among the recipient countries, see David W. Ellwood, *Italy 1943–1945* (Leicester: Leicester University Press, 1985), 103–4.
13 United Nations Archives, New York, USA (UNA), S-0520-0086, UNRRA, Bureau of Areas, Executive Office, Country Files, 1943–1949, file Italy 1944 – Observers' Mission – Report 1943–1949, 'Summary report of the UNRRA Observers' Mission to Italy', 15 September 1944, 1.
14 Ibid. See also *The Reminiscences of Spurgeon M. Keeny Sr.*, interview taken by Peter Jessup, Columbia University Oral History Research Office, 1982, 182–5.
15 Joël Glasman, *Humanitarianism and Quantification of Human Needs: Minimal Humanity* (London & New York: Routledge, 2020), 38–41.
16 'Summary report of the UNRRA Observers' Mission to Italy', 9.
17 UNA, S-0527-0863 Italy Mission: Chief of Mission: Subject Files 1944–49, file Welfare – Food Distribution.

18 See Luca Riccardi, *La «grandezza» di una media Potenza. Personaggi e problemi della politica estera italiana nel Novecento* (Roma: Società Editrice Dante Alighieri, 2017), 353–9.
19 UNRRA was supposed to provide Italy with 450 million dollars of supplies; Woodbridge, *UNRRA*, vol. II, 272.
20 Woodbridge, *UNRRA*, vol. III, 428. UNRRA spent the vast bulk of its resources in Europe, cfr. Jessica Reinisch, '"Auntie UNRRA" at the Crossroads', *Past & Present*, 218, supplement 8 (2013), 73.
21 UNA, S-1021-0039-04, UNRRA, Office of the Historian, Monographs, Country Area Missions and Offices, Italy 19, History of Welfare Division Italian Mission [by Phoebe Bannister], 'History of Welfare Division UNRRA Italian Mission Outline', 15.
22 See the paper she presented to the conference held in Tremezzo (Como) in 1946 and jointly organized by UNRRA and the Italian Ministero per l'Assistenza Post-Bellica; Phoebe Bannister, 'Previdenza sociale negli Stati Uniti', in *Atti del Convegno per Studi di Assistenza Sociale* (Milano: Marzorati, 1947), 11–17.
23 UNA, S-0556-10-15, UNRRA, Office of the Historian, Subject files, Welfare Division HQ, 'Welfare Division', 2.
24 UNA, S-1021-0183-02, UNRRA, Office of the Historian, Publications, Welfare, Background for Welfare Planning, Italy, 'UNRRA's Welfare Programme in Italy'; UNRRA – Italian Mission, *Survey of Italy's Economy* (Rome: UNRRA, 1947), 172–7.
25 Ibid.
26 Gianni Silei, *Lo stato sociale in Italia. Storia e documenti* (Manduria-Bari-Roma: Lacaita, 2004), 52–3; Chiara Giorgi, Ilaria Pavan, *Storia dello Stato sociale in Italia*, Il Mulino, Bologna 2021, 229–38.
27 Silvia Inaudi, 'L'assistenza nel secondo dopoguerra tra continuità e mancate riforme. Note a margine del dibattito storiografico', *Storica*, XVI:46 (2010).
28 UNRRA – Italian Mission, *Survey of Italy's Economy*, 173.
29 Large majority of UNRRA staff was from United Kingdom and United States: respectively 34 and 31 per cent. At the same date (31 December 1945) in Italy 46 per cent of the personnel was from the United States and 42 per cent from the United Kingdom (Woodbridge, *UNRRA*, vol. III, 415). Most important, the Chief of Mission was American as well as 15 out of the 22 people in service for the Welfare Division; UNA, S-0520-0087, UNRRA, Bureau of Areas, Executive Office, Country Files, 1943–1949, file Italian Mission – Personnel and Organization 1943–1949, 'Italian Mission Recruiting Schedule', 15 June 1945, 4.
30 UNA, S-1021-04-09, UNRRA, Office of the Historian, Monographs, Bureau of Administration, The Training Program.
31 Cfr. Silvia Salvatici, 'Professionals of Humanitarianism: UNRRA Relief Officers in Post-war Europe', in Johannes Paulmann (ed.), *Dilemmas of Humanitarian Aid in the Twentieth Century* (Oxford: Oxford University Press, 2016).

32 See the letter addressed by Genevieve Gabower (welfare officer based in Rome) to the Director of the Welfare Division in Washington, UNA, S-0520-0230, UNRRA, Bureau of Services – Division of Repatriation and Welfare – Country and Area Files 1943–1948, file Italy – Operations no. 2 – July '45–December '45, 'Letter to Mr. Charles Alspach', 30 November 1946.

33 Yi-Tang Lin, Thomas David and Davide Rodogno, 'Fellowship Programs for Public Health Development: The Rockefeller Foundation, UNRRA, and WHO (1920s – 1970s)', in Ludovic Tournès and Giles Scott-Smith (eds.), *Global Exchange. Scholarships and Transnational Circulations in the Modern World* (New York-Oxford: Berghahn, 2017).

34 Lynne M. Healy, *International Social Work. Professional Action in an Independent World* (Oxford: Oxford University Press, 2008), 135–49.

35 See Nicola Perrotti, *Le scuole per assistenti sociali* and Odile Vallin, *Problemi della formazione tecnica delle assistenti sociali e dell'organizzazione delle scuole di servizio sociale*, in *Atti del convegno per studi*.

36 'History of Welfare Division UNRRA Italian Mission Outline', 75.

37 See the letter addressed by Phoebe Bannister to the Lira Fund Control Committee, UNA, UNRRA, S-0527-0930 Italy Mission: Bureau of Requirements and Distribution: Sub-Bureau of Supply Operations: Program Coordination and Statistics Division – Subject files 1944–1947, file Welfare Feeding Project, 'Lira Fund Project – Welfare', 17 March 1947.

38 UNA, S-1021-0194-01, UNRRA, Office of the Historian, Publications, Countries, Italy, UNRRA Welfare Programme Operational Analysis No. 34, 'UNRRA's Welfare Programme in Italy Part II', 11–12.

39 'History of Welfare Division UNRRA Italian Mission Outline', 16.

40 UNA, S-0520-0087, UNRRA, Bureau of Areas, Executive Office, Country Files, 1943–1949, file Italian Mission – Child Care Program 1943–1949, 'Limited child welfare programme for Italy', 6 October 1944.

41 Delegazione del Governo Italiano per i Rapporti con l'UNRRA, *I risultati di una inchiesta sui consumi alimentari nelle convivenze assistite dall'UNRRA* (Roma: Failli, 1947), 9.

42 S-0520-0118, UNRRA, Bureau of Areas – European Mission Affairs – Country Files 1943–1949, file Italian Mission – Reports – Keeny letters II, 'Report of visit to Naples – Information and comments', 4.

43 UNA, S-1021-0041-07, UNRRA, Office of the Historian, Monographs, Country Area Missions and Offices, Italy 27, History of Activities of the Welfare Section – Emilia and Toscana Region [by Margaret Cullen], 'Activities of welfare section – Emilia and Toscana region', 10.

44 UNA, UNRRA, S-0527-0863 Italy Mission: Chief of Mission: Subject Files 1944–49, file Welfare Division, 'Istruzioni provvisorie per l'attuazione del programma UNRRA in Italia'.

45 Ibid., 8.
46 See the letters collected in UNA, UNRRA, S-00527-0828 Italy Mission: Chief of Mission: Regional Offices Correspondence 1944–1947, file Region D and S-0527-0863 Italy Mission: Chief of Mission: Subject Files 1944–49, file Welfare Division.
47 'Activities of welfare section – Emilia and Toscana Region', 9.
48 UNA, UNRRA, S-0527-0863 Italy Mission: Chief of Mission: Subject Files 1944–49, file Welfare 1, 'Extension and changes in the assistance programme and plans to carrying out the same', 2.
49 Delegazione del Governo Italiano per i Rapporti con l'UNRRA, *I risultati di una inchiesta*, 9.
50 UNA, UNRRA, S-0527-0863 Italy Mission: Chief of Mission: Subject Files 1944–49, file Welfare Division, 'Latte in polvere', 18 October 1945.
51 'Extension and changes in the assistance programme and plans to carrying out the same', 1–3.
52 On the American school lunch programme, see Susan Levine, *School Lunch Politics. The Surprising History of American Favourite Welfare Program* (Princeton and Oxford: Princeton University Press, 2008).
53 UNA, UNRRA, S-0520-0229 Bureau of Services – Division of Repatriation and Welfare – Country and Area Files 1943–1948, File Italy – Report on First Nutrition Conf. for Public Health Nurses held in Rome, 'Community Education in Nutrition, by Sue Sadow'.
54 UNRRA – Italian Mission, *Raccolta di 115 ricette per la preparazione dei viveri dell'UNRRA* (Venezia: Officine Grafiche Carlo Ferrari, 1947).
55 UNRRA – Italian Mission, *Guida pratica per la preparazione delle refezioni scolastiche* (Venezia: Officine Grafiche Carlo Ferrari, 1947).
56 UNA, UNRRA, S-0520-0229 Bureau of Services – Division of Repatriation and Welfare – Country and Area Files 1943–1948, File Italy – Report on First Nutrition Conf. For Public Health Nurses held in Rome, 'Lesson Edvige Fileti'.
57 UNRRA – Italian Mission, *Conferenza sull'alimentazione per le assistenti sanitarie del Veneto, Forlì, Ferrara e Ravenna* (Venezia: Officine Grafiche Carlo Ferrari, 1947), 48.
58 UNRRA – Italian Mission, *Survey of Italy's Economy*, 39.
59 Ibid., 41.
60 On the rise of this model in the United States, see Helen Zoe Veit, *Modern Food, Moral Food. Self-Control, Science and the Rise of Modern American Eating in the Early Twentieth Century* (Chapel Hill: University of North Carolina Press, 2013).
61 On the changes of Italian consumer behaviour in the 1950s, see Emanuela Scarpellini, *Material Nation. A Consumer's History of Modern Italy* (Oxford: Oxford University Press, 2011), 125–224.
62 Villani, *Dalla parte dei bambini*, 68–79.
63 *L'Amministrazione per gli Aiuti Internazionali*, 33.

64 UNA, UNRRA, S-00527-0828 Italy Mission: Chief of Mission: Regional Offices Correspondence 1944–1947, file Regional Offices – Regione E (Toscana Emilia), 'Confidential report'.
65 Ibid.
66 Elizabeth Borgwardt, *A New Deal for the World. America's Vision for Human Rights* (Cambridge, MA and London: Belknap Press of Harvard University Press, 2005), 119.

4

The muse of rural assistance in Greece for relief and rehabilitation: The Near East Foundation and United Nations Relief and Rehabilitation Administration, 1944–7

Joshua Thew

Introduction

The relief and rehabilitation narratives of the United Nations Relief and Rehabilitation Administration (UNRRA) following the Second World War approached nations, institutions and organizations as imperial legacies and introductions to Cold War internationalism.[1] In this vein, the Greek case illustrates how empires old (British) and new (Cold War divisions between the United States and Soviet Union) sought to ideologically reframe the nation through the philanthropic and voluntary actors that carried out UNRRA's mission. Attempts to assist the displaced, wounded, and sick reflect continued efforts to reconstruct the Greek village, polis region and nation closer to Europe.

Western assistance began with the birth of modern Greece in 1821 as it defined itself from the Ottoman Empire.[2] The Balkan Wars and the First World War continued to resolve Greece's 'Eastern Question' through expansion based on civilizational, national and religious separation that was imposed by Western relief and peace efforts.[3] The Western actors, some of whom were missionaries-turned-philanthropic administrators, created an enterprising network that attempted to fix communities and social groups (in this case, Christian) for the nation.[4] While philanthropy's etymology and original conceptualization came from classical Greece, Western organizations (British, American and Swiss) created a modern concept of the term by providing money for relief as Greece fought for independence.[5] From Greek independence in 1828 until the post-Second World War era, philanthropy remained dominated by external actors who played vital roles in defining assistance. These actors assisted with the national project for Greek reunification, known as *Megali Hellas*, which incorporated more territory and citizens into Greece on four different occasions.[6] The national project continued through UNRRA's use of external actors who aided those displaced in the Levant as they returned to Greece and fought to further homogenize the nation. This chapter will use the case of the Near East Foundation (NEF), an interwar agency that worked with UNRRA, to show how continuities in Anglo-led planning between the interwar and post-war periods focused on the 'rehabilitation' of educational systems.

The road to UNRRA's support began in 1941 when Axis forces occupied Greece. Although some fled, including the monarchy, the majority of the population was trapped under Axis occupation as they installed a puppet government that punished Greece and its remaining population for three years. The population was murdered, livestock was decimated through looting, and villages were burnt and destroyed. Greek monarchists returned to power in 1944, supported militarily and economically by the Allied Powers and the newly created United Nations. The UNRRA began implementing post-war programmes in late 1944, including health, sanitation and medical assistance. As UNRRA's post-war work commenced, the Greek monarchist regime oversaw the distribution of relief. Those who weathered the occupation in Greece expressed increased support for political plurality, including communism giving rise to new political actors who resisted the monarchist government's vision of Greece's future. Civil War (1943–9) broke out almost as soon as UNRRA's work began. The Greek monarchy, previously supported by the British, received continued support through US military aid, which helped claim military victory in 1949.

Many philanthropic organizations, such as UNRRA implemented relief and rehabilitation programmes throughout this period. First, this included health and medical relief following the Axis occupation. Second, during the Civil War, rehabilitation served as the Western international response to the communist threat. As Greece entered a socially and politically repressive post-war period, the programmes became models for various international and Western actors looking to stem communism's spread, including the Truman Doctrine. The Greek context illustrates how a flood of Western capital, military support and alliances, international actors, and philanthropic organizations helped bring Greece closer to the West.

UNRRA's international actors, mainly British, American and Greek, served as architects of UNRRA's Greece mission; they held civilizational vantage points continuing past Greek reconstruction, through and beyond UNRRA's work.⁷ The posture prescribed relief first followed by a socio-economic emergency rehabilitation that was framed spatially, racially, nationally and temporally. In this context, the NEF, a US philanthropic foundation specializing in rural education, exemplifies the continuities and changes in Greek assistance between the interwar and Cold War periods.⁸ Experts came to NEF with experiences connecting the segregated US South, urban immigrant populations, reservations of autochthonous US populations and US colonies as 'comparable' underdeveloped contexts.⁹ The educational programmes collectively retained urban political dominance over the rural by providing ladders that served to incorporate peripheral actors into the increasingly right-wing political system as opposed to political plurality. The programmes carried forward a language of socio-economic reconstruction, leaning into Western international markets through relief and rehabilitation goals, making Greece more economically suited to a Western political economy. The actions of UNRRA in post-war Greece thus utilized a logic where preservation of the nation came through relief while modernization of the country came through rehabilitation.

Exploring NEF's ethos of relief and rehabilitation is vital due to its collaboration with UNRRA's Greece Mission. This partnership effectively connects the interwar and Cold-War periods by providing a glimpse into joint relief and rehabilitation strategies through the lens of education. This chapter will thus examine the continuities, changes, and relevance of UNRRA's Greek Mission through analysis of the top-down articulation of UNRRA, NEF's civilizational education model and imagined conceptions of rehabilitation before concluding with a case study on Emilie Willms, a NEF nurse who worked on the ground.

The shadows of Greek interwar modernization

The international and national backdrop to UNRRA's Greek Mission centres on the combined interests of Western organizations during the interwar. At their core, these external actors articulated and addressed early categories of underdevelopment in urban, rural and civilizational terms. The work was part of a cooperative process of preservation and modernization at the same time.¹⁰ International and national actors of Greek modernization attempted to preserve the ideas of Classical Greece, notably its people and geography, by connecting them to the Greek nation-state and Western civilization. Modernization was pursued to expand rural land settlement allowing the state to redeem more Greeks from the surrounding nations. The Greek village thus became a location to stem the rural to urban population flow or situate them rurally. At the same time, however, the village and its people required socio-economic reconstruction to keep them rural. Nicole Sackley refers to these sights as transnational impositions where the village became a place for engineering and reengineering.[11] Collectively, missionary, philanthropic and voluntary actors attempted to carry out this mission through their expertise in rural education and US extension practices. Past civilizational education programmes were part of a welfare approach that continued with UNRRA.[12] In doing so, UNRRA inherited the ethos of former missionary work and philanthropic foundations, giving UNRRA a dominant Western and precisely US orientation.

Post-1945 relief and rehabilitation administered through UNRRA continued to address Greece's incomplete interwar modernization schemes. The interwar plans included socio-economic integration of the resettled population in newly acquired Macedonia, Greece, following the forced exchange of populations between Greece and Turkey, as part of the Treaty of Lausanne (1923). Additionally, the modernization schemes that continued the Greek national project incorporated Anglo-American political, trade and financial alignments. The Greek government took out loans from British and American banks to pay for assistance for the rural and urban modernization schemes. The infrastructure improvements included reclaiming rural land to settle most of the new population and improving Athens's water access; American construction firms carried both out. Then welfare needs of the population were addressed partially through Western philanthropic organizations, such as the International Red Cross, American Red Cross, American Women's Hospitals, Rockefeller Foundation and the Near East Relief (and the NEF, post-1930), working through the League of Nations' Refugee Settlement Commission (1925–30) and the Greek government. The ecumenical interests, Greek American interests, Anglo-American relations, US rural extension service, US land-grant college association and US Public Health education (and extension to Greece) gave UNRRA further distinct US interests. Many of these same actors continued their interwar work through UNRRA.

The interwar history of Anglo-American socio-economic leadership also continued to guide the Greek national project. Eftihia Voutira and Davide Rodogno regard the changes to interwar Greece assistance as part of a social and economic self-sufficiency language beginning with the Refugee Settlement Commission (RSC, 1925–30) of the League of Nations. The forced resettling of Ottoman Christians during the interwar, financial agreements with British and American banks, and philanthropic assistance transitioned ideas of humanitarian assistance to one of national development for a greater Greece, both geographic and demographic. The Anglo-American transition to nation-building left Greece economically and politically tied to Western actors for assistance in settling the new Greek population of 1.2 million, or a 20 per cent increase. The financial agreements ensured that Greece paid for its assistance, while philanthropy-funded programmes with the slogan 'helping Greeks help themselves'.[13] The international economic depression led to shrinking assistance programmes and national austerity as the Greek economy's rural/urban regional self-help was simultaneously pursued. Although limited, the modernization tethered Greece financially and politically to British and American goals, largely incongruent with the new population's geographic and economic familiarity.[14] Greece's political system was marked by clientelism and unable to achieve the national self-sufficiency goals complicating the situation further.[15] Then, following the Second World War, UNRRA's Greek Mission continued exogenous Anglo-American direction through financing relief and rehabilitation and guiding government legislation. The Greek government held the responsibility to distribute relief resources, increasing national political power and the ability to continue clientele relationships through relief breaking with interwar assistance.[16]

Regarding UNRRA's expertise in Greece, proximity to the Western institutions served as a path to access twentieth-century public health knowledge in medical, health education and sanitation practices.[17] NEF nurse Emilie Willms' work with UNRRA represents the evolution of a technical assistant prototype in the cyclical travel of knowledge, beginning during the interwar with American Women's Hospital.[18] Davide Rodogno and Francesca Piana follow the work of Willms' mentors and predecessors education through 'discriminatory and civilizational postures'.[19] The context amounted to sharing a schematic of the shape and form segregated education could take abroad as part of UNRRA's actions in Greece, continuing individual and organization civilizational postures. The continuation of Willms' interwar rural education work adapted to UNRRA's Greek Mission among populations in Eastern Levant refugee camps, Greek Islands and Greece's mainland. The circumstances included nursing education, human rehabilitation and children's education as three elements already embedded in NEF's model, illustrating how the civilizational divide would approach Greek reconstruction.

UNRRA's medical, public health and homemaking education outreach illustrate the conflict's international interests in rehabilitating the nation.

The implementation continues to hold relevance and power today, given that the interwar ideas for the 'strategic village' turned into Cold-War technical assistance.[20] Cooperation between NEF and UNRRA helped articulate the ideological war as the Western camp attempted to safeguard Greece's development and modernization from the threat of communism. During UNRRA's mandate, rural education took on new meaning as organizations, scenarios and difficulties transformed education programmes into inoculations against communism, becoming a defining element of the Cold War.

Top-down articulation of UNRRA's Greece mission and the first prisoner of the Cold War

Axis occupation treated Greece and its population as 'sources of raw materials, food, and labour rather than potential political associates'. The weak leadership induced famine and the collapse of the national economy.[21] Many Greek citizens also found refuge in the eastern Mediterranean where Greek royalist leaders remained alongside Allied planning in Cairo. The devastating Axis occupation and resistance left Greece's population fractured and ultimately unable to reconcile political representation with leadership, descending the Greek republic into civil war. The civil war and resistance serve as context to the Greece UNRRA mission (1943–7); they offer a view to better understand the continued Greek *metabolé* (revolution or transformation).[22]

Official US planning for assistance began as soon as Greece was occupied by Italian, German and Bulgarian forces in 1941. US President Franklin Delano Roosevelt appointed former New York Governor Herbert Lehman to initiate US plans for UNRRA in the Office of Foreign Relief and Rehabilitation Operations (OFRRO). Under Lehman, George Xanthaky served as head of the Southern Europe region and brought a history of working with Lehman in US war planning. As a Greek-American, Xanthaky was able to energize the Greek-American diaspora by serving as an extraterritorial ambassador for UNRRA's Greek Mission.[23] The US OFRRO field office in Cairo worked alongside the British military organization, the Middle East Relief and Refugee Agency (MERRA, 1942–4).[24] The organizations' coordination at war's end ensured Britain maintained focus on political and military restoration as well as Greek refugee relief. In contrast, the US OFRRO focused on initial relief leading to rehabilitation.[25] The United States therefore continued Anglo-American interests, which served to counter the growth of communism among the Greek resistance through rehabilitation. As a result, UNRRA remained constrained and operated through clientele relationships with the government unavoidably politicizing the mission.

The political future of Greece began showing the first signs of a conflict while it was still occupied in 1944. The occupiers faced resistance in the villages and mountains as the National Liberation Front (EAM), the Greek People's Liberation Army (ELAS) and National Republican Greek League (EDES) tried to establish their dominance. EAM/ELAS functioned as a left-wing communist coalition while EDES was supported and funded by the British. When the Germans fled Greece in 1944, it was due to the advance of Allied forces and the resistance movement's success in Greece. Meanwhile, the British oversaw and supported the Lebanon agreement establishing a temporary Greek coalition government permitting communist political representation among the National Liberation Front and National Popular Liberation Army. The political deal continued precedents of authoritarian governance through leaders who favoured Anglo-American assistance and shared a desire to shield Greece from further communist political engagement.[26] British and American support of Greek resistance during the occupation left Greece as a tinderbox when the resistance coalition attempted to form a separate post-occupation government.

At international level, the Cairo Agreement of 1944 established a consensus between Churchill, Stalin and Roosevelt confirming that Greece remained under Anglo-American influence.[27] When guerrilla warfare broke out in Greece, the Anglo-American camp framed the events as directed by the Soviets and Tito. The early-Cold-War posture resulted in UNRRA and NEF's work in Levantine camps, on the islands, and mainland as crucial locations to act if Greece was to remain intact and aligned with the United States and Western Europe. Between December 1944 and January 1945, the *Dekemvriana* began – a series of skirmishes between the communist and royalist forces backed by the British military. The initial phase of the Greek Civil War started following the demand for the disarmament of ELAS forces to participate in a unity coalition government between communists and Royalists. The communists resigned from the coalition government and began political demonstrations and strikes in Athens and Piraeus. The police used violence in response to the protests, after which EAM countered with their superior support and numbers by occupying Athens. British troops numbering approximately 25,000 intervened to liberate the Acropolis, resulting in two months of fighting.[28] Over 4,000 civilians died in the event, which concluded with the British aerial campaign that forced EAM to withdraw and disarm in exchange for amnesty. A brutal crackdown on leftists followed. Thousands were imprisoned on remote Greek Islands, and tens of thousands were wanted by Greek authorities over the next two years. These events drove the leftists back into the mountains and hardened their political positions. The elections of 1946 confirmed the return of King George II and initiated the final stage of the Greek Civil War, which lasted until 1949. The political breakdown and periods of terror hastened much-needed Greek relief as it narrowly averted famine during UNRRA's early relief assistance. Rehabilitation took a similar path through and following the Civil War.

UNRRA's Greek Mission originated from foundational organizations such as MERRA and OFRRO, providing continuity to a predominantly Anglo-American network of experts. Within UNRRA, cooperation existed alongside tension, where both British (illustrated by MERRA, a military organization) and American (OFRRO, a civilian organization) interests resisted the other's domination. The US role increased following the communists' occupation of Athens in 1944. Then, the British, short on funding, warned the Americans that a takeover was imminent without interference they could no longer provide. The United States responded by funding royalist military forces in the Greek Civil War alongside the bulk of UNRRA assistance. As the civil war ensued, US domestic politics debated funding; the need for security was increasingly incompatible with UNRRA, resulting in funding issues for programmes beyond initial relief assistance between 1944 and 1945.[29] The political relationship concerning rehabilitation increasingly fused it with Western security needs for post-war Greece, effectively securing it as the first prisoner of the Cold War.

NEF's civilizational education for reconstruction

NEF formed in 1930 utilizing Thomas Jesse Jones' ideas of civilizational education as a guide to their rural education.[30] Jones' education scheme focused on agriculture, health, sanitation, and recreational education to socio-economically assimilate people in US colonial contexts, including immigrants, African Americans and autochthonous populations.[31] NEF's use of the model attempted social and economic changes among the newly settled – redeemed – Greek population. In Macedonia and near Athens, where the population settled, Jones' educational ideas were implemented to 'uplift' or reconstruct the communities. The improvements provided meagre economic results and maintained social divisions. The Greek government became closely linked to Western consumption and industry patterns pushing associated assistance further into the countryside. In rural and domestic terms, the programmes formed gender norms. Men and boys worked the farm and received an agricultural education. On the other hand, women received home economics training in nutrition, midwifery, homemaking and recreation. Western ideas of civilization shared through philanthropy formed the ideal relationship between men, women, children, home and farm demonstrating 'the way up' via the NEF ladder.[32]

The Marathon Plains project in Athens' periphery served as an interwar demonstration of modernization, blurring the lines between urban and rural. Additionally, the programme serves as an early example of US international modernization, which brought nations, like Greece, into an American hierarchy of patronage conceptualized like the US frontier.[33] NEF's Marathon project included health, sanitation, agriculture and industry assistants responsible for demonstration work. Alice Carr, veteran AWH and NEF nurse, directed the health and sanitary extension work to control malaria. C. S. Stephanides, US-trained Greek agriculturalist, helped implement the rural agricultural extension projects, such as livestock and crop improvements. A third assistant Priscilla Capps Hill led Near East Industries, which provided work for women and the disabled by creating traditional garments with cultural and historical significance; after manufacturing, the vestments were sent to the United States and sold as traditional Near East attire in New York and Los Angeles. All the Marathon projects combined to create a community demonstration for redeemed Greek's integration.

The American Council of Voluntary Agencies for Foreign Service was established in 1943 to anticipate humanitarian needs and coordinate relief. NEF personnel located within the association's regional subcommittees focused on Greece and the Balkans. At OFRRO's request, NEF's Program Committee began creating lists of 'specialized personnel' to assist in 'relieving starvation, disease, and distress'.[34] Beyond relief NEF reports articulated 'reconstruction' as the approach utilized by their staff. The reconstruction language was used when corresponding with other US agencies, such as the American Red Cross, US department of agriculture and US board of economic warfare.[35] By mid-1943, NEF planning was published in the 'Public Policy Digest' for the National Planning Association. The publication called for US plans and US personnel in economic recovery, because 'the job of outright relief cannot be ended without aiding in getting the first crops in, the wheels of employment started, and the people work'. The plans identified 'six fields of reconstruction activity' in which they had experience: 'Health and sanitation, reconstruction of agriculture, rehabilitation of the rural family, rehabilitation of the urban child, rehabilitation of the working youth, and rehabilitation of the war disabled'.[36] Therefore, NEF's civilizational education work informed their reconstruction language and called for health and sanitation work to pilot relief. The former acted as a catalyst to follow on rehabilitation work.

NEF brought together American domestic interests in business, labour, agriculture, and academia to conceptualize their ambitions and published them with the National Planning Association. The Coordinating Committee of American Agencies in Greece, made up of 'American engineers, agriculturists, educators, bankers, town planners, ship operators, and welfare leaders', outlined and provided planning.[37] First to cooperate were US universities in New York, such as Columbia and Cornell. The universities provided training for international civil servants in relief and rehabilitation. As a national development plan, the cooperation connected US university knowledge with overseas assistance. The coordinated transatlantic plans pushed NEF's role further as a staffing agency. They helped train personnel as international civil servants, surveyed to increase food supplies, and planned how relief and rehabilitation assistance could be partnered with US and Western economies. The supply of experts to participate in NEF/UNRRA sanitation, public health relief as well as agriculture, industry and human rehabilitation therefore served a Western economic system. Additionally, the assistance served as avenues where the language and approach to development were implemented. NEF supplied technical assistance as the prescriptive antidote to the economic effects of war and the UN's inoculation for underdevelopment.[38] The OFRRO, MERRA and American Council of Voluntary Agencies for Foreign Service served as models in the conceptualization of UNRRA's Greek Mission to establish a base for reconstruction.

Veteran NEF staff such as Carr, Stephanides, Hill and others wrote reports planning Greek recovery.[39] Mrs Hill's report called for the transformation of the industry programme to ensure Greeks had adequate clothing, turning the locations into repurposing and redistribution centres. Alice Carr promoted the programme's possible rehabilitation qualities, linking health and industrial clothing workshops.[40] 'The workshops should work in close harmony and cooperation with the medical and health officials ... it is suggested that they might be made the centres of medical work.'[41] The combination of medical rehabilitation with industrial rehabilitation exemplifies how NEF viewed reconstruction as both relief and rehabilitation as UNRRA formed.

Processes of modernization and preservation used by NEF exemplify Greece's political and economic interest through UNRRA work. On the one hand, the latest medical sciences were used to train Greek nurses with updated skills and modern methods, making healthier and more knowledgeable Greek citizens. At the same time, however, they tried to preserve the region's traditional clothing through Near East Industries giving women opportunities to maintain their traditional dress designs. When the Second World War ended the Near East Industries programme, NEF staff reimagined the factories as facilities to sort and redistribute used Western clothing throughout post-war Greece. The programme attempted rehabilitation, where NEF imagined a place to rehabilitate the Greek citizen through the diligent work of reclothing the Greek nation. The used clothing donation came from America and Britain, donated through appeal campaigns. In the process, Greece became an economic extension of the US political economy, relieving the United States of interwar cycles of production. American clothing manufacturers helped Mrs Hill write her reclothing Greece report, which necessitated collecting, transporting and offloading clothing in Greece.[42] Near East Industries would not only provide relief to Greeks with used clothing, but it would also rid the United States of surplus clothing, a relief to US clothing markets. Thus, preserving the Greeks necessitated economic modernization through industrial assistance from the West.

The context allowed NEF's reconstruction language to pivot slightly, utilizing UNRRA's ideas of relief and then rehabilitation through an educational language. The education equated to technical assistance through relief in medical care, sanitation improvements, and then socio-economic rehabilitation training new nurses, sanitarians and youth teachers for the nation's reconstruction. NEF sowed the fabric of US domestic policy to an international role placing Greece's domestic development in dialogue with US internationalism. The domestic practice of civilizational education turned into foreign policy, and in the process 'othered' people and nations labelling them as 'undeveloped', continuing the Greek process of renewal and redemption. The language of education and technical assistance institutionalized a language of progress for others to 'develop' into the modern age.[43] NEF experts, alongside UNRRA planners, continued to provide relief, while developing ideas under the guise of rehabilitation to bring the nation's economy closer to the West. The result was a peculiar form of reconstruction.

Once finalized, three of NEF's six fields of 'reconstruction activity' came to fruition as cooperative programmes with UNRRA. The first area of cooperation included NEF staff implementing health and sanitation in the Eastern Mediterranean MERRA refugee camps for Balkan refugees as MERRA work transitioned to UNRRA. NEF nurse Emilie Willms' UNRRA relief work began in the camps and continued in the Cyclades (Greek Islands) before transitioning to the rehabilitation of Greek hospitals. The second area of cooperation cantered on physical and mental rehabilitation. The final programme began as a cattle rehabilitation programme that transitioned to an artificial insemination programme most closely associated with agricultural technical assistance.[44] All three of these programmes defined and then redefined the role of relief and rehabilitation in NEF cooperative programmes.

Philanthropic visions of post-war Greece: NEF's imagined wartime rehabilitation of *Kali Panagia* (Good Mother) village

NEF communicated a message to its donors and stakeholders which imagined Greece reconstructed. NEF labelled the destruction in Greece as Axis retribution for delaying Hitler's schedule and equated it to a 'vacuum-cleaning policy'. Livestock was looted, villages destroyed and families broken. The view reflected that the Axis occupation of Greece caused a famine and the collapse of the national economy.[45] Greek food reserves, motor transportation, factories, retail, raw materials, hospital and medical supplies were targeted as booty. Most of the Greek countryside, farmers and villagers, were unable to leave, and NEF reported over 1,700 villages destroyed or partially destroyed, lacking roofs due to fire.

Additionally, it meant there were plenty of children without families and homes. As a response, NEF appropriated the work of the Hellenic Branch of NEF, a Greek national organization established following NEF's international staff exodus and as part of Greek nationalization of relief efforts. NEF named the Greek staff who remained 'Hellenic Near East Foundation'.[46] The sister organization helped establish temporary hostel care for children during the occupation. They utilized hostels known as 'Eagle's Nests' as orphanages for children from mountain villages. As the Hellenic Branch focused on essential relief, the NEF concerned itself with 'salvaging children' through nutritional and moral rehabilitation based on 'new knowledge in health and decency'. NEF saw this as an 'educational reconstruction' opportunity among the reported 4,000 schools lost. NEF's international staff believed that Greek villages were redeemable with NEF rehabilitation assistance.

Figure 4.1 illustrates the idea of turning the destruction of *Kali Panagia* into a reconstructed Greek village. The Greek village was redeemable with NEF assistance, which NEF communicated to its donors and stakeholders. The village in the Macedonia region of Greece served as a starting point for NEF to

Figure 4.1 Greece: Relief and Rehabilitation Propaganda, 1942. (C) Near East Foundation – (FA) 406-(RG) 1-(B) 109-(F) Graphs – Burned villages, Greece, 1943–46. Rockefeller Archive Center.

project an image of the village's death, destruction and emptiness that could be reconstructed and made better. The top drawing is set during the occupation, and the other is the rehabilitated village assisted by NEF. The image utilizes children for emotional appeal and as a symbol for the future of Greece. In occupied Greece (top half of the drawing), children were orphaned, parents lost children, spouses were widowed and the village was near disrepair. The new village imagined by NEF presents a different Greek village. In this village, children play, learn and socialize. Their clothes look more orderly with the boys' shirts tucked in, and the girls' hair put up. The village is socially organized, and stability is afforded through well-engineered homes and buildings, including a church and school. NEF's imagination extended beyond the village, envisioning it as part of a more extensive geography with a horizon leading upward, connected to other villages by roads and automobiles along the way. In the conceptualization of the afterimage, the vehicle coming to *Kali Panagia* arrived with technical assistants transporting books, medical supplies, sanitation equipment and seeds, enabling the village to flourish even more.

The relief and rehabilitation of health education: The case of Emilie Willms

Emilie Willms first arrived in Greece in 1929, recruited by the American Women's Hospital (AWH); it was her first time back in Europe since her childhood immigration from Germany. Before she arrived in Greece, she worked in a large US settlement house for Italian immigrants. She applied to a newspaper ad looking for nurses and began working in healthcare rehabilitation in Macedonia, Greece. She worked among Greece's newest population following the phasing out of relief work during the 1920s. Willms' interwar experiences included work alongside NEF's Macedonia plan of 'rural life improvement'. She worked in the AWH American Women's Training School for Nurses in Salonika, Greece. Then, she taught nurses at the Athens Schools of visiting nurses and the Kallithea Normal school. At the latter, Willms' protégés joined the same home welfare centres built by NEF in the Macedonian frontier, transferring the knowledge, and attempting to uplift the population through improved health.[47] By 1938, Willms became AWH head of nursing in Greece. Willms' climbed a socio-economic ladder, beginning work in US settlement houses and then becoming head nurse of AWH in Greece.[48] The educational stages were a common feature of NEF's employees and reappeared through Willms' work with the UNRRA Greece mission.

As the tensions in Europe escalated, Willms' work transitioned from the Macedonian frontier to the hospitals of Athens. During the German occupation, she worked in a hospital under German authority, a difficult task given that Willms herself was a German immigrant to the United States. When her safety became of concern, she returned to the United States, working in the Jersey City Medical Center. She became the medical department supervisor and an instructor of advanced medical nursing at the Jersey City Medical Center School of nursing. The US intermission served as a steppingstone and preparation for the passage back to Greece on a new mission; Willms signed a contract with NEF in 1943, which served as recruitment to UNRRA work where her past experiences in United States, settlement houses, Macedonia and Athens provided an upward trajectory and basis on which to hire her for post-war relief and rehabilitation.

The post-war Greece Willms returned to included physical wreckage, human displacement and economic destruction, all of which found common ground as categories of underdevelopment and needing rehabilitation. Willms' post-war experiences provide a window into the organizations, region and period where she, persistently, because of her expertise, tried to expand, improve and renew a Greek Healthcare system through improved nursing education outside and throughout Greece. UNRRA's Greece mission rooted in Anglo-American and Greek interests presented Willms with early ideological hurdles of the Cold War. As she arrived in late 1943, MERRA still led the relief and refugee efforts as authority transitioned to UNRRA in the Balkans and Eastern Mediterranean.[49] Beginning with her journey back to the region, we get a snapshot of how Emilie Willms perceived the colonized, protectorate and mandated social world.

The journey by plane, ship and lorries retraced British Colonial lines from the British West Indies to South Africa up the Rift Valley of British East African Colonies to the Mediterranean. The travels brought to Willms' attention the reality of indirect rule and perceptions of races different from what she had previously experienced. The experiences were noticeably different enough to reflect on them in her unfinished memoir. In Trinidad, Willms commented on the mixing of races and the excellent position held by several 'Negros and Indians' and that some were allowed to attend nursing schools. In South Africa, Willms noted the differences compared to Trindad in the British West Indies, where South African racial restrictions served as civilizational signposts reading 'For Europeans Only' and 'non-European'. She also noted that the native Zulus and other 'tribes' intermingled with East Indians and 'Mulatos'.[50] The journey through British colonies was noticeably different in her writing, where various forms of segregation merited explication more than a mere mention. Willms' first appointment with her new NEF contract took her to another British Colonial setting. In Cairo, Egypt, the headquarters of both MERRA and OFRRO, Willms' perception of Egyptians centred on behaviour and less on physical characteristics. Egyptians as Muslims were referred to with tropes of the time such as being 'backward', 'lazy', and 'untrustworthy', the reuse of tropes, and derogatory comparisons within the Near East and specifically Greece, were common despite being predominately Orthodox Christian. The civilizational posture paralleled other American NEF employees and perpetuated views of Colonized Africans (a descendant or otherwise) and Muslims (or those who previously lived in Muslim empires) in similar 'underdeveloped' and 'backward' categories.[51] Post-war assistance and colonialism found common ground in the early Cold War to distinguish, rank and segregate.

When Willms arrived in Cairo, she was assigned to work in the Balkan refugee camps throughout the Levant as their administration shifted to UNRRA. The headquarters were in Cairo, but the organization operated refugee camps throughout the region beginning in June 1942, following the occupation of Eastern Europe and the Balkans by the Axis Powers and the Soviet Union. Those who fled Greece to the Eastern Mediterranean were transported to segregated camps in the Eastern Levant, depending on where they came from in the Balkans. The camps were Moses Wells on the Red Sea in Egypt, El Shatt east of the Suez Canal in Egypt, Nuseirat, Gaza in Palestine, and a sorting camp near Aleppo, Syria. Two camps were explicitly used for Greek refugees, Moses Wells and Nuseirat. Moses Wells previously operated as a quarantine camp for Mecca pilgrims, while Nuseirat functioned as an Australian and Polish military base during the war. Willms first travelled to Moses Wells under the Greek management of Commander Major Ralli and noted the camp as 'well organized and disciplined, it was kept clean and had a cheerful atmosphere'.[52] Willms viewed conditions like this as ideal to implement at Camp Nuseirat, in Palestine, her destination.

At Camp Nuseirat (Figure 4.2) in Mandate Palestine's Gaza, over 10,000 (predominately) Greek refugees arrived from Samos and the Dodecanese Islands. The latter were interwar Italian-occupied islands with a substantial Jewish population. The camp population was selected by excluding all men of military age. Boys as young as twelve years old were removed from the population and sent to the Greek armed forces.[53] The MERRA Camps in the Eastern Levant were established by the British military with voluntary agencies (NGOs) operating alongside as UNRRA started work. For example, the Friends Ambulance Unit (FAU) ran the camp's welfare division distributing clothing and shoes, possibly sorted at a former Near East Industries facility. Willms, however, began her work alongside Dr Ruth Parmelee, another former NEF employee, in Camp Nuseirat shortly after refugees started pouring in. The two conducted an

Figure 4.2 Tents at Nuseirat, Southern Palestine. UNRRA's Biggest Camp for Greek Refugees United Nations Relief and Rehabilitation Administration, 1945–8. UNRRA, Photographs, Country Mission Photographs, Middle East – Displaced persons, S-0800-0008.

initial survey finding the camp population had both lice and scabies illustrating poor sanitary conditions and a need for organization and tidiness. The two called for the creation of a receiving area for new camp members. They noted barbed wire was required to fence off the camp, creating a barrier between the local population and the displaced; material to fly-proof nursing stations was needed; and electrical lighting was needed to illuminate the camp. Additionally, diseases such as typhus fever and typhoid concerned Willms and Parmelee as potential health concerns.[54] All medicine was requested for UNRRA to purchase as it took over relief operations.[55]

The camp functioned as a demonstration of health relief and social/national hierarchy. Parmelee and Willms' 'organization and coordination' efforts resulted in three clinics established, each with a Greek nurse and an Italian orderly for the Italian-speaking population. Parmelee and Willms then built up the camp's medical capabilities. Two examples are the disinfection of new residents and their inoculation from smallpox. The disinfection process had to be done the 'old-fashioned way' without DDT, working with disinfectors, injectors and scabies scrubbers. In the second example, after completing an initial vaccination effort of smallpox in the camp, an outbreak occurred in the surrounding Arab population; accordingly, the vaccination had to be re-administered among the displaced island population. The local Gazans' fate was not mentioned. Parmelee and Willms sourced the medication locally from Tel Aviv to do so. Willms and UNRRA's attempts to create order and sanitation in the Camp alongside fixing bodies through vaccination and medication clarifies how a segregated camp served as an initial sight of relief demonstration and social rehabilitation. Camp Nuseirat as an orderly space illustrated 'the way up' through American and British organizations and health science initiated by governing Greece's redeemable bodies.

Willms' memoir noted the need for education among the refugees – both general youth and adult health education – with schools and classes still needing to be established. In this regard, Willms noted that a 'Greek-born nurse', Penelope Kalergi, who studied at New York Presbyterians Training School, organized classes to help train nurses in the camp. Then Greek Red Cross set up a system to rotate nurses throughout the camps in the eastern Levant. Regarding youth education, the President of Pierce College (a school close to Athens, Greece) arrived at the camp and organized classes and training for boys and girls under fourteen, roughly 1,500 in total. Among the remaining refugees, instructors and former teachers were chosen. In Camp Nuseirat segregated education initiated Greek rehabilitation for Greece.

A final situation in Nuseirat indicates how the demarcation of relief and security in a wartime camp is easily blurred. One day after returning from a medical supply run from Gaza to Tel Aviv, Willms and Parmelee were asked to speak to Camp Nuseirat's commanding officer, who told them of a communist uprising in the camp while they were away. Those responsible for causing the uprising were taken to jail in Gaza, outside the centre. The camp's commanding officer asked the American nurses if they would be willing to search and question the women, and both accepted the task. It was peculiar to ask nurses to perform security tasks, but they were chosen because they were the only women 'available' to do so; they were also the only women trusted to do the interview. Nursing for Willms was a privileged position as an American. Because of this, she was entrusted with the governance of the camp. Security measures such as searching and questioning the camp's women obscured her role as a nurse and pointed to the possibility of new gendered roles NEF women could serve. The example clarifies how the lines between relief, rehabilitative education and security were often blurred.[56]

Between 1944 and 1945, two changes occurred. First, the transition of the camps from MERRA to UNRRA was completed, so members of the various organizations like NEF with employees seconded to MERRA continued their work with UNRRA. As a result, both Parmelee and Willms made their way to Cairo, waiting for their next assignment. Second, the Dodecanese islands were liberated in 1945, with the surviving population, excluding the Jewish people, eventually returned to Greece.

> To the refugees, now in better health, Spring [1944] brought a little more joy of living. They walked straighter and stronger with an air of self-respect and renewed hope. Rehearsals for Greek Independence Day (March 25th) and plans for the Greek Easter filled the air. From the fields near by dandelion greens were gathered and then stored on tent floors. Later they would be washed bit by bit and made into a salad or cooked vegetables. Strung on the barbed wires around the compound were freshly laundered clothes, their varied bright colors making a cheerful contrast against the dead white sand and tents.[57]

A final point on the Nuseirat camp that should not be lost is that NEF's participation in governing Dodecanese Islanders into Greek citizens occurred within the British Mandate of Palestine as tension and conflict between Jewish and Palestinian populations reached a crescendo. The ephemeral experience of NEF employees working there throughout 1944 was the third time NEF's American employees cooperated with the British in colonial contexts and the second segregating within mandate Palestine.

The nexus of relief and security provides clear continuity from one colonial context to the next for social reconstruction intent on homogenizing or accommodating segregation. As the displaced Balkan population was relocated, the British implemented a policy of admitting as many Jewish refugees as possible to Palestine. It was noted, 'for security, checking these refugees occurred in the Palestine Camps'. UNRRA inherited this policy and continued sorting people in the name of security. In the years to come, the location became the Gaza refugee camp (and later the Gaza strip as part of a future Palestine). From far beyond the village, Palestinians sought refuge as Israel used the site to confine and settle those who didn't fit within their homogenized borders.

The mobility of UNRRA's work played a crucial role in providing relief in the eastern Mediterranean. A ship named IMERRA, constructed in Egypt, arrived in Greece in 1944 to escort Willms on her next journey from the camps to Greek Island relief. The mercy ship, a fair-weather schooner, was intended to fill the diverse needs of UNRRA and other agencies as they administered health relief and surveyed for rehabilitation. A series of surveys indicated the Greek islands' populations suffered from tuberculosis, malaria, tick fever, oedema and malnutrition. The island of Naxos received DDT, for which NEF paid, and Atrabrin (anti-malaria medication) was provided on the island of Areos. The last of the Cyclades to be freed was the Island of Milos. Willms joined the US Navy, British military and other UNRRA staff who met the 600 captured German soldiers on the island. It was the first assistance that included clothing and medicine for the island's 6,500 inhabitants since the occupation began. The UNRRA staff surveyed the population finding many residents had been living in the island's caves. The island's hospital staff was diminished and lacked nurses or midwives. There were six doctors, of whom five were retired and a few physicians. NEF and UNRRA following relief proceeded to medical rehabilitation as a priority. Immediately, a graduate nurse was left on the island, as had also been done on the island of Syros. Relief work occurred through fixing the population proceeding directly to training future nurses intended to rehabilitate the island population.

Willms' departure from Milos was not the end of her work with the island's population. In Athens, she directed the Civilian Rehabilitation Center for the Physically Disabled. Over 10,000 mines were deposited on the island by the Germans, and Willms continued work among the Milos population as they came to the centre with missing limbs. Milos Island, like Camp Nuseirat, represented an isolated yet clear vision of what rehabilitation beyond relief in the aftermath of war looked like. The remainder of NEF's work in Greece as part of UNRRA was located on the peninsula and, therefore, was broader and more directly related to developing Cold-War security.

In 1945, UNRRA was funded to extend the organization's operation through 1946 and 1947.[58] By then, Britain was unable to finance or support Greece's recovery. Anglo-American cooperation in Greece indicates that the United States was 'suspicions Britain was using UNRRA as a till [bank] for proxies in Greece and elsewhere'.[59] The frustration was held by NEF Foreign Director Laird Archer, who eventually quit UNRRA and retired from NEF.[60] In this context, Willms' work in Greece continued after UNRRA's mandate in rehabilitation at the centre for the disabled in Athens. NEF also established an Athens boys home based on a US model for homeless boys. The ends of the Second World War and Greece's Civil War are complicated by how children are portrayed in these homes. They attempted to be secular on paper while participating in political segregation of the population through othering. For instance, communists required isolation in post-Second World War situations, including camps and rehabilitation centres. Parallel camps administered by NEF implemented industrial rehabilitation using the clothing distribution centres as places to heal physical harm and repair the individuals for the Greek nation allied to the West.

NEF and UNRRA sources clearly illustrate shifting tensions in Greece between German occupation, liberation and the post-war ideological battle. In Athens, Willms' UNRRA work repeatedly attempted to establish improved nursing schools. Yet, in the new context, she was attacked for not accomplishing what she set out to do. One heated discussion over the improvement work resulted in Willms being told by a Greek co-worker to 'Remember your job at "Elpis" is no longer pre-war but post-war … You push for supplies and equipment, but keep your hands off nursing and nurses'.[61] She was now being relegated to relief as Greeks took on rehabilitation work. Willms reacted to the situation by trying to improve facilities. With the help of Laird Archer and his replacement Harold B. Allen at NEF, they managed to get NEF to pay for the plumbing and sanitary repairs in the Nurses' Residence, including supplies and labour. UNRRA's Colonel Wright and malaria experts used DDT on the entire facility as part of the Rockefeller Foundation's cooperation with UNRRA to implement the most extensive Malaria control programme throughout Greece.[62] Nonetheless, criticism increased, and she called a meeting of the nurses. During the meeting, a coup was orchestrated against her, to which she was far outnumbered. Then, there was vandalism at night, destroying nursing equipment. She had a meeting with the instigating party, indicating she had acquired many supplies (paid for by NEF and the department of nurses at Columbia University) that were on their way over from the United States. She hoped the shipment would address the group's grievances if it arrived. After the event, Willms continued to implement planned work and received apologies for bad behaviour. 'We don't know what got into us', they said, to which she responded, 'That's all right … I do. Communism is bred from misery and you've had more than your share. Let bygones be bygones and forget it.'[63] Willms was again transferred at the needs of Greece and the request of Queen Sophia and the president of the Children's Hospital board of managers.

At the new hospital, Willms' implemented a series of improvements after arriving and being very unhappy with the conditions. She again tried and improved the level of the training at the school at the same time expansion was underway. She was again accused of mismanaging this programme. However, this time, she was charged with placing training nurses in housing for maids, an affront to the hierarchy she helped construct. However, issues in UNRRA between the British and Americans stalled funding, and NEF was not able to continue the project.[64] Relief and rehabilitation work that NEF performed primarily reflected those avenues of domesticity afforded to American women; Willms' actions reflect improvement in socio-economic opportunities for women, where rehabilitation work offered Western women a civilizational platform that both empowered them and allowed them to replicate similar patriarchal gender relations with other cultures.[65] The rhetoric used reflected Americanization at home and US civilizing abroad as part of a much larger American frontier.

Conclusion

Davide Rodogno illustrates that Greek rehabilitation carried out during the interwar served as a 'mantra of Promethean state-builders, empire builders, and colonial rulers' with shared architectural goals among humanitarian and development actors.[66] American Philanthropy in Greece included the Near East Foundation's view of reconstruction work as the rebuilding of places, regions, and societies – such as the US South following the Civil War – as well as a socio-economic undertaking from rural to urban.[67] The rollout of first relief and then rehabilitation as part of UNRRA's mandate in Greece amounted to political preservation and socio-economic reconstruction. The language of self-help, long utilized by scientific philanthropy, empowered through training and 'building ladders for the aspiring' to 'help them help themselves'.[68] At the same time, self-help was used politically to isolate and reform communist sympathies through a 'carrot and stick' approach as the Greek economy was marshalled from one of resistance to Western economic cooperation and social submission. The post-First World War lesson of planning and coordination combined with interwar economic activity aligned Greece with the West internationally. Internally, however, rising support for communism paralleled increased resistance to post-war programmes of relief and rehabilitation, necessitating modification and continuation. Thus, technical assistance became the educational school within the ecosystem of reconditioning individuals, communities and societies to the Western socio-economic model.[69]

A year after NEF's experience with UNRRA ended, H. B. Allen started creating a new document that outlined ideal qualities of workers best suited to join NEF as they participated in the Cold War. New American employees needed to work with 'like minded Europeans' to counter fears imagined of a Greece not part of the 'the Free World'. NEF's work, referred to as 'the way up', assumed there was always a higher pinnacle for the local population. The training was provided first to NEF's US staff and only then extended to local staff through training centres. The process allowed the slow transfer of knowledge but kept paths nationally inspired, gendered and separated by age. Thus, NEF training became a key component of what would become a Western ladder.

Within NEF, H. B. Allen, the foundation's unofficial historical biographer of inter-war and early-Cold-War programmes, described their work with UNRRA in Greece as a choice of either an 'evolution from within or revolution from without'.[70] The language served as a post-factual justification for NEF's programme success in Greece, including health guidance and medical training. The new post-war programmes in Greece portray an evolution of NEF's interwar concentrations in health, agriculture, sanitation and home economics. The change came in education, which increasingly served a security role within foundations. The resulting programmes compromised their creativity with national security needs creating a blend of assistance to address the threat of communism and the influences of the Soviet Union.

NEF's work as part of UNRRA's mandate were not the first-time that employees sought to give short-term relief to avoid perpetuating penury conditions. Similarly, the continuation of humanitarian work among the blind, deaf and handicapped children shifted to training Greeks, further sharing of the Hull House model coupled with a Western economy.[71] The Kaisariani community field Recreation demonstration also became a site for creation and re-creation following the war. Recreation and sporting activities took on new roles as places where NEF fears of communism could be addressed.[72] By the end of 1947, NEF staff set up summer camps and youth welfare centres to direct youth towards employment. NEF noted that 'unemployment, hunger, frustration, and despair provided fertile ground for communism', necessitating sites like Kaisariani as a 'chief point of attack'. The rehabilitation ideas coming from the rehabilitation of amputees in the United States played a role in establishing repair for those who fell victim to the long guerrilla war between communist insurgents and those Greek and Western forces fighting for capitalism. One implication of the type of work then promoted and provided by NEF in Greece for these recoverees included employing them in sorting centres for donated clothes from the United States to Greece.

As an organization ahead of its time, NEF set standards for flexibility in working with communities. At the time, corporate social responsibility was not yet an industry standard. Yet, the projection of the relationships between the social and economic ecosystems enabled NEF to remain adaptable to changes and constantly propagate a view of their work that was not always representative. While NEF was not a humanitarian organization, they continued to appropriate a language of relief and a humanitarian mission, claiming new terminology based on science, planning and management. The alchemy of past humanitarian assistance, missionary work and extension of technical assistance from the university amounted to 'proto-development'.[73] The proto-development also included elements of technical assistance, creating proto-social responsibility *sans frontiers* for US and Western business and industry interests.[74] Unfortunately, the Western-constructed 'free world' remained full of barriers.

NEF, aware of its status as one of the few organizations with a pre-existing legacy of relief and rehabilitation, instrumentalized these in UNRRA to promote work, actors and significance. For example, relief served as a strategic tool for NEF, enabling it to draw on past experiences when needed. In doing so, NEF secured an ethos of compassion regardless of performed work. In the spectacle of post-war rehabilitation, funding and programmes became tokens that NEF and the United States were on the right side of history. NEF actors viewed relief programmes as a necessary base for socio-economic reconstruction. To the corporate donors and architects of NEF programmes, philanthropy and international organizations helped find a compromise between US and local actors, alleviating the responsibility of official US actions. To the consumers of propaganda, primarily the American religious communities, including Greek-Americans, UNRRA served as a promotional platform to raise awareness for preserving 'an ancient land's people'. The label became a mantra of 'under development' in NEF language used to describe its work in Greece and the Near East.

Additionally, in this narrative, the redeemable Greeks as victims in this region had to be preserved to not come under the influence of communism. US philanthropy became a way to socio-economically rehabilitate and modernize their relationship with their environment based on US economic security. Ultimately, work in Greece would also help build a foundation of knowledge and expertise for organizations like the World Health Organization and the Food and Agriculture Organization. Additionally, the security needs of the Economic Cooperation Administration (ECA) that began its work in Greece in 1948 continued UNRRA's work. A US economic mission went on to study Greece's needs, resulting in the Truman doctrine, and enabled large amounts of aid to continue rehabilitating Greece and win the civil war.[75] American rhetoric towards the region was hardened by taking a security approach that would lead to the ECA and, succeeding it, the Mutual Security Administration. In the process, Greece was ruled by right-wing governments for the next twenty-five years, which contributed to Cold-War policies throughout.

Notes

1. Mark Mazower, 'Reconstruction: The Historiographical Issues', *Past & Present*, 210, no. suppl_6 (1 January 2011), 17–28; F. Cooper, 'Reconstructing Empire in British and French Africa', *Past & Present,* 210, no. Supplement 6 (1 January 2011), 196–210; Jessica Reinisch, 'Internationalism in Relief: The Birth (and Death) of UNRRA', *Past & Present*, 210, no. Supplement 6 (1 January 2011), 258–89; Jessica Reinisch, 'Introduction: Relief in the Aftermath of War', *Journal of Contemporary History*, 43:3 (2008), 371–404; Silvia Salvatici, '"Help the People to Help Themselves": UNRRA Relief Workers and European Displaced Persons', *Journal of Refugee Studies*, 25:3 (1 September 2012), 428–51.
2. Davide Rodogno, *Against Massacre: Humanitarian Interventions in the Ottoman Empire, 1815–1914: The Emergence of a European Concept and International Practice, Human Rights and Crimes against Humanity* (Princeton, NJ: Princeton University Press, 2012).
3. Davide Rodogno, *Night on Earth: A History of International Humanitarianism in the Near East, 1918–1930* (Cambridge: Cambridge University Press, 2021).
4. Karine V. Walther, *Sacred Interests: The United States and the Islamic World, 1821–1921* (Chapel Hill: The University of North Carolina Press, 2015); Joseph L. Grabill, *Protestant Diplomacy and the Near East: Missionary Influence on American Policy, 1810–1927* (Minneapolis: University of Minnesota Press, 1971).
5. Mark Mazower, *Greek Revolution: 1821 and the Making of Modern Europe* (London: Allen Lane an imprint of Penguin Books, 2021), 418–19; Robert H. Bremner, *Giving: Charity and Philanthropy in History* (Taylor and Francis, 1994), https://doi.org/10.4324/9780203790724.
6. Walther, *Sacred Interests*, 51; Eric D. Weitz, 'From the Vienna to the Paris System: International Politics and the Entangled Histories of Human Rights, Forced Deportations, and Civilizing Missions', *The American Historical Review*, 113:5 (2008), 1333; Brenda L. Marder, *Stewards of the Land: The American Farm School and Modern Greece*, East European Monographs, no. 59 (Boulder : New York: East European Quarterly ; distributed by Columbia University Press, 1979), 66.
7. Mitchell L. Stevens, Cynthia Miller-Idriss and Satanāy Ḫālid Šāmī, *Seeing the World: How US Universities Make Knowledge in a Global Era*, Princeton Studies in Cultural Sociology (Princeton: Princeton University Press, 2018), 9–26; Walther, *Sacred Interests*, 5–23.
8. Merle Eugene Curti, *American Philanthropy Abroad*, Society and Philanthropy Series (New Brunswick, NJ: Transaction Books, 1988); Robert L. Daniel, *American Philanthropy in the Near East, 1820–1960* (Athens: Ohio University Press, 1970).
9. Mona Domosh, 'Practising Development at Home: Race, Gender, and the "Development" of the American South', *Antipode*, 47:4 (2015), 915–41.

10 Amalia Ribi Forclaz (ed.), 'Shaping the Future of Farming the International Labour Organization and Agricultural Education, 1920s to 1950s', *Agricultural History Review*, 65:2 (2017), 339; Cyrus Schayegh, 'The Interwar Germination of Development and Modernization Theory and Practice: Politics, Institution Building, and Knowledge Production between the Rockefeller Foundation and the American University of Beirut', *Geschichte Und Gesellschaft*, 41:4 (2015), 649–84.

11 Nicole Sackley, 'The Village as Cold War Site: Experts, Development, and the History of Rural Reconstruction', *Journal of Global History*, 6:3 1 January 2011, 481–504.

12 Dimitra Giannuli, '"Repeated Disappointment": The Rockefeller Foundation and the Reform of the Greek Public Health System, 1929–1940', *Bulletin of the History of Medicine*, 72:1 (1 March1998), 47–72.

13 Rodogno, *Night on Earth*, 259; citing Voutira, Eftihia, When Greeks Meet other Greeks: The Long Term Consequences of the Lausanne Treaty and Policy Issues in the Contemporary Greek Context, Paper presented at the conference The Compulsory Exchange of Populations between Greece and Turkey: Assessment of the Consequences of the Treaty of Lausanne, 75th Anniversary, September 1998.

14 Rodogno, *Night on Earth*, 432.

15 Georgios Kritikos, 'The Agricultural Settlement of Refugees: A Source of Productive Work and Stability in Greece, 1923–1930', *Agricultural History*, 79:3 (2005), 321–46.

16 George Woodbridge, *UNRRA: The History of the United Nations Relief and Rehabilitation Administration*, vol. II (New York: Columbia University Press, 1950), 101–3.

17 Health Organization of the League of Nations, Rockefeller Foundation's International Health Board, American Red Cross, and American Women's Hospital; Giannuli, 'Repeated Disappointment'.

18 Rodogno, *Night on Earth*, 114.

19 Rodogno, *Night on Earth*, 288; Francesca Piana, 'Maternalism and Feminism in Medical Aid: The American Women's Hospitals in the United States and in Greece, 1917–1941', in Esther Möller, Johannes Paulmann and Katharina Stornig (eds.), *Gendering Global Humanitarianism in the Twentieth Century: Practice, Politics and the Power of Representation*, Palgrave Macmillan Transnational History Series (Cham: Palgrave Macmillan, 2020), 85–114.

20 Sackley, 'The Village as Cold War Site'.

21 Mark Mazower, *Inside Hitler's Greece: The Experience of Occupation, 1941–44* (New Haven: Yale University Press, 1993).

22 Kostas Kalimtzis, *Aristotle on Political Enmity and Disease: An Inquiry into Stasis* (New York: State University of New York Press, 2000), 105.

23 Specifically Xanthaky dealt with the transition from military to civilian control, voluntary assistance actors like NEF, and, subsequently, the Soviets; George

Woodbridge (ed.), *U.N.R.R.A. The History of the United Nations Relief and Rehabilitation Administration*, vol. I (New York: Columbia University Press, 1950), 200–214; Woodbridge, *UNRRA*, vol. II, 3–16.

24 Woodbridge, *UNRRA*, vol. II, 81–4.
25 Woodbridge, *UNRRA*, vol. II, 86–9.
26 Bruce Robellet Kuniholm, *The Origins of the Cold War in the Near East: Great Power Conflict and Diplomacy in Iran, Turkey, and Greece* (Princeton, NJ: Princeton University Press, 1980).
27 Woodbridge, *UNRRA*, vol. II, 3.
28 Laird Archer, 'Activities of the Commission during the Insurrection. (December 1944–January 1945)', 1946, Laird Archer Papers, MC 454, Box 5, Folders 1, University of Arkansas Special Collections.
29 Richard Clogg, *A Concise History of Greece*, 2nd ed., Cambridge Concise Histories (Cambridge: Cambridge University Press, 2006), 122–41.
30 Thomas Jesse Jones, *Essentials of Civilisation: A Study of Social Values* (New York: Henry Holt, 1929).
31 Robert Vitalis, *America's Kingdom: Mythmaking on the Saudi Oil Frontier* (London: Verso, 2009), 39–40; Jonathan Zimmerman, *Innocents Abroad: American Teachers in the American Century* (Cambridge, MA: Harvard University Press, 2008), 195; Andrew Zimmerman, *Alabama in Africa: Booker T. Washington, the German Empire, and the Globalization of the New South*, America in the World (Princeton, NJ: Princeton University Press, 2010), 179, 202–4, 207, 218; Kenneth James King, *Pan-Africanism and Education : A Study of Race Philanthropy and Education in the Southern States of America and East Africa*, Oxford Studies in African Affairs (Oxford: Clarendon Press, 1971), 22–3, 180, 207–8, 251.
32 *The Way Up: Near East Foundation at Work in Underdeveloped Areas* (New York: Near East Foundation, 1952).
33 David Ekbladh, *The Great American Mission: Modernization and the Construction of an American World Order*, America in the World (Princeton, NJ: Princeton University Press, 2010); Vitalis, *America's Kingdom*.
34 Laird Archer and Edward C. Miller, 'Personnel Training for Reconstruction Service in the Near East', 26 February 1943, (C)Near East Foundation-(RG)1-(S)10-(FA)406-(B)126-(F)Personnel Training, Rockefeller Archive Center.
35 Gunn Selskar, 'Selskar Gunn to Laird Archer', 19 July 1943, S-1271-0000-0161 (NEF – Mr Archer, etc.), United Nations Archives, United Nations Relief and Rehabilitation Administration.
36 'Near East Foundation Planning', *Public Policy Digest – National Planning Association*, June 1943, Near East Foundation Files-RG1-S10-FA406-B164-F5, Rockefeller Archive Center.
37 Carl W. Blegen, 'The United States and Greece' (1948), 172, Series V: Miscellaneous Box 28 – Folder 1 & 2 Political Manuscripts, American School of Classical Studies

at Athens, Archives, Carl W. Blegen Papers (Αμερικανική Σχολή Κλασικών Σπουδών στην Αθήνα, Αρχείο Carl W. Blegen).

38 Ekbladh, *The Great American Mission*, 87–8.
39 Henry A. Hill, 'Emergency Relief in Greece after Liberation, Preliminary Plan', 1943, UNA, S-1271-0000-0036 (Mission Report); Priscilla Capps Hill and Alice G. Carr, 'General Study of the Problem of Reclothing the Greek People after the War', 1943; Alice G. Carr, 'Emergency Medical Centers as an Aid to Relieving Congestion In Public Dispensaries' (UNRRA, March 1943), UNA, S-1247-0000-0036 (Mission Report Emergency Medical Centers), United Nations Archives, United Nations Relief and Rehabilitation Administration; Robert E. Monks, 'Memorandum on Restoration of Communications in Greece' (UNRRA, December 1942).
40 Hill and Carr, 'General Study of the Problem of Reclothing the Greek People after the War'.
41 Ibid., 55.
42 Ibid.
43 Jan Nederveen Pieterse, 'Dilemmas of Development Discourse: The Crisis of Developmentalism and the Comparative Method', *Development and Change*, 22:1 (1991), 5–29.
44 Laird Archer, 'Laird Archer to George Xanthaky', 22 July 1943, UNA, S-1241-0000-0179 (Executive Office).
45 Mazower, *Inside Hitler's Greece*.
46 Laird Archer, 'Foreign Director's Report', Annual Report (Athens: Near East Foundation, May 1945), 8.
47 Emilie Willms, 'A First Graduating Class: At the American Women's Hospitals School in Greece', *The American Journal of Nursing*, 30:10 (1930), 1281–3.
48 'News about Nursing', *The American Journal of Nursing*, 38:4 (1938), 478–90.
49 MERRA operated until May 1944, when UNRRA absorbed it.
50 Ethel S. Beer and Emilie Willms, *The Greek Odyssey of an American Nurse: Adapted from the Unfinished Autobiography of Emilie Willms, R. N* (Mystic, Conn: L. Verry, 1972), 45–7.
51 Rodogno, *Night on Earth*, 289.
52 Beer and Willms, *The Greek Odyssey of an American Nurse*, 49.
53 'Nuseirat Camp' (MERRA & UNRRA, 10 May 1944), UNA, S-1312-0000-0022-00001 (Middle East Relief and Refugee Administration, MERRA).
54 Beer and Willms, *The Greek Odyssey of an American Nurse*, 49–54.
55 Lt. Col. Green, 'Perimeter Fencing – Nuseirat Refugee Camp' (MERRA & UNRRA, 10 June 1944), UNA, S-1309-0000-0050-00001 (Headquarters Balkan Mission – Policy Nuseirat).
56 Rodogno, *Night on Earth*, 172; 457–61.
57 Beer and Willms, *The Greek Odyssey of an American Nurse*, 52–3.
58 Reinisch, 'Internationalism in Relief', 103.

59 Ekbladh, *The Great American Mission*, 88.
60 Laird Archer, *Balkan-Tragedy*, Military Affairs (Manhattan, KS: Military Affairs, 1977).
61 Beer and Willms, *The Greek Odyssey of an American Nurse*, 69.
62 Katerina Gardikas, 'Relief Work and Malaria in Greece, 1943–1947', *Journal of Contemporary History*, 43:3 (1 July 2008), 493–508, https://doi.org/10.1177/0022009408091837.
63 Beer and Willms, *The Greek Odyssey of an American Nurse*, 74.
64 Ibid., 78.
65 Rodogno, *Night on Earth*, 275 Citing; Louise Michele Newman, *White Women's Rights: The Racial Origins of Feminism in the United States* (New York: Oxford University Press, 1999), 7–8.
66 Rodogno, *Night on Earth*, 10–12.
67 Domosh, 'Practising Development at Home'; Barclay Acheson, 'A New Approach to Old Problems', 1930s, (C)Near East Foundation-(FA)406-(RG)1-(S)12-(B)001-(F)008, Rockefeller Archive Center.
68 Robert H. Bremner, *American Philanthropy*, 2nd ed., The Chicago History of American Civilization (Chicago: University of Chicago Press, 1988), 173.
69 Rodogno, *Night on Earth*, 278.
70 H. B. Allen, *Rural Reconstruction in Action, Experience in the Near and Middle East* (Ithaca, NY: Cornell University Press, 1953).
71 Rodogno, *Night on Earth*, 272.
72 Ibid., 498.
73 Schayegh, 'The Interwar Germination of Development and Modernization Theory and Practice'.
74 Rodogno, *Night on Earth*, 467.
75 C. M. Woodhouse, *Modern Greece: A Short History*, 5th ed., revised (London: Faber and Faber, 1998), 258.

5

Looking at refugees: Relief and rehabilitation in UNRRA/CNRRA photographic representations of refugees in post-war China†

Caroline Reeves

Introduction

Since the Second World War the image of the refugee has become well known in the West. What constitutes refugee-ness is clearly recognized: masses of humanity pressed together in abject neediness or in active flight, individuality blurred and 'raw humanity' in stark relief.[1] Since the early twentieth century, photography has been integral in creating this vision of refugee-ness. Bolstered by the media, non-governmental organizations (NGOs) and other humanitarian institutions have promulgated and popularized this visual repertoire. In the past two decades, however, this image of dislocation and its implications for humanitarian agencies and action have been confronted and interrogated.[2] Critics cite humanitarians' complicity in presenting refugees as nameless, helpless victims without agency or individual voice and have condemned this genre of photography.[3] Although the media continues to shorthand the refugee experience through certain visual tropes – masses of displaced persons crowded together; dusty travel; piles of dishevelled luggage; careworn or frantic faces, particularly of children and/or mothers; and more recently, boats spilling humanity into perilous seas – many humanitarian agencies and other humanitarian institutions have tried to move away from this visual stereotyping of suffering to allow refugees their own agency and voice.

But what of arguably the most extensive refugee crisis of the past century, one in which the most significant photographic archives of the event pointedly

† Special thanks to Mr MA Xiao-He at Harvard University's Yenching Library for his extraordinary research aid.

ignores the chaos, tragedy, uncertainty, need and loss of displacement, instead presenting an intentionally filtered and optimistic view of the situation? In the late 1930s and early 1940s, the Chinese experience of the Second World War lasted for eight years (1937–45) and resulted in the dislocation of 80 to 100 million Chinese civilians and the death of 14 to 20 million more.[4] Yet, the photographic record of this crisis created by the United Nations Relief and Rehabilitation Administration (UNRRA)'s national counterpart in China, the Chinese National Relief and Rehabilitation Administration (CNRRA), almost completely excludes images of the hardships and misery caused by these years of war (known regionally as the Second Sino-Japanese War, and in China, as the War of Resistance).[5]

Instead, UNRRA and CNRRA's photographic archive presents a sanitized humanitarian narrative. It is centered not on victims, but on the providers of aid; not on misery, but on materiel; not on suffering, but instead on science; not on far-flung famine, but on a far better future. This imbalance in the photographic record reflects the relative importance that UNRRA and CNRRA leaders from China placed on the two eponymous imperatives of UNRRA's mission: relief and rehabilitation. Although tasked with the succour of refugees, neither UNRRA nor CNRRA focused on the plight of displaced persons as the primary lens of their visual propaganda in China. Both agencies had other public relations and political agendas to further through the presentation of their work. As humanitarian scholar Silvia Salvatici writes about UNRRA's photographic work in Europe, 'UNRRA "public relation stories" were aimed at shaping an altogether different type of narrative [of the WWII refugee experience]. They did not seek to stir up stark emotions. Instead, their purpose was to explain their mission and persuade, reassure, and familiarize the post-war public with a new vision of humanitarians as modern, professional, and thoroughly international.'[6] China's CNRRA had yet another mission: to use the international aid and technology available through UNRRA to build a new China out of the ashes of war, a China more like the countries from which it was taking aid (the United States and Britain). Instead of featuring the distress of the victims, these agencies thus created images that emphasized the agents of relief, the forces of rehabilitation and the bigger, brighter future of a China-to-come.

UNRRA and CNRRA were not alone in downplaying the significance and depths of China's wartime crisis. Although China's involvement in the Second World War is not unknown to world audiences, the extent of suffering and dislocation borne by China's populace during the war has been subsumed by other narratives of the same era. For example, the European refugee crisis became the definitional refugee crisis of the period, so much so that it changed the language surrounding displacement. The legal exclusion of internally displaced people from the 1951 Geneva Convention Relating to the Status of Refugees became so normative that China's roughly 100 million refugees were no longer considered 'refugees' and were thus subsequently systematically excluded from 'refugee history'.[7] Furthermore, the advent of Chinese Communism and the start of the Cold War after 1949 made China's wartime experiences less credible to the West, while in China, the new Chinese Communist Party (CCP) focused on leaving the past, and any Nationalist Party (such as Guomindang, GMD, formerly KMT) involvement, behind. Their focus was instead on the CCP's successes. Although the scale of wartime suffering in China dwarfed that of the European theatre across an equally extensive, culturally and linguistically diverse geographical area, this moment of mass displacement and this refugee experience did and still do not command the same attention or scholarship as the post-war refugee crisis in Europe, nor as other more recent refugee crises.[8]

This lacuna is a serious one. These archives and photographs constitute what Michael Ignatieff calls 'a regime of visual authority'.[9] The marked absence of suffering in this historical 'record' obscures the true history of the period. Yet these images do provide profound insights into contemporaneous attitudes towards China's post-war relief and rehabilitation and what those values meant in action. As we move forward in thinking how we want to portray refugees in the contemporary world – a problem that is not going away any time soon – the CNRRA case provides a cautionary tale for today's revisionists of refugee representation. Bringing China and CNRRA back into the story of UNRRA and the treatment of refugees reveals how not only language but also imagery is manipulated to influence political and administrative action and world opinion. Importantly, it also shows how the amelioration of suffering ('relief') can be subsumed by other prerogatives.

This chapter explores the photographic holdings of CNRRA with special focus on its refugee archive, comparing it to earlier genres of Chinese disaster relief imagery and the wider œuvre of humanitarian photography. In so doing, it reveals the tensions between relief and rehabilitation in post-war Asia as in Europe and uncovers how 'rehabilitation' was understood by the Chinese actors of UNRRA and the CNRRA.

UNRRA in China and the CNRRA

UNRRA was intended to become the main instrument of post-war reconstruction in Europe and Asia. It was mandated to provide 'relief and help in rehabilitation for the victims of German and Japanese barbarism'.[10] Although later historiography would highlight the European efforts of the group, Asia was integral to the UNRRA mission from the start. At the insistence of the United States, China was a founding member in the new administration's central committee, alongside the United States, Britain and the Soviet Union. The inclusion of China in this group was an important coup for China's Nationalist leaders, intent on enhancing China's sovereignty and international status.[11] This concern with China's image to the world would become an important factor in the CNRRA story and the relative balance given to 'relief' versus 'rehabilitation' in the CNRRA photographic lexicon.

UNRRA was formed as the humanitarian arm of a new international order, slated to bring modernization, science and technology to bear on healing the wounds of the war. Headquartered in Washington, DC, with its European regional office in London, UNRRA and its staff worked through country missions, originally including a UNRRA China Mission opened in November 1944 that operated in concert with the Chinese Nationalist government. In January 1945, however, a Chinese partner of UNRRA, the CNRRA was established. Backed by Nationalist president Generalissimo Chiang Kai-shek, American-trained UNRRA Central Committee member Jiang Tingfu (T. F. Tsiang) insisted on this unique arrangement in order to ensure China's sovereignty in determining priorities for and distributing UNRRA aid.[12] The United States, primary funder of the organization, championed the deal, and CNRRA was born. Financier and Nationalist official T. V. Soong, chair of the Special Cabinet Committee on Relief and Rehabilitation, oversaw the organization for the Chinese government.

UNRRA's arrangement in China was unique in the UNRRA administration. As contemporary critic George Kerr notes, 'In Europe the international organization, cooperating with the host countries, retained control of all material supplies for relief and rehabilitation until they reached the point of "end use." Not so in China.'[13] The CNRRA distributed UNRRA aid through a controversial programme of direct sales as well as through relief aid distributed through fifteen regional offices across China and Taiwan; it also managed the agenda of rehabilitation. Meanwhile, UNRRA's own China Office continued to operate first in Chongqing and then from Shanghai, receiving supplies to be transferred to CNRRA, observing CNRRA operations, and providing expertise and personnel to work with CNRRA and the Nationalist government. Both organizations created photographic archives documenting their work.

In its remarkably brief four years of operation UNRRA distributed over $4 billion globally. Of this total, the largest portion, $515 million (primarily in commodity aid) went to China. European nations also received significant aid – for example, in the top five, Poland, $477 million; Italy, $418 million;

Yugoslavia, $416 million; and Greece, $347 million.[14] Despite China's position as recipient of the biggest slice of UNRRA's largesse, the distinction is misleading. China's size and population meant that UNRRA's *per capita* expenses in China were actually much lower than those of other top national beneficiaries. As UNRRA scholar Jessica Reinisch points out, 'the DP programme in Germany was over three times as expensive as a similar programme in China (costing $7,531,200 and $2,385,800 respectively) and had the largest staff of all UNRRA units. There was a clear disparity in the resources assigned to UNRRA in Europe compared with the rest of the world'.[15]

China's government also funded UNRRA/CNRRA operations, including financing the coordination and administration of in-country operations and the distribution of UNRRA-provided aid. Particularly due to the destruction of China's transportation networks during the war, this task itself was expensive. Post-war calculations put China's own contributions to the UNRRA/CNRRA efforts at about $190 million. These were monies the Nationalist government was reluctant to commit, thus resulting in the unusual and controversial 'direct sale of aid' arrangement with UNRRA which took some of the financial burden off the GMD.[16]

As in all countries, the amount of money available to China's government for relief and rehabilitation was woefully inadequate. China needed over $3.5 billion in aid, of which it asked UNRRA for $1 billion, and of which it ultimately received half.[17] Director General of CNRRA Jiang Tingfu himself recognized this problem, estimating that the country's entire relief budget could support at most 5 per cent of the population who needed aid.[18] This discrepancy was pivotal, forcing decisions about how the money would be allocated and revealing Jiang's and other Chinese leaders' intentions for China's post-war period.

Other UNRRA aid came was to come in the form of human capital. As in other countries ravaged by the war, there was an urgent need for personnel to carry out the massive post-war undertaking, whether it be for relief or rehabilitation. Jiang Tingfu took advantage of the situation to further his own agenda for China's future, requesting the dispatch of over 1,000 professional experts from twenty-five countries to be assigned to roles in the Chinese government, including advisory, technical and administrative positions.[19] From 1945 to 1947 this joint enterprise employed over 1,300 specialists, Chinese as well as other nationalities.[20] Some of the foreign experts brought in from overseas questioned the need for their skills and presence in China. For example, some of the 'survey missions' noted that 'it seem[s] clear to officers on the spot that corpses on the street signified undernourishment, and that trucks and rice, not more V.I.P.'s, were the prime need' to be addressed by UNRRA funds.[21] This disconnect between the aid China requested (and often received) and the aid China most clearly needed highlights the emphasis Jiang Tingfu and his colleagues decided to place on rehabilitation as opposed to relief.

From the start, this tension between the twin exigencies of relief and rehabilitation in the UNRRA/CNRRA mission was apparent at many levels of the operation in China, just as it was across Europe. UNRRA's new vision of humanitarianism was intended to encompass more than 'mere "soup kitchen" charity' focused on the 'relief' of immediate suffering.[22] UNRRA and its experts explicitly promoted a humanitarianism that was to be marked by efficiency, modernity and professionalization, a 'rehabilitation' which was to go far beyond the distribution of relief supplies. This vision dovetailed neatly with the political agenda of China's ruling party, the Nationalists.[23] The word for 'relief' in UNRRA's title translates into Chinese as *jiuji* – the age-old Chinese term for disaster relief. Attracting the same kind of disdain as 'soup kitchen charity' did in the West, *jiuji* was dismissed as neither modern nor scientific, and certainly did not signal the future that China's Nationalists saw for their post-war nation. *Shanhou*, however (the term used for 'rehabilitation') was something that Jiang Tingfu and his cronies, at least, understood as much more forward-looking. In English, the two Chinese characters that make up the word for rehabilitation translate into 'care (*shan*) after (*hou*)'. But what *shanhou* came to mean in Chinese slid almost indiscernibly from something amorphous into a very concrete agenda of rebuilding and reconstruction during the post-war period.[24] In a pivotal article from 1946 called 'CNRRA: What Should It Do and How Should It Do It?' ('*Shanhou jiuji zongshu: gan shenme? Zenme gan?*')[25] the head of CNRRA Jiang Tingfu writes:

> Normally, many of our people have blind faith in relief. Actually, relief is the worst of social policies. Our way out of difficulties, therefore, does not lie in relief, but in reconstruction ... This is the thing in which the UNRRA can help us and it constitutes the principal mission of the CNRRA.[26]

The conflation of 'rehabilitation' and 'reconstruction' in China was foreseeable almost from the start.

China's situation on the ground

As scholar Tehyun Ma has demonstrated, Chinese leaders of the 1930s and 1940s – from the Nationalists to the growing Chinese Communist Party – had become increasingly aware of the international imperative for the modern nation state to provide more comprehensively for its people, either along the lines of the 1942 British Beveridge Report, the American New Deal, or, in the CCP's case, the tenets of Marxism.[27] Yet plans for national construction to turn post-imperial China into a modern state were precarious even before the Japanese invasion in 1937, buffeted as they were by continuing civil war, empty coffers and a worsening international situation.[28] With the wholesale destruction wrought by the Japanese occupation, exacerbated by the Nationalists' own strategies to halt the Japanese advance, the material reality confronting UNRRA, CNRRA, the Chinese state and the Chinese people in the early 1940s was dire. Relief was a challenge in and of itself. Was rehabilitation a bridge too far? The CNRRA combated this reality with a propaganda legerdemain: its photographic 'record'.

How bad was the situation on the ground in China when UNRRA first arrived and CNRRA was formed? The years of the Japanese war were exceptional in their brutality and the extent of their destruction, but China had already been consumed by war and hardship – at least on a regional scale – for decades before the 1937 Marco Polo Bridge Incident had marked the official start of the Second World War in China. The Sino-Japanese War of 1894–5, the Boxer Uprising in 1900, the Russo-Japanese War of 1904–5 (despite its name, fought on Chinese soil), the Xinhai Revolution that toppled the Qing Dynasty in 1911, and the ceaseless local battles of the Warlord Era (1920–6) had left a China crippled by war. This parade of military destruction was followed almost immediately by the first phase of the civil war between the Communists and the Nationalists (1927–37), as well as by innumerable battles in western China involving minority peoples and/or invading Russians/Soviets. In 1931, even before the official start of the Second World War in China, the Japanese had already subjugated north China, impacting the people of Manchuria and surrounding regions. Coupled with the famines that had decimated swathes of China roughly every seven years from the beginning of the century, these countless wars had left China's people in a precarious position long before the Second World War and UNRRA came to China. China's reality was that there was not much to rehabilitate; reconstruction, although explicitly not part of the UNRRA mission, would have to be from the ground up and without any dedicated budget.[29]

Scholars have suggested that during the Second World War, 20 to 25 per cent of China's population (80 million to 100 million people) was displaced. This massive dislocation of China's populace was unprecedented, even in a country where civil disturbance, famine and other natural disasters were commonplace. Even in the Taiping Rebellion of 1850–64, which convulsed China in a civil war that left 30 million to 50 million dead, the number of migrants fleeing the war reached only 30 million and was concentrated along China's eastern corridor. At the beginning of the war in China, the Japanese invasion quickly and indiscriminately brought devastation to every Chinese political, cultural, economic and industrial centre, emptying China's major cities onto its roads. In the Japanese total war, civilians suffered alongside soldiers. Japanese deployed chemical and biological weapons in population clusters strategically followed by aerial incendiary bombs, scattering China's people in a campaign that overpowered China's twenty-one provinces within twelve months and left Mainland China engulfed in a sea of refugees.[30]

Drought and famine, particularly in Henan Province in central China in 1942–3, exacerbated the suffering of local populations and led to widespread death and the creation of yet more refugees. Estimates range up to three million refugees from the Henan Famine alone.[31] During the Japanese invasion the Nationalist government actually added significantly to the trauma and devastation of the Chinese people through its desperate attempts to stop the advance of the Japanese offensive. In 1938, Chiang Kai-shek ordered the demolition of all Yellow River dikes north of Zhengzhou in central China to try (quite literally) to wash the Japanese forces away. This action was taken without any warning to the local population. The strategy caused over a million Chinese deaths, laying waste to over 2,300 square miles of arable land, and making it impossible for local civilians to feed themselves, once again creating yet another wave of refugees.[32]

The competition between the demands of relief and of rehabilitation with destruction on this scale led to very real consequences in China. 'There was a tension between UNRRA's desire to relieve very immediate suffering, and the aim of CNRRA (as a body of the Chinese government) to use wartime relief as a means of reconstructing the state', explains historian Rana Mitter. American observers recognized the lack of progress in refugee relief and resettlement and commented on it, although privately.[33] 'James Johnson, American legal counsel to UNRRA, declared in a private letter that a major problem was the "slow and sometimes imperceptible progress" of CNRRA in dealing with refugee matters.'[34] This observation highlighted a truth in action. Without other sources of financing and well aware of their delicate situation in appearing as a credible state in the eyes of the international community, the Nationalist government took the decision to focus its UNRRA aid on building infrastructure – its interpretation of the rehabilitation agenda – rather than on providing immediate relief to China's destitute and shattered civilians. The CNRRA photographic archive reflects that decision, obscuring the poignant and distressing situation of China's 100 million refugees.

UNRRA/CNRRA photography

In reviewing the CNRRA Refugee Collection in the United Nations archive, the scale and depth of China's Second World War tragedy are barely evident.[35] Viewing the archive as a whole, it is clear that the CNRRA refugee photographs, as part of an entire narrative consisting of almost sixty folders and over 600 photographs, were meant less to document Chinese refugees' plight and need of immediate relief, and more to provide evidence of CNRRA's commitment to modern rehabilitation, or better, reconstruction. Modern accoutrements, effectiveness and accountability are on display here. The archive is dominated by photos of heavy machinery, scientific and biomedical materiel, and attractive Western advisors and observers interacting with often smiling Chinese refugees and officials. Interestingly, the archive also contains photographs of European refugees in Shanghai in disproportionate numbers to photos of Chinese refugees; despite their small numbers relative to the number of Chinese displaced persons, the Europeans receive significant attention.

One set of photographs in the CNRRA collection does not feature human subjects at all. Photographs such as Figure 5.1, foregrounding an enormous barge with trucks emerging from its open doors, showcase the modern materiel

Figure 5.1 'Trucks are unloaded from a river barge at Changsha, capital of the famine-stricken province of Hunan. Low water level of the Siang River, prime artery of transport to Hunan, has prevented adequate food shipments. (Photo by Wipperman.)'[38]

Figure 5.2 'LW Nelson, of Seattle, shows students in the UNRRA-sponsored food processing training school in Shanghai how to pack fish in a tin for cooking. Also watching him are William Green, left, head of UNRRA's Agricultural Rehabilitation Division in China, and ER Henson, center, head of UNRRA's agricultural rehabilitation program in Washington. Fish canned at the plant have been caught by the UNRRA-sponsored Fisheries Rehabilitation Administration. (Photo by Wipperman.)'[39]

CNRRA was using to tackle China's post-war crises. Boats, planes, trucks and a variety of machinery, from tractors[36] to cranes unloading slabs of steel plate to be turned into farm tools are featured in these photographs, often framed by open expanses of sky which put the materiel into stark relief.[37] People are absent or dwarfed by the machinery they are operating. In these photographs, the equipment itself (modern, expensive, imposing) is the hero, promising a future for China that transcends the frailty of man – which is pointedly excluded from view.

Another genre of photograph features China's engagement with international science and technology. Instead of focusing on the famine confronting China's refugees, these images often display a cornucopia of the-next-best-thing in food science, agribusiness and aquaculture coming from the West. Figures 5.2 and 5.3 show Western experts in these areas helping eager groups of Chinese students

Figure 5.3 'CNRRA 466 home food preservation specialist Mrs Anne K Weaver from San Francisco discusses vegetable canning with Miss Ma Teh-Yin, one of the fifty trainees who will graduate today from the first six-week course in food preservation conducted by UNRRA's recently instituted canning school in Kiangwan Road. Each graduating student will take back to his home district the knowledge and equipment necessary for the setting up of community food preservation centres where farmers of his region will can their surplus food produce to save it for the lean winter season. (Photo by Wipperman.)'[40]

learn how to use the most modern technologies to move into their new, post-war future – a future flush with 'surplus food'.

Scholars have recently argued that UNRRA was meant to be an overseas extension of President Franklin Delano Roosevelt's New Deal, and 'inherited its reliance on photography to document and persuade' from the Farm Security Administration (FSA) information apparatus as well as some of its personnel.[41] For example, Arthur Rothstein was one of the original photographers for the FSA documentary project. After working briefly for *Look* magazine, Rothstein joined the Office of War Information and then the US Army as a photographer. The Army took him to China, where he served as the chief photographer for the UNRRA China Mission between 1945 and 1947.[42] His photographs appear frequently in the CNRRA archive.

The image shown in Figure 5.4 is a typical Rothstein action shot. On the left, a Chinese refugee appears, opening his shirt to be anointed by a spray gun of DDT by an official-looking CNRRA worker, well dressed in a dark jacket. This miracle chemical is clearly intended to solve the problem of lice and bedbugs (featured prominently in educational posters displayed behind the refugee's head); the posters tell the story of what is happening in the photo even if/when the caption cannot provide the details. The recipient of this attention seems to be grinning broadly: CNRRA is taking care of even his most intimate problems. The two men are alone in a well-defined space; there are no onlookers gawking or crowds waiting for their own turn to be deloused. If there is suffering or discomfort, it is about to be dispelled by the modern magic of chemistry. The duster's resemblance to a hypodermic aimed at the heart of this smiling and willing subject provides a symbolic paean to science.

Similarly, Figure 5.5, the Rothstein photograph 'Mrs. Wang Koo Shee being treated with a kindness' presents a refugee image that is a far cry from the faceless, unnamed masses often associated with refugees today. The photograph's cheery

Figure 5.4 'Refugees are thoroughly dusted with DDT after taking a shower soon after their arrival at the refugee camp in Wuchang, which is operated by CNRRA and supplied by UNRRA. (Photo by Rothstein.)'[43]

portrayal of an older, named female refugee, individually welcomed, well treated according to her station in life, clean and well fed is a heart-warming one. The composition of the photograph is defined by two women, one bending down to serve the other, as well as by the vertical railings that highlight the women's actions of giving and receiving. Mrs. Wang's small bound feet are foregrounded, emphasizing her years. Again, even without the detailed caption, the message of the photograph is clear: here are women being well cared for in an uncrowded, hygienic setting (note the white apron on the server). Although the image is a heartening one, it is clearly out of sync with the harsh realities of the refugee experience abundantly captured by contemporaries and scholars. Harriet Zurndorfer has pointed out the exceptional hardships endured by women refugees, many documented in oral histories taken after the war, including the threat of rape or coerced prostitution, the birth of unwanted children, separation from family members, the pain of choosing between starvation for themselves and their children or complicity with the enemy, as well as the daily terror of

Figure 5.5 'Mrs. Wang Koo Shee being treated with a kindness due to her years, is given a cup of tea and a piece of steamed bread when she arrives at the Nantao refugee camp in Shanghai supplied by UNRRA and operated by CNRRA. (Photograph by Rothstein.)'[45]

aerial attack, bombardment and other physical harm.⁴⁴ Although Mrs Wang Koo Shee's reality might have been different from that of Zurndorfer's subjects, her embodiment as the quintessential older woman refugee in this portrait is eminently suspect.

In contrast, a photograph (Figure 5.6) by *New York Times* war photographer Harrison Forman *not* included in the CNRRA archive, entitled 'Henan Province (China), elderly refugee woman waiting in the crowd' presents a very different vision of an older, female refugee from the same period.⁴⁶ Unnamed, this woman is presented almost filling the frame of the photograph with her lined, careworn face and stained peasant coat, eyes downcast and body bowed. Behind her, the photographer reveals glimpses of other women (perhaps carrying babies?), conveying the personal plight of this individual, as well as suggesting the representativeness of her situation to other women around her. Although she is not alone in the frame, her position in the middle of the portrait and the cast of her head suggest that she is indeed very alone. Unlike Mrs Wang, this solitude occurs in a 'crowd'. The two women's experience of refugee-ness could not be more different.

Even the CNRRA photograph below (Figure 5.7), taken by an unknown photographer and showing a much less rosy picture of refugee life does not

Figure 5.6 'Henan Province (China), elderly refugee woman waiting in the crowd.'⁴⁷

Figure 5.7 'Refugees from the famine stricken parts of Henan Province.'[48]

capture the extreme destitution or total devastation of famine refugees. The family in this photo is still intact, women and children unsold; their goods are with them; and they are clothed and relatively healthy, rather than skeletal. These refugees will make excellent recipients of aid, and the story begun with this photograph is sure to end well in CNRRA hands.

Alternate visions

This focus on the positive work being done by UNRRA and CNRRA in China for appreciative and wholesome refugee-recipients was not the dominant mode of humanitarian photography at the time. Sensationalism, the fetishization of suffering and the presentation of the needy as powerless victims were already well-established tropes in Euro-American visual humanitarianism by the early twentieth century.[49] As in print journalism, where the mantra of the day was 'if it bleeds, it reads', the spectacle of suffering had already been established across the world as the most effective way to move audiences to compassion and to generate funds for worthy causes.[50]

In 1919, Eglantyne Jebb had shockingly but enduringly popularized picturing the starving baby to raise money for her newly founded Save the Children Fund. Although originally, she was arrested for passing out 'treasonous' leaflets showing starving Austrian babies, her message and its medium were to create a lasting legacy.[51] Western missionaries also helped set the trend for fundraising photography, sending gruesome and shocking photos of wretched victims from exotic field locations to galvanize home congregants into supporting missionaries and their work overseas.[52]

The growing international humanitarian community recognized the power of this visual trope. As early as 1919, when the newly formed League of Nations tried to raise money and sympathy for its work among Mediterranean refugees in the aftermath of the First World War, those in charge of publicity were clear on what kind of photos of refugees was effective as propaganda. Misery and destitution would sell their cause. These League of Nations workers despaired of obtaining what they termed 'the right kind of photograph', ones that would arouse emotions and thus support for their work among the refugee population. 'Grinning refugees' were not ideal subjects; 'really acute distress' was the preferable focus. As one aid worker wrote to another:

> Thank you for your letter of the 5th, re photographs of refugees. This is not so easy a matter as you might suppose: the refugees all look too cheerful, they have mostly got sufficient clothes and food, the weather is perfect, and there is very little really acute distress. Moreover, it is quite impossible to find anyone here who really understands how to take the right kind of photographs – they take groups of grinning refugees, and so forth! However, I have now obtained quite a good camera myself, and hope to get something useful – but it will take time. You really should have a 'publicity man' travelling round, photographing and reporting. That would be the only way of getting really comprehensive information and pictures.[53]

Refugees' lives were not all misery. Yet, these were not Christmas card snapshots or selfies meant to present life at its rosiest. The aim of these photographs was to raise awareness of the plight confronting these individuals in need. The multiplicity of possible themes, attitudes and implications of refugee photography made the choice of subjects and how they were portrayed a necessarily conscious and deliberate one, a choice most often mission-driven.

In the Second Sino-Japanese War, Western photographers of China – and Chinese photographers snapping photos for a Western audience – further fed viewers' appetite for suffering, following this interpretation of humanitarian photography. The iconic photo 'Bloody Saturday' of a Chinese infant crying and abandoned on railroad tracks after a 1937 Japanese bomb attack on a Shanghai rail station is one such photo. Taken by a Chinese photographer explicitly for a Western audience, this image intentionally plays on an emotional register well established in the West. The 'usefulness' of such photographs in convincing far away audiences to take notice of and respond to the plight of distant sufferers and to donate to their relief became a fundamental of humanitarian imagery, but one explicitly missing from the CNRRA archive. The CNRRA photographic mission was a different one. Portraying China in terms such as 'Bloody Saturday' suggested China as a weak victim, rather than as the nascent Great Power China's Nationalist government wanted their country to be considered.

Themes in earlier Chinese humanitarian imagery[54]

The more positive image of refugees espoused by CNRRA was not unknown in China before the 1940s, however. Traditional Chinese charitable organizations had long dealt with displaced and destitute people in China, and by the 1940s, photographs of refugees and of relief efforts on their behalf were commonplace. As we shall see, some focused on the positive and some on the negative side of the refugee narrative.

Chinese print technologies had long been used in the service of philanthropy, and vivid imagery had always played a significant role in representing China's needy. As early as 1594, a Confucian official had submitted an illustrated report to the emperor about famine in his province, enlivened by fourteen woodblock pictures of his constituents' suffering. The pictures, successful in their mission, were meant to move the emperor and his court women to understand the depth of the crisis and to open their purses for famine relief.[55]

The use of graphic illustration to document need, and to move hearts surfaced repeatedly in China's elite circles. Another famous example came in 1864 at the end of the Taiping Rebellion. Confucian scholar Yu Zhi produced a pamphlet called *A Man of Iron's Tears for Jiangnan*, featuring forty-two images directed at raising money for refugee relief in the Southern Yangtze area. These illustrations ranged from scenes of decapitation and cannibalism (Figure 5.8) to utopian images of Southeast China rebuilt and of Confucian order restored.[56] Deliberately shocking, these images combined text and stark lines to present a strikingly disturbing visual narrative on the one hand, and a vision of a China restored on the other.

Figure 5.8 Woodcut: *Cannibalism*.⁵⁷

Yu Zhi's influential work became an inspiration for future philanthropists, and in the Great North China Famine of 1876, concerned observers intentionally cribbed both the name of Yu's pamphlet and many of his illustrative tropes for a deliberately similar charitable appeal.⁵⁸ The 1878 version of *Tears from Iron* inspired a front-page article in the Chinese-language, Chinese circulation newspaper *Shenbao*, particularly for its use of images. The power of the image to inspire charitable action was apparent to all, in nineteenth-century China as in the twentieth-century global arena.

With the increasing availability and affordability of photography in China by 1900, photography quickly replaced the hand-drawn image in many Chinese publications.⁵⁹ The introduction of modern printing presses imported by missionary groups in the 1870s, the technology of half-tone printing, and the development of the portable camera (George Eastman's Kodak, available after 1888 in the West and shortly thereafter in Asia) opened the door for the new art.⁶⁰ Relief groups such as the Chinese Red Cross Society (founded in 1904) used these technologies and their resultant images to establish credibility as charitable organizations and to create an identity as modern, national organizations.⁶¹ By the 1920s, vivid photographs from China's battlefields and disaster zones and their aftermaths animated Chinese charitable appeals and publications. The Chinese Red Cross Society, created by local Chinese elites and recognized by the International Red Cross Society in 1912, aided refugees from its inception and actively photographed these efforts.⁶² The Society published these photographs in local newspapers and magazines as well as in its own fundraising and informational materials in order to publicize and fund its activities, to attract members and donors, and to inform the national and world community about its work.⁶³

Interestingly, Red Cross imagery in China did not take its antecedents from earlier Chinese or Japanese woodblock prints. Instead of depicting dramatic scenes of human trauma or the pitiful plight of victims as in the earlier *Tears from Iron* pamphlets or in Japanese imagery, the Chinese Red Cross Society launched its pictorial debut on a celebratory note, featuring detailed photographic portraits of its celebrity principals: high officials, presidents, and diplomats serving as honorary and actual officers of the Chinese Red Cross Society.⁶⁴ The departure from portraying suffering victims was to be a hallmark of Chinese Red Cross photography from that time on, and a precursor to the CNRRA strategy for its own photographic record. These are photographs documenting hope and accomplishment, not despair.

Precedents of refugee photography in China

Not all individuals pictured in Red Cross publications retained or proclaimed their individuality like the cameo dignitaries smiling from Red Cross periodicals' frontispieces. Some individuals appear in group portraits: doctors and nurses in front of Western-style hospitals as well as well-dressed members gathered in voting halls.⁶⁵ Another group pictured *en masse* in China's Red Cross and other publications is refugees. For example, this rather standard portrait of Chinese relief recipients facing the camera in 1921 (Figure 5.9) appears in a 1934 county gazetteer.⁶⁶

Figure 5.9 The Beijing Buddhist Relief Society working with a Shanghai Merchants Organization to deliver relief to the stricken mountainous region of west Zhili by the Shanxi border.

Photographs of refugees in China taken by Chinese photographers for Chinese audiences mostly picture refugees *not* in their 'raw humanity', as Malkki terms it, but rather in situations already well under control.[67] These refugees are purposefully gathered. They are going to be fed or housed; the images suggest a group being handled, not a surging 'sea of humanity' (another Malkki phrase).[68] And although they are not the scrubbed and grinning refugees of CNRRA photography, they certainly do not look like victims on the verge of death who we know existed in the 1920–1 North China Famine. These are victims who can and will be helped, and who are, in fact, in the process of so being.

The Chinese Red Cross took this visual convention to the next level, making it even more clear in their photographic narratives that these refugee situations are being actively *managed* under the Red Cross flag (Figure 5.10). Rather than portraying refugee groups as indicative of a breakdown of order and civilization, these refugees are part of a narrative of Red Cross rescue and relief, of a future better than the past. The omnipresence of the Red Cross symbol and flag, sometimes patently added into the photograph, is a key element and signifier in these images. Sometimes the photos tell a story of dramatic rescue; more often they indicate the 'next stage' in the refugee aid process: men sitting at tables with ledgers documenting the refugees massed in front of them; refugees being fed or cared for medically; refugee children all dressed in the same uniforms; refugees in front of a temporary shelter, where men, women and children are finally able to put down their bundles.

Figure 5.10 The Chongqing Chapter of the Chinese Red Cross.[69]

Although no individuals are separately identified in these photographs – in other words, both refugees and aid providers are non-distinct characters in a narrative, rather than individuals whose unique personalities and life stories specifically add to the narrative – the narrative of rescue and of aid emerges clearly from these pictures (Figure 5.10 and 5.11). People in need are being helped by people who care. Both parties are engaged as actors. And the future is bright.

In many Red Cross photos, as in CNRRA photographs, the accoutrements of relief also play a significant role as actors: modern technologies such as trains, boats, ambulances and biomedical intervention are part of the Red Cross arsenal of rescue. These items feature prominently in the pictures, suggesting modernity and performing semiotically (Figure 5.12).

Thus, the organization's mandate of modern humanitarianism is concretized through these photographs, making the abstract notion of 'providing aid' literally 'image-inable'. This is a visual documentation of order and efficiency, of modern technologies harnessed to an age-old imperative, a record of concerned compatriots (often in modern white uniforms) reaching out professionally and capably to help the needy. A better future awaits the subjects of these lenses, rather than the spectre of more suffering. Photos like these put the Chinese Red Cross Society at the very forefront of modern humanitarianism in China, creating an argument about the need for and efficacy of the new organization and its new kind of disaster relief. The CNRRA drew on similar tropes and created its photographic archive for similar reasons and for similar effect.

Figure 5.11 The Tianjin Red Chapter of the Chinese Red Cross, Longting Refuge.⁷⁰

Figure 5.12 The Medical Ship of the General Office of the Chinese Red Cross arriving in Shanghai from Henan Province.⁷¹

Conclusion

Thus, we can see there is precedent for the visual language the CNRRA photographic archive uses to document post-1945 China. Not all refugee photography insists on portraying recipients of aid as abject victims, even when they were. In fact, UNRRA/CNRRA photographs resemble the early-twentieth-century Chinese style of portraying disaster: focusing not on needy victims, but on the relief-providing aid workers and on the modern, scientific, efficient technologies and materiel they are using to get the job done, a future-forward vision of disaster relief that continues to mark China's humanitarian photography today, as Chinese photographs from the 2008 Sichuan earthquake demonstrate.[72] This convergence in visual tropes reflects a shared desire to present an optimistic narrative of the humanitarian endeavour that legitimates and celebrates aid providers and the future they promise, a narrative that ironically often downplays the actual conditions of the recipients of aid and the world they are living in.

This photographic focus on a rosier future has its positive sides, yet it is also not without its negatives. I would argue that the CNRRA photographs with their clothed and sanitized and debugged refugees, and their focus on an aspirational rehabilitation of infrastructure, rather than on immediate relief to the needy, take the imperative to downplay suffering too far, skewing the visual record away from the very real human tragedy occurring in the moment. Whether or not this contemporary record reflects what was actually happening on the ground for China's sufferers of the moment, the cumulative image we are left with today obscures the actual conditions of post-1945 China.

Denis Kennedy has characterized humanitarian photography as 'the veritable commodification of suffering'.[73] But there are other tropes in humanitarian photography, including instrumental ones that have less to do with human suffering and more to do with presenting evidence in support of particular narratives of relief or, in post-1945 China, rehabilitation-cum-reconstruction. As in any narrative device, the elements and actors in the photographic story can be manipulated and enhanced to advance a multiplicity of agendas and arguments: political, exhortatory, social, cultural or aspirational.

Today we face pervasive issues of preserving (or not) visual reminders of the ugliness of the human record. Although a cameo shot of child's irrepressible joy even in the face of hardship is a real moment in the refugee narrative and should indeed be celebrated, should we not still communicate the larger tragedy of 100 million lives turned on end and 14 million to 22 million civilian lives lost, as they were in China from 1937 to 1945?

Susan Sontag has written:

> Though an event has come to mean, precisely, something worth photographing, it is still ideology (in the broadest sense) that determines what constitutes an event. There can be no evidence, photographic or otherwise, of an event until the event itself has been named and characterized. And it is never photographic evidence which can construct – more properly, identify – events; the contribution of photography always follows the naming of the event.[74]

'Naming the event' of 'refugee-ness', to use Sontag's terms, has been contested from the start. Are smiling children playing in the sun 'worthy' of being designated refugees? Are the most needy refugees worth calling attention to *qua* refugees since they cannot be helped because they are too needy? Is excising, or emphasizing, the suffering of refugees from the photographic record justified in the service of other, perhaps more worthwhile goals? Is Sontag wrong, and has photography actually been constitutive of refugee-ness in meaningful ways? And finally, what is the photographer's responsibility to historiography? Whereas photographs which cause viewers to wonder how the photographer could fail to intervene in the immediate suffering in front of their lens are, perhaps, prurient, and photographs of faceless, nameless crowds of refugees perhaps do not do justice to the humanity of individuals, is it not still a worthwhile endeavour to document moments and regimes of suffering simply to say, 'this happened'?

The creation of CNRRA's authoritative visual narrative concealing Chinese refugees' lived experiences has helped skew the historiographical record of the Second World War and its aftermath. Recently, scholars of Chinese history have themselves tried to 'rehabilitate' the Chinese Nationalists' vision of a post-war future for China – the same vision furthered by the CNRRA and captured in the UNRRA-CNRRA archive.[75] Yet, as the photographic collection suggests, a focus on rehabilitation/reconstruction without providing for immediate relief, or on rebuilding for the future without acknowledging the reality of immediate suffering led to a disconnect between the agency and the post-war situation that not only lost lives, but also the hearts and minds of the Chinese people and, in fact, the very international community that the GMD and its agents at CNRRA were trying to join.

Notes

1. Liisa Malkki, 'Speechless Emissaries: Refugees, Humanitarianism, and Dehistoricization', *Cultural Anthropology*, 11:3 (1996), 377–404, 387. Peter Gatrell also takes up the theme of anonymity and timelessness in *The Making of the Modern Refugee* (Oxford: Oxford University Press, 2013), 10–11.
2. Jonathan Benthall, *Disasters, Relief and the Media* (London: I.B. Tauris, 1993).
3. For an interesting recent discussion of this issue, see Sean O'Hagan, 'The photographs that moved the world to tears – and to take action', *The Guardian* (September 2015), https://www.theguardian.com/commentisfree/2015/sep/06/photograph-refugee-crisis-aylan-kurdi.
4. Rana Mitter puts the number of deaths at least 14 million. *Forgotten Ally: China's World War II, 1937–1945* (Boston, MA: Houghton Mifflin Harcourt, 2013), 5.
5. The CNRRA archive can be found in the United Nations Archives (UNA) in folder S-0801, https://search.archives.un.org/chinese-national-relief-and-rehabilitation-administration-cnrra-photographs.
6. Silvia Salvatici, 'Sights of Benevolence: UNRRA's Recipients Portrayed' in Heide Fehrenbach and David Rodogno (eds.), *Humanitarian Photography: A History* (New York: Cambridge University Press, 2015), 200–22, 211.
7. The estimates of numbers of refugees vary, although recent understanding of the scale of displacement puts the number at the higher end. See Harriet Zurndorfer, 'Wartime refugee relief in Chinese Cities and Women's political activism, 1937–1940', in Billy K. L. So and Madeleine Zelin (eds.), *New Narratives of Urban Space in Republican Chinese Cities* (Leiden: Brill, 2013), 65–91: 66 and Pamela Ballinger, 'Entangled or "Extruded" Histories? Displacement, National Refugees, and Repatriation after the Second World War', *Journal of Refugee Studies*, 25:3, (2012), doi: 10.1093/jrs/fes022 discusses the definitional lacuna.
8. For example, googling 'biggest refugee crisis' in 2021 brings up MSN's slideshow 'The Biggest Refugee Movements in History', which includes sixteen events and concludes that 'The Second World War and its aftermath led to the largest refugee crisis of the 20th century, with more than 50 million people displaced across Europe.' https://www.msn.com/en-gb/news/photos/the-biggest-refugee-movements-in-history/ss-BBDqNM0?fullscreen=true#image=16. See also Zurndorfer, 'Wartime Refugee Relief', 70.
9. Michael Ignatief, *The Warrior's Honor: Ethnic War and the Modern Conscience* (New York: Henry Hold & Company, 1998), 26.
10. 'Address of the President of the United States', *United Nations Relief and Rehabilitation Organization Journal*, 1, 10 November–2 December 1943, 1.
11. Rana Mitter, 'Imperialism, Transnationalism, and the Reconstruction of Post-war China: UNRRA in China, 1944–7', *Past & Present*, 218, Supplement 8 (2013), 51–69, https://doi.org/10.1093/pastj/gts034, 10.

12 Rana Mitter, 'State-Building after Disaster: Jiang Tingfu and the Reconstruction of Post-World War II China, 1943–1949', *Comparative Studies in Society and History*, 61:1 (2019), 176–206, doi:10.1017/S0010417518000531.
13 George Kerr, *Formosa Betrayed* (Boston, MA: Houghton Mifflin, 1965). See Chapter 8, 'The UNRRA CNRRA Story'.
14 Katrine R. C. Greene, 'UNRRA's Record in China', *Far Eastern Survey*, 20:10 (16 May 1951), 100–102, https://www.jstor.org/stable/3024444, 101–2.
15 Jessica Reinisch, '"Auntie UNRRA" at the Crossroads', *Past & Present*, 218, Supplement 8, (2013), 70–97, https://doi.org/10.1093/pastj/gts035.
16 Kerr, *Formosa Betrayed*, Chapter 8.
17 Mitter, 'Imperialism', 61.
18 Jiang Tingfu, 'Shanhou jiuji zongshu: gan shenme? Zenmo gan?' (UNRRA: what should it do and how?), in Zhang, *Jiang Tingfu*, 242, cited in Mitter, 'State-building', 182.
19 Greene, 'UNRRA's Record in China', 101–2.
20 Ibid., 100–2.
21 Ibid., 100.
22 *Helping the People to Help Themselves: The Story of the United Nations Relief and Rehabilitation Administration* (London, 1944) cited in Reinisch, "Auntie UNRRA", note 1.
23 Salvatici, 'Sights of Benevolence'.
24 In fact, contemporary China scholars writing about CNRRA also use the words 'reconstruction' and 'rehabilitation' interchangeably in describing the CNRRA mission. For example, Oxford/Harvard historian of China Rana Mitter tellingly titles one of his articles on UNRRA in China 'Imperialism, Transnationalism, and the Reconstruction of Post-war China: UNRRA in China, 1944–7'. In another, 'State Building after Disaster' he uses the words 'reconstruction' and China 'rehabilitation' interchangeably to describe CNRRA's work. Mitter, 'Imperialism', and Mitter, 'State-building'.
25 Tsiang, T.F. (Jiang Tingfu), 'Zhongguo shanhou jiuji zongshu, China National Relief and Rehabilitation Administration C.N.R.R.A. What does it do? How does it do it?' (International Publishers, Shanghai, February 1946).
26 Ibid., 8.
27 Tehyun Ma, '"The common aim of the Allied Powers": social policy and international legitimacy in wartime China, 1940–47', *Journal of Global History* (2014), 9, 254–75, doi:10.1017/S1740022814000060.
28 For a particularly negative – and influential – account of the pre-war years, see Lloyd E. Eastman, *Seeds of Destruction: Nationalist China in War and Revolution, 1937–1949* (Stanford, CA: Stanford University Press, 1984).
29 Reinisch, 'Auntie UNRRA', note 1.
30 Zurndorfer, 'Wartime Refugee Relief', 68.

31 Mark Baker, 'Spaces of Starvation: State and Province in the Henan Famine, 1942–43', Yale University Agrarian Studies Spring Series, 5 June 2016, 4. https://agrarianstudies.macmillan.yale.edu/sites/default/files/files/Spaces%20of%20Starvation%20-%20BAKER.pdf. UNRRA/CNRRA investigations in the area three years later noted the extent of the famine and its effects. UNA S-0528-0058 (Hunan, 1944–9), (Vera H. McCord, Famine Survey Team, Welfare survey, Ling-ling area, Hunan province, July 1945) cited in Mitter, 'Imperialism', 66.
32 Diana Lary, 'The Waters Covered the Earth: China's War-Induced Natural Disasters', in Mark Selden and Alvin Y. So (eds.), *War and State Terrorism: The United States, Japan, and the Asia-Pacific in the Long Twentieth Century* (Maryland: Rowman & Littlefield, 2004), 143–70. Edward Dreyer, *China at War, 1901–1949* (New York: Longman House, 1995), 228.
33 Mitter, 'Imperialism', 62.
34 Ibid., 63.
35 The archive can be found in the United Nations Archives as part of the UNRRA Fonds (Fonds United Nations Relief and Rehabilitation Administration [UNRRA] 1943–1946, AG-018), Subfonds UNRRA Photographs (AG-018-041), Series CNRRA – Photographs (S-0801) in Folder S-0801-0001-21 – China – Refugees and Folder S-0801-0009-0001 – Refugees. https://search.archives.un.org/refugees-3 These two folders seem to hold the same photographs. CNRRA Photo archive can also be easily accessed through: http://www.flickr.com/photos/70217867@N07/8553009284/in/set-72157629204775474/.
36 UNA, S-0801-0005-0001 CNRRA/247 Honan, China – July 1946.
37 UNA, S-0801-0005-0001 CNRRA/294 Shanghai, China – December 1946.
38 UNA, S-0801-0011-0001-00005 CNRRA/249 Shanghai, China – August 1946.
39 UNA, S-0801-0006-0003-00006 CNRRA/488, Shanghai, China – July 1947.
40 UNA, S-0801-0006-0003-00017 CNRRA/466, Shanghai, China – June 1947.
41 Salvatici, 'Sights of Benevolence', 2, cites E. Borgwardt, *A New Deal for the World: America's Vision for Human Rights* (Boston, MA: Belknap Press, 2005), 118–21.
42 Oral history interview with Arthur Rothstein, 25 May 1964, Archives of American Art, Smithsonian, http://www.aaa.si.edu/collections/interviews/oral-history-interview-arthur-rothstein-13317.
43 Ibid. S-0801-0007-0001-00036 CNRRA/137, Wuchang, China – May 1946.
44 Zurndorfer, 'Wartime Refugee Relief', 69.
45 Ibid. S-0801-0009-0001-00073 CNRRA/52, Shanghai, China – April 1946.
46 Harrison Forman, 'Henan province (China), elderly refugee woman waiting in the crowd', from the Harrison Forman Collection-China, Harrison Forman Diary, China, December 1942–March 1943, Forman Nitrate Negatives Box 2, https://collections.lib.uwm.edu/digital/collection/agsphoto/id/4566. From the American Geographical Society Library, University of Wisconsin-Milwaukee Libraries.

47 Harrison Forman, 'Henan province (China), elderly refugee woman waiting in the crowd.'
48 Ibid. UNA, S-0801-0009-0001-00066 CNRRA/552, Honan, China – July 1947.
49 Cf. Kevin Rozario, '"Delicious Horrors": Mass Culture, The Red Cross, and the Appeal of Modern American Humanitarianism', *American Quarterly*, 55:3 (September 2003), 417–55, and Julia Irwin, *Making the World Safe: The American Red Cross and a Nation's Humanitarian Awakening* (Oxford: Oxford University Press, 2013), 87–8.
50 Japanese Red Cross authority and international jurist Ariga Nagao famously told a group of Shanghai philanthropists that publishing photos of 'flesh flying about' would encourage donations. Speech to Chinese philanthropists, Shanghai, 19 November 1912, *Zhongguo Hongshizihui Zazhi* 1 (May 1913).
51 For more on Eglantyne Jebb, please see: http://herstoria.com/?p=663, 'Eglantyne Jebb.'
52 Heather Curtis, 'Depicting Distant Suffering: Evangelicals and the Politics of Pictorial Humanitarianism in the Age of American Empire', *Material Religion*, 8:2, 154–83.
53 League of Nations archives, Box R1762, Refugees from Asia Minor. Probably Lionel Fielden, a translator for LON, to Mr. Phillip British (?). Lionel to Phillip, titled 'Photographs of Refugees', Athens, 12 December 1922. Thanks to Davide Rodogno of IHEID for this document.
54 My working definition of humanitarian imagery is the mobilization of imagery in the service of humanitarian initiatives, including fundraising and awareness. Some would add 'across state boundaries', but I would not.
55 Tobie Meyer-Fong, *What Remains: Coming to Terms with Civil War in 19th Century China* (Stanford, CA: Stanford University Press, 2013), 52; 226.
56 Meyer-Fong, 51–63 for images and a detailed description of this pamphlet.
57 *Woodcuts, from The Famine in China, Illustrations by a Native Artist, with a Translation of the Chinese Text* (by the Rev. James Legge), (London: China Famine Relief Fund/Kegan Paul & Co., 1878).
58 Kathryn Edgerton-Tarpley, *Tears from Iron: Cultural Responses to Famine in Nineteenth-Century China* (Berkley, CA: University of California Press, 2008), 132–41.
59 There is a growing literature on indigenous Chinese photography. See Claire Roberts, *Photography and China* (London: Reaktion Books, 2013); Oliver Moore, *Photography in China: Science, Commerce and Communication* (New York: Routledge, 2022); Jeffrey W. Cody and Frances Terpak (eds.), *Brush and Shutter: Early Photography in China* (Hong Kong: Hong Kong University Press in association with The Getty Research Institute, 2011).
60 Roberts, *Photography and China*, 53.

61 For a revealing cross-cultural comparison of Red Cross societies' entry into publication, cf. Julia Irwin, *Making the World Safe: The American Red Cross and a Nation's Humanitarian Awakening* (Oxford: Oxford University Press, 2012), 83–90, which discusses the origins and rise of the American Red Cross magazine.
62 For a brief history of the Chinese Red Cross, see Caroline Reeves, 'The Chinese Red Cross: Past, Present, and Future', in Jennifer Ryan, Tony Saich and Lincoln Chen (eds.), *Philanthropy for Health in China* (Indiana: Indiana University Press, 2014), 214–34.
63 For example, in the *Dongfang Zazhi* 10:2, 1 August 1913.
64 See 'Throwing Off Asia III' by John W. Dower – Chapter Two, 'Old Media, New Enemy' 2-2 Massachusetts Institute of Technology, 2008 Visualizing Cultures http://visualizingcultures.mit.edu.
65 Caroline Reeves, 'Developing the Humanitarian Image in Late Nineteenth – and Early Twentieth-Century China,' in Fehrenbach and Rodogno (eds.), *Humanitarian Photography: A History*, 115–39.
66 Jingxing County Gazetteer, 1934 (np). 'The Beijing Buddhist Relief Society working with a Shanghai Merchants Organization to deliver relief to the stricken mountainous region of west Zhili by the Shanxi border', with many thanks to Pierre Fuller, Science Po.
67 Malkki, 'Speechless Emissaries', 390.
68 Ibid., 377.
69 *Zhongguohongshizihui ErshiJiniance* (Chinese Red Cross Society 20th Anniversary Commemorative Edition), (Shanghai, 1924), photographic section (np).
70 Ibid.
71 Ibid.
72 It is important to distinguish the origins and destinations of the photos from this event before analysing them.
73 Denis Kennedy, 'Selling the Distant Other: Humanitarianism and Imagery – Ethical Dilemmas of Humanitarian Action', *The Journal of Humanitarian Assistance* (28 February 2009), 2.
74 Susan Sontag, *On Photography* (New York: Penguin, 1979).
75 Ma, 'The common aim of the Allied Powers'; Mitter, *Forgotten Ally*.

6

The forgotten 'R': UNRRA's Central Tracing Bureau and the recovery of missing persons in post-war Germany, 1945–7†

Katherine Rossy

'On the walls of the Deutsches Museum in Munich DPs scribble names and messages in a variety of different languages, giving the latest news of themselves and their friends', announced a radio broadcast by the United Nations Relief and Rehabilitation Administration (UNRRA): 'Each day thousands pass through this transit centre and scan the unofficial wall lists, hoping against hope to find news of a lost relative or friend. Then they themselves add their messages and pass on.'[1] The broadcast reflected the reality of millions of displaced persons who were lost in the shuffle of the post-war tide. Tasked with the unenviable responsibility of restoring order to the chaos in occupied Germany, the Allies quickly realized that there was an urgent need for an international tracing system.[2] UNRRA emerged in the wake of this crisis by launching the Central Tracing Bureau (CTB) in November 1945. The Bureau coordinated the mass recovery of victims of Nazi atrocities in Germany until UNRRA shut its doors in 1947, launching a new chapter in international tracing operations.

Tracing was not a mere humanitarian formality. While UNRRA concentrated much of its efforts on relief and rehabilitation, the two 'r's in its acronym, tracing marked a penultimate step towards repatriation and resettlement and therefore played a vital role in rehabilitating persons and reconstructing states. Immediate, short-term relief through food, shelter, and medical care and long-term rehabilitation through vocational training, repatriation and resettlement were

† The author would like to extend her sincerest thanks to the *Histories of Internationalism* series editors – Jessica Reinisch and David Brydan – as well as Becky Taylor, Itay Lotem, Samantha Knapton and the anonymous reviewers for their many helpful comments on earlier drafts.

key pieces of the puzzle, however these aspects of UNRRA's mandate would not have reached fruition had it not been for the CTB. Without a successful recovery operation, many displaced persons would not have been located and sent home.

The relationship between recovery, relief and rehabilitation has been unclear since UNRRA's inception. Careful research in the records of the Central Tracing Bureau, housed within the United Nations Archive in New York, reveals few references to relief and rehabilitation. This suggests that for UNRRA's tracing experts, recovery was a standalone humanitarian process. One reason for the lack of understanding surrounding the interaction between recovery, relief and rehabilitation is that the contributions of the Central Tracing Bureau have been largely forgotten. There is no comprehensive study on the CTB and therefore no consideration of the way in which early United Nations' tracing efforts impacted post-war reconstruction or shaped later operations by other agencies. The opening of the International Tracing Service's (ITS) archives in 2009, one of CTB's successor agencies, generated a new wave of research on the tracing of victims of Nazi persecution. As a result, the ITS has received the lion's share of scholarly attention even though it inherited many of the CTB's practices and resources. Höschler, Borggräfe and Panek's edited volume on the ITS provides useful insights on the CTB but does not go into major detail.[3] Suzanne Brown Fleming's foundational account on the ITS dedicates only several pages to the predecessor organization.[4] This exclusion extends to recent literature on the recovery of lost and stolen children after the war. Dan Stone's work on the ITS and the forced removal of children from German institutions provides in-depth discussion on UNRRA without delving deeply into the role that the CTB played in this process.[5] The same can be said of Lynne Taylor's work on unaccompanied children in the US Zone of occupied Germany, which explores the interaction between the military authorities and humanitarian agencies that recuperated children without much discussion of the CTB.[6]

Such lacunae raise questions that beg attention. How did UNRRA's search for missing persons interact with other humanitarian processes on the ground, and in what ways did the CTB contribute to their relief and rehabilitation? What precedent did CTB policy set for international cooperation once UNRRA shut its doors in 1947? Finally, was the recovery of displaced persons through mass tracing operations a distinct humanitarian process within UNRRA's broader mandate? This chapter argues that the mass recovery operations of UNRRA's Central Tracing Bureau were an integral part of early United Nations humanitarian intervention. An often-forgotten component to the Administration's broader relief and rehabilitation efforts, it facilitated the reunion of families and reconstruction of nation states left shattered by Nazi atrocities. By excavating the history and functions of the CTB, this study will determine the ways in which the post-war recovery of missing persons launched a new international precedent in post-war tracing operations.

Mass tracing: A political problem

The process of tracing missing persons during and after the war changed hands many times. Although nobody knew how many people were missing, a concerted effort to locate displaced persons was well underway before the spring of 1945. As Christine Schmidt notes, the British Red Cross headquarters in London established a tracing bureau to help victims of Nazi persecution in 1943 that ran parallel to the one run in Geneva by the International Committee of the Red Cross.[7] When it morphed into the United Kingdom Search Bureau in May 1944, it housed a central index that contained the names and information of missing persons that would later fall under the mandate of the Supreme Headquarters Allied Expeditionary Force (SHAEF) as of the spring of 1945.[8]

SHAEF focused its tracing efforts on Allied-occupied Germany. Its tracing initiatives, such as the SHAEF Tracing Unit and the Combined Displaced Persons Executive Central Tracing Bureau, were established to locate missing Allied nationals through traditional military channels in each German occupation zone.[9] But while the military authorities could assist those in need in the short term, they were not equipped to provide long-term relief to the millions of refugees and displaced persons left behind in their occupation zones. Amongst SHAEF's broader objectives in Germany was a commitment to alleviate 'conditions of destitution among displaced persons', which included the provision of immediate, urgent services such as food, clothing, shelter and medical attention. It also pledged to set up a system that would 'affect the rapid and orderly repatriation of displaced persons', that quickly proved to be a massive political and humanitarian problem.[10]

Since none of the occupation authorities was willing to assume total responsibility for tracing, it became clear that there was a need for an independent organization. The most logical solution was to recruit an existing agency, such as the International Committee of the Red Cross (ICRC). It possessed a wealth of experience in the registration and logging of information about prisoners of war and had highly qualified staff at its disposal.[11] But since it was the only international agency permitted to work behind enemy lines during the war, the Allies felt that this disqualified it from carrying out post-war tracing activities on behalf of the newly created United Nations.[12] Instead, the Allies entrusted the task to UNRRA, an agency of 'international character of which was satisfactory for all the powers'.[13] On 26 November 1945, UNRRA and the Allied military authorities created the Central Tracing Bureau, headquartered in Bad Arolsen, and appointed British staff member Colonel John B. Bowring as its director.[14]

While Germany was the epicentre of UNRRA tracing operations, its civil structures and institutions were immediately excluded from operations. The Allied Control Council in Berlin, particularly the French and Soviet representatives, denied Bowring's request to use existing German services to facilitate the search, such as German postal and police services.[15] They felt that the recovery of Allied nationals missing due to German aggression was an international matter best handled by an international organization. By 30 May 1946, there were approximately 3,585,000 United Nations nationals still unaccounted for.[16] This included 3 million Poles, 200,000 Czechs, 200,000 French, 100,000 Greeks, 60,000 Dutch, 21,000 Belgians and 4,000 Luxembourgers. Since UNRRA could only assist United Nations nationals who were internally or externally displaced as of 1 September 1939, anyone who did not belong to a UN member state, was from a neutral state, or was deemed an 'enemy or ex-enemy national' was excluded from international protection.[17] This meant that Germans could not use CTB's services. Those who wished to track down missing persons were invited to contact the German Red Cross offices in Hamburg and Munich, which contained the information and last known whereabouts of approximately 7 million people.[18]

The Central Tracing Bureau had a sole function: to work with zonal and international tracing bureaux who were searching for missing United Nations nationals in Germany. It worked as a 'clearing house' between its partners and was tasked with the 'processing and transmission of records of mixed nationalities and the preservation of those which, owing to their nature, [could not] be decentralised, and for the transmission of individual inquiries to the zones and the performance of other search functions'.[19] In many ways, the CTB was a last resort. As UNRRA Chief of Operations in Germany Frederick E. Morgan pointed out in a November 1945 memorandum, parties would have better luck if they first sent enquiries about individuals thought to be in Germany to national tracing bureaux.[20] Since these bureaux already possessed much of the available information regarding their missing nationals, it would eliminate the need for UNRRA involvement and prevent backlogs. If no record existed, then one could ask the CTB to launch an investigation.

The key to CTB operations lay in its central index of records, a vast inventory of millions of captured German documents, letters, photographs and field reports.[21] It retained information about stateless persons, persons of undetermined nationality, and those whose home countries had no national tracing bureau of their own.[22] It had a bipartite function. Zonal bureaux in Germany passed on leads uncovered in Germany to national bureaux while national bureaux transmitted enquiries through CTB to zonal bureaux in the field.[23] Once an enquiry reached CTB headquarters, staff searched its central index for existing clues before forwarding unsuccessful cases to the appropriate zonal field office. The results of each query were then sent back to CTB headquarters, who then transmitted it to the national tracing bureau whose responsibility it was to contact the enquiring party.[24]

The CTB's insistence on zonal and international cooperation is a broader reflection of UNRRA's emphasis on what Jessica Reinisch calls 'the importance of the principle of national sovereignty to the administration's mandate and constitution'. She states that 'in areas not under military control, consent for relief work had to be obtained from the national authorities': 'National governments were UNRRA's clients and it worked through and for them, and only at their request'.[25] While the tracing bureaux in occupied Germany were subject to the regulations of each zone's military commander, the CTB did not interfere in national tracing operations. Most nations had deployed search teams in Germany during the immediate post-war period that collected documentary evidence, reviewed lists of names of those who had been deported to concentration and forced labour camps, and carried out searches and interviews with local Germans and German civil authorities.[26] Such was the case with France, whose Ministry of Prisoners of War, Deportees and Refugees issued its own search and tracing directives in Germany as early as August 1945. It instructed French military officers to comb German hospitals and institutions to 'note the identity of all French nationals (both continental and colonial) and of foreigners who resided in France before the outbreak of hostilities in September 1939'.[27] Similar instructions were issued for German prisons, military bases and amnesiac institutions. To process the overwhelming number of enquiries it received each week, Poland set up a Polish Red Cross Search Bureau in Germany along with its own index card database. The Polish government quickly realized that it could not process the overwhelming number of enquiries it received each week and asked CTB to procure and distribute 200,000 evidence cards and 150,000 enquiry cards to DP camps around Germany.[28] But while the CTB respected the 'national sovereignty' of its partnerships, it excluded anyone who did not fall within its mandate. Such was the case when the Swedish National Tracing Bureau requested help locating the last known whereabouts of Baltic nationals in Germany in November 1945. 'We are not in a position at the present time to accept enquiries where the enquirer is a neutral,' Morgan replied: 'Enquiries are not accepted from ex-enemy enquirers although an ex-enemy national will be traced if the enquirer is a United Nations national.'[29] Such restrictions, which lay at the heart of the UNRRA mandate, meant that many displaced persons cases could not be solved.

Recovery: The ill-defined forgotten 'R'

The mass recovery of missing persons after the war was a mission of unprecedented scope and scale. Post-war tracing was by no means a new phenomenon, as national agencies had been collecting the dead and searching for the missing long before the Second World War. Yet, the practice of tracing was effectively internationalized when UNRRA took the reins from SHAEF. An 'agent of internationalism', Reinisch argues, 'UNRRA was the biggest, boldest, best-funded international organization working on refugee matters the world had seen. In its five-year lifespan it organized the repatriation of millions of people [...] and thereby helped to define and redefine mid-century approaches to rehabilitation, repatriation and resettlement.'[30] While UNRRA certainly 'defined' and 'redefined' such practices, mass recovery remains largely absent from the larger narrative. Where exactly does 'recovery', the ill-defined and often forgotten other 'r', fit into this equation, if at all?

The relationship between tracing and UNRRA's broader mandate of relief and rehabilitation remains undefined. Much of this ambiguity stems from confusion surrounding UNRRA's own definition of 'rehabilitation'. One seldom finds specific references to 'rehabilitation' in CTB records in the United Nations Archives, which begs the question of whether recovery was a distinct UNRRA phenomenon or whether it was linked to the two 'r's in its acronym. A June 1945 UNRRA report on the tracing of missing persons in Germany suggests that there is a connection to be made between physically locating the displaced and providing them with humanitarian assistance:

During its first phase, the problem was viewed largely as a humanitarian one. The reunion of deported families, the return of children to their parents, and the re-establishment of contacts disrupted by years of occupation and war were viewed as a necessary prerequisite for any sound program of repatriation or resettlement. In a larger sense, social reconstruction could not be attempted in any major sense until the basic human relationships had been restored.[31]

Curiously enough, the report does not refer to 'rehabilitation' by name, citing instead 'social reconstruction'. If one could 'restore' social networks, relationships and contacts through mass tracing operations, then tracing could facilitate the 'social reconstruction' of entire communities and states.

UNRRA contemporaries struggled to define 'rehabilitation' in their own terms. As Samantha K. Knapton points out earlier in this volume, 'rehabilitation' was mentioned eleven times in the November 1943 UNRRA Agreement without ever offering an actual definition: 'Without a clear definition of what the term rehabilitation was meant to imply, it is difficult to discern to what extent rehabilitation had, or had not, been completed.'[32] Explanations offered in archival records, such as a June 1945 UNRRA welfare guide, are often contradictory: 'Rehabilitation has three aspects: (i) mental no less than physical recovery from physical illness and starvation [...] (ii) recovery from serious emotional loss [...] (iii) recovery, by "resocialisation", from apathy, restlenessness or unreality feelings.'[33] In CTB documents, 'recovery' is used to signify the physical discovery of missing persons. Here, however, it is used to describe the physical and psychological reconstitution of an individual. The term 'resocialization' is equated with strategies used to promote rehabilitation, such as education, vocational training, repatriation and resettlement, although 'rehabilitation' is not referenced by name.

UNRRA scholars have also wrestled with its possible interpretations. As Laure Humbert posits in her study on humanitarian aid in the French occupation zone, rehabilitation through work was emphasized even though rehabilitation was a complex process that involved many approaches. Ideas about what constituted 'successful rehabilitation were based on gendered assumptions', as welfare workers 'tried to "retrain" DP mothers to care *for* (via nurturing) their children, and DP fathers to care *about* (via breadwinning) their children'.[34] New Deal policies also shifted the meaning of what rehabilitation was supposed to look like, Silvia Salvatici argues, even though few in attendance at UNRRA's first meeting in Atlantic City in 1943 seemed to understand what the term actually meant as 'the famous motto "help the people to help themselves" was supposed to summarize the programme of rehabilitation that UNRRA aimed at carrying out, but beyond it remained vagueness and ambiguity'.[35] Rehabilitation could have also been interpreted through the lens of new psychological theories and ideas, Tara Zahra argues: 'UNRRA workers did not simply understand their mission in terms of providing shelter and preventing starvation and disease, though these were formidable tasks. In a shift from earlier relief efforts, post-WWII humanitarian workers anointed themselves agents of psychological reconstruction.'[36] While each of these contributions offers insight into the various dimensions of UNRRA's rehabilitation policies, the second 'r' in UNRRA's acronym remains difficult to define.

'Social reconstruction', 'resocialization', 'recovery' and 'rehabilitation' are used interchangeably in UNRRA records without much regard for their individual meanings. Each seems to suggest a similar aim: the ability for displaced persons to transcend traumatic wartime experiences through physical and psychological avenues, and often through humanitarian assistance, to return to a state of pre-war normalcy. Recovering from such emotional and physical wounds was a long and arduous process that required skilled relief workers and humanitarian agencies. The key to beginning such a process lay in the restoration of social ties through mass recovery operations. Only then could 'social reconstruction', to borrow UNRRA's term, truly begin.

Gathering evidence

From the very beginning of its mandate, CTB workers attempted to piece together the wartime fates of missing persons. They mapped out death marches, combed German orphanages, hospitals and institutions, and searched refugee camps. As one April 1946 memorandum points out, 'the full extent of the tracing problem did not present itself until the Allied Governments came to realise the thoroughness and brutality with which Fascist agencies extirpated their enemies. The problem of identifying the dead and establishing the fate of those who cannot be found alive has come to be the purpose of many national governments'.[37] Since the search was often an exercise in determining who was still alive, the memorandum continues, it relied heavily on the 'exploitation of records and documents'.

Tracing took on an entirely new meaning in the wake of the Second World War. It was a painstaking process based on several strategies, such as collecting documentary intelligence, conducting search operations in the field and issuing public appeals. The easiest method was the study of captured German documents, or 'documentary intelligence'. 'In the midst of conquering Germany and the liberation of surviving victims of Nazism', Rebecca Boehling notes, 'the Allies, in particular the British and Americans, collected documents that survived the attempted destruction of records of concentration camps, prisons as well as forced labour.'[38] Many of UNRRA's branches, including the CTB, amassed troves of German documents used not only for tracing but also for the pursuit of international justice. Many of the records in CTB's Central Index of Records were first acquired by the Allied War Crimes Commission to prosecute German war criminals at Nuremberg. Such records included affidavits from victims and witnesses, POW camp registries, nominal rolls from death camps, hospitalization records, and *Arbeitskommando* and Gestapo records.[39] Upon obtaining and filing these documents into its central index, CTB was able to share documentary intelligence with zonal and national partners in the hopes of covering as much ground as possible.

Concentration and death camp records, which were available in abundance, usually included 'known facts on death marches, their routes and distances, known facts about concentration camps and other installations and other similar material'.[40] By June 1945, UNRRA had tracked down the death records of 50,000 victims from Buchenwald and 100,000 records from Nordhausen, mostly from German index cards on which the names, nationalities, birth and death dates of Holocaust victims had been callously recorded.[41] But the post-war search was complicated by the fact that the Nazis had destroyed much documentation at the end of the war. Such was the case in Cologne, where American military authorities learned that the Gestapo had seized and destroyed the death certificates of foreigners executed at Klingelpütz prison.[42] Another instance involved a July 1946 visit to former Gestapo headquarters in Berlin by Eyre Carter, Deputy Director of UNRRA's DP Division in Germany. Upon arrival, he was told that 'all the central records had been destroyed either by bombing or by the Security Police themselves'.[43] He received similar information from an employee at the former Ministry of Labour in Potsdam, where he learned that all documents had been incinerated as the Russians advanced on Berlin.[44] And then there were instances of pure negligence, one UNRRA telegram to the US zonal bureau in Wiesbaden reveals: 'Information received that original documents of the Gestapo being used as toilet paper in "Prinz Ludwig" Gasthaus Kochel near Munich. Send representatives to collect documents immediately.'[45]

In the absence of German documents, the CTB began to rely on duplicate records from other sources. Such was the case when UNRRA workers managed to track down copies of records from local police and employment offices, arranged neatly on alphabetized index cards, after discovering that all records at a regional labour office had been destroyed. They even found Allied POW records by searching the hospital archive of the German army information office.[46] There were also fortuitous finds. In August 1945, 2,758 captured German documents were recovered from Kreis Eichstätt in Bavaria that contained the information of Polish, Ukrainian, Yugoslav, Russian, Serbian, Italian and Lithuanian displaced persons.[47] In another instance, the War Crimes Commission supplied the names of individuals who were gassed at Neuegamme concentration camp as well as records from different *Stalag* (Nazi prison camps) nearby.[48] A search in the backyard of a house in Hamburg turned up a significant number of death records from Bergen-Belsen concentration camp spanning from January to April 1945, when the camp was liberated by British and Canadian forces. And then there was the *Mauthausen Camp Book*, a logbook that had recorded the names of concentration camp inmates in pencil.[49] The document was under possession of the Czech government who was unwilling to hand it over to UNRRA but offered to microfilm it at the cost of approximately seven pounds sterling.

Once documentary intelligence was received, it was checked against CTB's central index using a strategy called the 'meeting of the cards principle', a method that was often used by the International Red Cross and national search bureaux:

> According to this method, when 'A' enquires after 'B' their names are carded into an index where they wait until 'B' or possibly 'C' enquires after 'A'. As the names of 'A', 'B' and 'C' are added to the index a considerable body of information is accumulated against which to screen subsequent enquiries. Nevertheless, there can be no known locations, i.e., persons found, until there is a junction or 'meeting' of 'A' with 'B' or 'C'. Consequently, many enquiries are never answered, and, in any event, except in the rare case, a great lapse of time occurs before any answer is forthcoming.[50]

The 'meeting of the cards principle' meant that matches could only be made if there were two or more parties alive to submit enquiries. This was problematic in cases where family members were exterminated, especially for children who did not have surviving relatives to ask for them. The Bureau's unaccompanied children operation is a prime example of the limitations of UNRRA's mass tracing approach. The Child Search Branch (CSB), described as a 'miniature of the Central Tracing Bureau', was created in January 1946 with a three-person staff.⁵¹ By March 1946, 1,000 children of United Nations nationality were found, a number that reached 10,000 by June. By July, there were six child search teams composed of up to fifteen members who spoke twenty-seven languages combined. Despite this, the CTB was hampered by a lack of staffing and resources. Of the 5,372 UNRRA employees in Germany, which included 2,041 in its headquarters and 3,242 in the field, only eighty-nine worked in child search.⁵² The unavoidable backlog of cases that resulted generated tensions between UNRRA and Allied military authorities in Germany. By the end of 1945, the French military authorities had complained that UNRRA's search bureau was 'completely inefficient and should be abolished'.⁵³ While the British agreed with their French counterparts, the Americans felt that the CTB was an important resource that simply needed more personnel.

Although the CSB carried out tracing in all ex-enemy nations, Germany was undoubtedly the 'nodal point in the search for children'.⁵⁴ It carried out physical searches in German institutions and foster homes and used enquiries received by families as well as clues submitted by German authorities. One August 1945 inter-zonal policy ordered all German mayors to submit information regarding unaccompanied children living within their jurisdictions. By December of that year, however, only 20 per cent of the US Zone and 50 per cent of the British Zone had sent in results.⁵⁵ UNRRA realized that another approach was needed if the Bureau hoped to track down missing nationals before the end of its mandate in 1947. This prompted the CTB to issue public appeals across Europe and North America through radio broadcasts, news and film reels, and the press. Together, these petitions mobilized public opinion. As Heide Fehrenbach and Davide Rodogno point out in their study on humanitarian photography, 'the effectiveness of humanitarian rhetoric appears to depend on its apparent simplicity and directness of emotional address. It focuses viewer attention on suffering, framing it as unjust yet amenable to remedy'.⁵⁶ Such was the case in an undated radio broadcast on Genevan airwaves, during which UNRRA's CTB made the following appeal:

> This is UNRRA Central Tracing Bureau, Child Tracing Branch, Arolsen, near Kassel, Germany, broadcasting over Radio Genève by courtesy of the International Committee of the Red Cross. We are calling on all peoples of the world to help in finding members of scattered families and tracing the unrecorded dead. In this programme we ask listeners to give us any information they can which may help to reunite unaccompanied children with their lost families.⁵⁷

The broadcast, which was repeated weekly, listed the names of missing children along with other pertinent details. CTB also sent nominal rolls of missing children to be included in a daily programme on Radio Genève from 1:45pm to 2:00pm.

Such appeals were crucial to the way in which UNRRA portrayed its humanitarian mission. As Johannes Paulmann argues, 'media are an essential feature of humanitarianism – and they have been ever since individuals or organizations began to undertake humanitarian action over long distances and across frontiers'.[58] UNRRA produced over a dozen films and numerous newsreels to play throughout Europe and North America.[59] It also published the names of missing persons in over one hundred German newspapers and aired broadcasts on twenty-three European radio stations. One could also find informational videos playing in German cinemas as well as posters plastered on the walls of DP camps and German assembly centres.[60] In frequently airing radio broadcasts to wider audiences, such as the one below, UNRRA could garner the sympathy of the public by showcasing the horrendous crimes of the Nazis:

> This is UNRRA Central Tracing Bureau, Arolsen near Kassel, Germany, broadcasting over Radio Luxembourg. A famous waxwork exhibition in London has an underground department known as 'The Chamber of Horrors', for there are depicted life-size effigies of notorious criminals and murderers, together with mediaeval torture instruments and the gear of executioners. In comparison the Records Division of UNRRA Central Tracing Bureau might be likened to a spiritual chamber of horrors, for in its archives are thousands of records of sadistic cruelties practiced by the Nazis. These records have to be checked and searched as much of the information contained in them refers to missing people. The study of the documents makes gruesome readings. One report on the investigation of war crimes describes Flossenburg Concentration Camp where so many innocent victims were murdered as 'a factory dealing in death'.[61]

These blunt and emotional broadcasts provided UNRRA with an opportunity to display the noble work it was carrying out on the ground. As Paulmann ascertains, such kinds of media 'play a crucial role in providing information about other people's plight and setting public agendas'.[62] By exposing the shocking details of Nazi crimes alongside public pleas for help, UNRRA oriented the narrative of its relief and rehabilitation programmes through tracing, a long process that led displaced persons one step closer to home.

A forgotten legacy

Few UNRRA contemporaries would argue that the Bureau had successfully met its objectives by the time it shut its doors in 1947. In a note to a colleague, CTB Director Bowring expressed his pessimism toward future recovery operations in Germany:

> Although we have not been as successful as we could have been had we received more help and understanding from some of the organisations and individuals also engaged in tracing, I think that the best possible results in the existing circumstances have been obtained. I do not view the future of tracing activities in Germany with any confidence, and even if I had not decided to resign for personal reasons would have done so in view of the re-organisation now taking place.[63]

In an earlier memo of April 1946, CTB Deputy Director R. M. Trachtenberg expressed similar reservations by pointing out that the Bureau's rigid eligibility criteria hampered what could have otherwise been an effective mission: 'It would seem that the application of such strict rules would be contrary to the humanitarian principles that should head in our tracing activities and thus reduce considerably the utility of the existence of the Tracing Service.'[64] Despite these criticisms, however, the Bureau marked the first step in the rehabilitation of victims of Nazi persecution. Without it, many would never have made it home.

This chapter has excavated the history of the CTB along with its policies and practices. Careful study of CTB records in the United Nations Archives reveals some fascinating insights. First, the broader components of UNRRA's programme, namely relief and rehabilitation, are seldom mentioned or defined in CTB documents. This omission reveals two truths. First, it implies a lack of consensus amongst UNRRA contemporaries on the role that relief and rehabilitation played in post-war reconstruction processes. Second, it suggests that recovery, the ill-defined forgotten 'r', operated as a separate humanitarian phenomenon beyond the realm of UNRRA's relief and rehabilitation policies.

While the work of the CTB ended when UNRRA shut its doors, its legacies continue. The recovery of missing persons after war became a recognized international problem that required 'the strengthened continuation of the coordinating and centralizing function under a strong international body'.[65] The Bureau's tracing operations and central index were absorbed by the International Tracing Service (ITS), the International Refugee Organization

(IRO), and the Allied High Commission for Germany. In 1955, an agreement stipulated that the ITS would operate under the structure of the International Committee of the Red Cross and be managed by a Swiss delegation.[66] This arrangement persisted until 2009, when the International Commission for the International Tracing Service opened its doors to the public and made its archives accessible to all. Now part of UNESCO's Memory of the World Register, the ITS is a living testimony to millions of victims of Nazi atrocities.

These tracing milestones would not exist had it not been for the painstaking efforts of UNRRA's CTB. Although tracing changed many hands between 1943 and 1955, it was a practice that was shaped, structured and internationalized by UNRRA. Its recovery operations led to many tearful reunions and sobering moments of closure and thus provided individuals with the information needed to begin the long process of rehabilitation. Despite its short mandate, UNRRA's CTB carried out its mandate against the backdrop of a new kind of United Nations humanitarianism, whose successor agencies would continue its work for much of the post-war period. A new chapter in mass recovery operations, the CTB redefined humanitarian practice and policy for decades to come.

Notes

1. 'Luck Plays a Part', UNRRA radio broadcast transcript, undated, The United Nations Digital Archives and Records Management Section, New York, USA (hereafter abbreviated as UNA), S-0413-0001-06.
2. The Central Tracing Bureau, 'The Tracing of Missing Persons in Germany on an International Scale with Particular Reference to the Problem of U.N.R.R.A.', July 1946, UNA, S-0413-0001-05. The Allied powers, the United States, the Soviet Union, Great Britain and France were the four occupation authorities in Germany.
3. Christian Höschler, Henning Borggräfe and Isabel Panek, *Tracing and Documenting Nazi Victims Past and Present* (Berlin: De Gruyter, 2020).
4. Suzanne Brown-Fleming, *Nazi Persecution and Post-war Repercussions: The International Tracing Service Archive and Holocaust Research* (Lanham: Rowman & Littlefield, 2016).
5. Dan Stone, 'The Politics of Removing Children: The International Tracing Service's German Foster Homes Investigation of 1948', *Contemporary European History*, 30 (2021), 77.
6. Lynne Taylor, *In the Children's Best Interests: Unaccompanied Children in American-Occupied Germany, 1945–1952* (Toronto: University of Toronto Press, 2017).

7   Christine Schmidt, 'Those Left behind: Early Search Efforts in Wartime and Post-war Britain,' in Christian Höschler, Henning Borggräfe and Isabel Panek (eds.), *Tracing and Documenting Nazi Victims Past and Present* (Berlin: De Gruyter, 2020), 104–5.
8   Ibid., 105, 111. In the spring of 1945, Germany was occupied and divided into four zones: the US Zone in the south, the British Zone in the north, the French Zone in the west and the Soviet Zone in the east. Berlin, located in the Soviet Zone, was carved up into four sectors.
9   'The Tracing of Missing Persons in Germany on an International Scale with Particular Reference to the Problem of U.N.R.R.A.'
10 UNRRA Welfare Guide, 15 February 1945, The Archives Nationales de France, Pierrefitte-sur-Seine, France (hereafter abbreviated as AN), AJ/43/16.
11 'The Tracing of Missing Persons in Germany on an International Scale with Particular Reference to the Problem of U.N.R.R.A.'
12 *Activities of the Joint Relief Commission of the International Red Cross* (Geneva: November 1943), pp. 3–5, AJ/43/14. During the war, the International Committee of the Red Cross operated in Allied, Axis and neutral territories, where it created evidence logs, central indexes and carried out investigations for missing civilians and prisoners of war. It was precisely this work behind enemy lines that disqualified it from becoming the main Allied tracing apparatus after the war. For more information, see Christian Höschler, Henning Borggräfe and Isabel Panek, 'Introduction,' in *Tracing and Documenting Nazi Victims Past and Present* (Berlin: De Gruyter, 2020), 3.
13 'The Tracing of Missing Persons in Germany on an International Scale with Particular Reference to the Problem of U.N.R.R.A.'
14 Allied Control Council to UNRRA, 'Central Tracing Bureau', 26 November 1945, UNA, S-0413-0005-04.
15 Allied Control Authority, 'Points from Quadripartite Meeting', 21 November 1945, UNA, S-0413-0001-13.
16 Central Tracing Bureau Documents Intelligence, 'Notes on discussion between Captain T. Shaughnessy (British Search Bureau) and Captain R. Flohr (CTB)', 26 April 1946, UNA, S-0413-0002-09.
17 'Statement on Displaced Persons', 24 January 1946, AN, AJ/43/16. 'Ex-enemy states' included Austria, Bulgaria, Germany, Hungary, Japan, Romania and Siam. Also excluded from UN aid were ex-Wehrmacht personnel, war criminals, traitors and collaborators from any country, race or religious background, ethnic Germans (*Volksdeutsche*) and Germans Balts from Latvia, Lithuania and Estonia. Stateless persons and Italian nationals were eligible for UNRRA assistance. 'Order No. 52: Eligibility for UNRRA Assistance', 24 June 1946, AN, AJ/43/18.
18 Dorothy de la Pole, 'Enquiries which are not accepted by Central Tracing Bureau', 16 November 1945, S-0413-0005-04; 'The Tracing of Missing Persons in Germany

on an International Scale with Particular Reference to the Problem of U.N.R.R.A.'; Bowring to Flexner, memorandum, 10 July 1946, UNA, S-0413-0005-09.
19. The Central Tracing Bureau, 'The Tracing of Missing Persons in Germany on an International Scale with Particular Reference to the Problem of U.N.R.R.A.'
20. Morgan to the Swedish National Tracing Bureau, 23 November 1945, UNA, S-0413-0006-03.
21. Morgan, 'Central Tracing Bureau'.
22. 'Proceedings of a board of survey held in the Central Tracing Bureau', 1 March 1946, UNA, S-0413-0005-05.
23. 'The Tracing of Missing Persons in Germany on an International Scale with Particular Reference to the Problem of U.N.R.R.A.'
24. Morgan, 'Central Tracing Bureau'.
25. Jessica Reinisch, '"We Shall Rebuild Anew a Powerful Nation": UNRRA, Internationalism and National Reconstruction in Poland', *Journal of Contemporary History*, 43 (2008), 459.
26. The national search bureaux with whom CTB worked closely included the *Bureau National Français des Recherches* in France, the *Service d'identification et de Recherches* in Belgium, the *Informatiebureau Van het Nederlandsche Rood Kruis* in the Netherlands, the *Commissariat au Repatriement* in Luxembourg, the *Biuro Informachyne* in Poland, the *British Red Cross* in the United Kingdom and the *Central Location Index* in the United States. UNRRA European Regional Office, 'UNRRA Tracing Procedure in Different Countries', undated, S-0413.
27. Ministry of Prisoners of War, Deportees and Refugees, 'Instruction No. 1', 21 August 1945, UNA, S-0413-0004-12.
28. Polish Red Cross Chief Tracing Officer to Director of Central Tracing Bureau, 2 August 1946, S-0413-0004-15.
29. Morgan to the Swedish National Tracing Bureau, 23 November 1945, UNA, S-0413-0006-03.
30. Jessica Reinisch, 'Introduction: Agents of Internationalism', *Contemporary European History*, 25:2 (May 2016), 200; Jessica Reinisch, 'Old Wine in New Bottles? UNRRA and the Mid-Century World of Refugees', in Matthew Frank and Jessica Reinisch (eds), *Refugees in Europe, 1919–1959: A Forty Years' Crisis?* (London: Bloomsbury, 2017), 147.
31. 'The Tracing of Missing Persons in Germany on an International Scale with Particular Reference to the Problem of U.N.R.R.A.'
32. See Chapter 1 in this volume.
33. Welfare Division of the European Regional Office of U.N.R.R.A., 'Psychological Problems of Displaced Persons', June 1945, UNA, S-0413-0001-05.
34. Laure Humbert, *Reinventing French Aid: The Politics of Humanitarian Relief in French-Occupied Germany, 1945–1952* (Cambridge: Cambridge University Press, 2021), 330.

35 The national search bureaux with whom CTB worked closely included the *Bureau National Français des Recherches* in France, the *Service d'identification et de Recherches* in Belgium, the *Informatiebureau Van het Nederlandsche Rood Kruis* in the Netherlands, the *Commissariat au Repatriement* in Luxembourg, the *Biuro Informachyne* in Poland, the *British Red Cross* in the United Kingdom and the *Central Location Index* in the United States. UNRRA European Regional Office, 'UNRRA Tracing Procedure in Different Countries', undated, S-0413.

36 Tara Zahra, *The Lost Children: Reconstructing Europe's Families after World War II* (Cambridge: Harvard University Press, 2011), 89.

37 'Notes on discussion between Captain T. Shaughnessy (British Search Bureau) and Captain R. Flohr (CTB)'.

38 Rebecca Boehling, 'From Tracing and Fate Clarification to Research Center: The Role of International Players and Transnationalism in Shaping the Identity of the ITS', in Höschler, Borggräfe and Panek (eds.), *Tracing and Documenting Nazi Victims Past and Present* (Berlin: De Gruyter, 2020), 246–7.

39 Central Tracing Bureau Records' Centre, 'Gestapo Material', March 1946, UNA, S-0413-0005-06.

40 UNRRA European Regional Office, 'UNRRA Tracing Procedure in Different Countries', undated, UNA, S-0413-0005-04.

41 'Source Material: Report No. 1, War Crimes Commission, U.S. Zone'; UNRRA Central Records Office, 'Source Material: Report No. 1, War Crimes Commission, U.S. Zone', 30 June 1945, UNA, S-0413-0002-10.

42 Grötzner to Bruman, memorandum, 29 November 1945, UNA, S-0413-0001-07.

43 Eyre Carter, 'Report No. 8: German Central Records', 16 July 1945, UNA, S-0413-0004-06.

44 'Report No. 8: German Central Records'.

45 UNRRA to U.S. Zone Bureau, 6 August 1946, UNA, S-0413-0002-10.

46 Kocur to Bowring, 'Records', 28 January 1946, UNA, S-0413-0005-09.

47 'German Records of Displaced Persons', 25 August 1945, UNA, S-0413-0004-06.

48 'Notes on discussion between Captain T. Shaughnessy (British Search Bureau) and Captain R. Flohr (CTB)'.

49 E. Longley, 'Mauthausen Document in the Possession of the Czech Ministry of Social Welfare', 20 August 1946, UNA, S-0413-0004-10.

50 'Notes on discussion between Captain T. Shaughnessy (British Search Bureau) and Captain R. Flohr (CTB)'.

51 'Meeting of the Central Tracing Policy Board in Berlin'; 'UNRRA Fifth Session of the Council', 8 July 1946, AN, AJ/43/19.

52 'Appendix VII', 8 July 1946, AN, AJ/43/19.

53 Memo, 1 December 1945, AN, AJ/43/18.

54 'Child Search Programme', 13 October 1950, AN, AJ/43/302.

55 'Meeting of the Central Tracing Policy Board in Berlin'.
56 Heide Fehrenbach and Davide Rodogno, 'Introduction: The Morality of Sight', in Heide Fehrenbach and Davide Rodogno (eds.), *Humanitarian Photography: A History* (Cambridge: Cambridge University Press, 2015), 6.
57 Central Tracing Bureau radio transcript, undated, UNA, 13 October 1950, S-0413-0001-06.
58 Johannes Paulmann, 'Humanitarianism and Media: Introduction to an Entangled History', in *Humanitarianism & Media: 1900 to the Present*, vol. 1 (Oxford: Berghahn Books, 2019), 1.
59 Suzanne Langlois, '"Neighbors Half the World Away": The National Film Board of Canada at Work for UNRRA (1944–47)', in *Canada and the United Nations: Legacies, Limits, Prospects* (Kingston: McGill-Queen's University Press, 2017), 46.
60 Luxembourg Radio Script No. 50, 25 April 1947, UNA, S-0413-0001-06.
61 Luxembourg Radio Script No. 42, 28 February 1947, UNA, S-0413-0001-06.
62 Paulmann, 'Humanitarianism and Media', 1.
63 Bowring to Abbott, memorandum, 15 January 1947, UNA, S-0413-0005-09.
64 Trachtenberg, memorandum, 8 April 1946, UNA, S-0413-0005-09.
65 'The Tracing of Missing Persons in Germany on an International Scale with Particular Reference to the Problem of U.N.R.R.A.'
66 Brown-Fleming, *Nazi Persecution and Post-war Repercussions,* ix-x.

7

The Pate Reports and UNRRA: The beginning of UNICEF, 1946

Lisa Payne Ossian

Introduction

'We took no satisfaction that our repeated warnings over the years had come true,' ex-president Herbert Hoover reminded his Carnegie Hall audience on V-E Day (8 May 1945). Despite the Second World War ending in Europe on that day, Hoover's speech began with the haunting details of the increased 'starving and stunting of the bodies and minds of the children of the democracies', lamenting 'it is now 11:59 on the clock of starvation'.[1] In his speech, he made the desperate desire for some type of humanitarian action clear. Even at the beginning of the war in Europe, Hoover never relented the humanitarian ideals he had developed during the Great War. He 'campaigned for extensive cross-blockade relief' for the 'Five Small Democracies' [Poland, Belgium, Finland, Netherlands and Norway], yet his relief strategies were ignored in both London and Washington during 1940 and into 1941. He ultimately had to concede that relief efforts of emergency food rations, even for the children within occupied countries, would not be a possibility due to military concerns that the German enemy could confiscate those supplies for their own use, thus prolonging the war.[2]

This chapter will analyse the development of United Nations International Children's Emergency Fund (UNICEF) to show the direct link between it and the United Nations Relief and Rehabilitation Administration (UNRRA). In doing so, alongside highlighting the central role UNRRA played in UNICEF's creation, this chapter will also examine the often-overlooked contributions of Herbert Hoover's Famine relief survey and subsequent Pate Reports to the organization's creation. By February 1945, shortly after the Yalta Conference, Hoover expressed his misgivings about the structure, function and future of UNRRA: 'UNRRA and its failure to provide adequate relief are due for a thorough investigation by Congress and probably by Parliament,' he wrote to a colleague and publisher of the *Army and Navy* journal, John Callan O'Laughlin.[3] He continued that the 'organization must be overhauled if it is to function on the large scale desired, and that its relations with the Armies must be established upon a more workable and harmonious basis'. This was something which was later agreed upon by the Big Three at Yalta, but the planning process and its execution were two completely separate things. Promises were made to those in need that, through UNRRA, Hoover claimed, 'they would get everything they required both for sustenance and rehabilitation'. In reality, however, many of these promises went unfulfilled. According to Hoover, 'UNRRA's excuse is that it would enter into a liberated country only upon the invitation of the Government, and such invitations were not extended by either France or Belgium.'[4]

Although Hoover had initially been supportive of UNRRA's initiation in November 1943, pleased that 'preparatory action for the inevitable famine had been undertaken', he immediately identified several weaknesses of the UNRRA structure. From his experience when initiating the Commission for Relief in Belgium (CRB), during the Great War and the American Relief Administration (ARA) for Soviet famine relief in the early 1920s, Hoover lamented that the whole structure of UNRRA's organization would be cumbersome to say the least. Firstly, UNRRA's director would have to act through committees (thus slowing efficiency and immediacy), and secondly the 'internal distribution of supplies' would be controlled by recipient countries which potentially allowed for possible black markets. Devastatingly and most importantly, however, the quantity and availability of food would not be sufficient for those countries able to pay for supplies.[5]

Hoover's ideas and ideals of scientific efficiency and economic possibilities culminated from his experience with CRB and ARA into a 'payment-for-aid' procedure in which countries with financial resources, but not immediate food supplies created 'a precedent of promise of payment'. As UNICEF historian Jennifer Morris explains, 'to provide relief assistance without extracting funds countered the idea that aid was a form of temporary relief, meant solely to help a return to self-sufficiency'.[6] Hoover, however, was already familiar with criticism of his relief methods. Some thought his ideas for ARA in the Soviet Union were based upon the belief that 'his principal motives in Russia were political, for which his humanitarianism served principally as a cover'.[7] An international organization would ultimately be the result of Hoover's experience and research feeding children in the aftermath of war when it was clear UNRRA could not maintain the long-term focus needed to meet the needs of international children.

UNICEF is therefore the lasting legacy of several relief organizations before it: the CRB, the ARA and UNRRA.

This chapter will utilize a broad range of personal and professional papers of former president Herbert Hoover to track the genesis of post-war famine relief while focusing on the work of his long-term associate Maurice Pate. While providing an overview of the Pate Reports and their findings, this chapter will show how the Famine survey in 1946 influenced the establishment of an organization specifically for children in the post-1945 world. Hoover's own memoirs, published and unpublished alike, are often laudable of his own achievements without proper recognition of what others in the United States, and indeed elsewhere, were doing towards the issue of preventing a post-war famine. Read alongside the contributions to this volume, what Hoover's notes do, however, is provide a unique and interesting insight into wartime and post-war dynamics in Washington, pulling between protectionism and ideas of 'relief for sale' and the larger long-term ambitions of post-war recovery linked so closely to UNRRA's own conceptions of 'rehabilitation'. Hoover was also uniquely positioned to direct post-war famine relief due to two main factors: firstly, his past expertise in post-war famine relief, and secondly his status as a former president of the United States which thus afforded him a platform, both in public with the press, and in private amongst the current government to influence ideas at the top level. He was also a staunch critic of UNRRA who believed the organization's temporariness from the outset hindered the work it was able to complete. The chapter will therefore establish how UNRRA's unwieldy organization necessitated the development of another organization dedicated to the specific welfare of children: UNICEF. Although works have been published on the creation of UNICEF in recent years, there is little addressing the impact of the famine survey conducted in 1946 by Maurice Pate at the behest of Herbert Hoover.[8] One of UNRRA's foundational principles underpinning 'rehabilitation' was tied to the organization's mantra of 'helping the people to help themselves', but for the starving and destitute children of post-war Europe self-sufficiency was not a feasible option.

Hoover, UNRRA and the need for famine relief

Criticism of UNRRA's inability to provide long-lasting relief for children in the post-war world re-emerged after the Second World War, but Hoover found surprisingly bipartisan support from the new US president in the spring of 1945.

Just six weeks after taking office, President Harry Truman requested that Hoover visit the White House to offer his advice about the proposed Army's emergency action for the liberated countries. During that summer, the War Department would furnish a million tonnes of rations per month, but the starvation scenario seemed destined to worsen. This initial visit would be courteous but brief. Truman was trying to end two wars – the overwhelming six-year global war as well as a simmering personal political war of the previous twelve years. On 28 May 1945, Hoover returned to the White House after newly sworn-in President Harry Truman recognized the need for the former president's expertise. Rejecting old partisan rivalries, Truman requested the help of Hoover's engineering mind and humanitarian touch on a number of post-war subjects; 'I naturally raised the problem of rehabilitation of children with him,' recalled Hoover. 'I recited Mr. Roosevelt's refusals to allow us to protect them during the war. We canvassed the whole question of food relief as related in previous chapters and as he had asked me for a memorandum, I included it.'[9] Truman, who practised writing memorandums to himself during difficult situations, had sincerely requested Hoover's written summation of their first crucial meeting to further clarify the new direction for post-war famine relief. 'A program should at once be provided', Hoover's memo began, 'for undernourished children by feeding from soup kitchens and canteens, many of which already exist over these areas'.[10] Still, this initial meeting remained rather short, as there was too much to discuss in too little time.

Hoover's food relief involvement began just weeks after the Second World War ended but quickly stalled during the summer of 1945. He delivered a speech on 17 September 1945, to the Executive's Club in Chicago on 'Post-war Foreign Loans'. In the midst of his talk, he emphasized the funding needed for urgent post-war relief work stating, 'we have already pledged billions of post-war aid to foreign countries, through the International Bank, the Stabilization Fund, and the Export-Import Bank. We have rightly assumed great burdens to feed the hungry through UNRRA'.[11] In his memoir, Hoover later explained the dreaded pause on his relief effort, stating 'the President was too much engaged, and UNRRA was not interested … Therefore, I could get no attention to the subject until February 1946[…]'.[12] Yet, it was clear that by 1946 the situation of children in displaced persons (DPs) camps around Europe, and indeed the world, was continuing to worsen as the effects of wartime starvation could not be ameliorated by UNRRA's measured hand. Hoover recalled he was tasked by Truman to 'take that gigantic famine in hand. Peace and progress will not be restored if those who survive are to be infected by a generation of men and women stunted in body and distorted in mind.'[13] Famine concerns had emerged at the beginning of the Second World War with terrible echoes and reverberations from the Great War's famine largely reflected in revised food relief pamphlets with such titles as 'Our Hungry World' and 'Food, Famine and Relief'.[14] The emotional propaganda and poignant photographs collected and developed during 1946 presented no exaggeration: 'Fill His Cup First', or even more explicitly biblical, 'Bread is Life'. Hoover, a former humanitarianism and food relief expert from the Great War, had learned that children must be at the heart of the post-war story. The public must know and feel if they were to act and although Hoover was critical of UNRRA and their expenditure, he admitted they certainly both knew that the best way to ensure that a topic receives due attention is by getting the public on side. He dedicated the seventh chapter of his memoir titled *The Four Horsemen in World War II* to the necessity of preparing for famine in war's aftermath during wartime. Hoover believed Churchill and Roosevelt only delivered 'vast promises' to the world during these critical years and, 'such promises were hardly encouraging to a mother watching her children wilt before her eyes'. He remembered from his past experience that agricultural exhaustion would often occur in war areas, resulting in a 'gigantic famine'.[15] It was a haunting reminder that history may, repeat itself.

The initial plan for UNRRA had been developed by Dean Acheson, Assistant Secretary of State, who, as Hoover detailed in his memoir with a recounting that certainly was not without personal or professional bias, had 'neither food, economic, nor international experience'. Representatives from Great Britain, the USSR and China gathered two weeks after Pearl Harbour for this first discussion on 21 December 1941 and drafted a preliminary document for the proposed relief organization. What concerned Hoover as he read the notes from this meeting, however, was (and he italicized this point in his typeset memoir) – that the organization would function when '*unanimous in every decision*'. Effectively this meant 'the birth of a veto by a single member'.[16] Just one vote could undo all logical plans, and Hoover was wary of the Soviet Union due to his second humanitarian organizational feat, famine relief in the Soviet Union during 1921–3.

Hoover would continue to criticize this United Nations' organization before it even began as yet another 'New Deal futility', believing that the United States would be paying over '95 per cent of the bill'.[17] The lack of a cooperative, coordinated structure as well as fair financing for this proposed relief organization made no sense to Hoover – it was too theoretical and certainly not practical.[18] President Roosevelt had announced on 25 September 1943 that a relief agreement to be named UNRRA would be signed by forty-four nations during a White House Ceremony on 9 November.[19] The location of the signing and the stipulation that UNRRA's Director General be an American, all furthered Hoover's negative opinion about UNRRA: 'It was obvious to any child', he later wrote, 'that the vast majority of both the money, food and supplies for UNRRA would come from the American people'.[20] When UNRRA's Deputy Director General Haskell resigned in August 1946, he communicated his misgivings of the organization's structure, offering to Hoover 'a wealth of material on the wastes and incompetence already going on'. Years later Hoover expressed strong misgivings about the fate of UNRRA, claiming that 'in 1946, I was to see with my own eyes the rottenness of the organization and its failure to meet the world problems'. One of his biggest criticisms was that 'over $400 million had been expended in overhead, as compared to $2 million in 1919–1920 when we fed more people'.[21] Hoover's opinion of UNRRA, although critical and perhaps a little too harsh, was in line with many at the time who had already seen the vast organization undergo administrative restructuring in 1944 as the whole mess had entangled itself. UNRRA's promise of delivering both relief and rehabilitation in the aftermath of war was, by 1946, seen as somewhat of a figment of the planner's imagination. As detailed at the beginning of this volume, what 'rehabilitation' actually meant was so thoroughly contested by administrators, donors, field workers and the displaced themselves that understanding what was wanted became an impossible task.

To Hoover, the problem of separating relief from rehabilitation was not an issue. While analysing his memoirs, it was clear his focus was solely on the child and what they needed after immediate relief had been provided. In war's aftermath, the time had come again to raise this poignant problem, or, in Hoover's dramatic words, 'a world-wide crusade'. When Hoover first delivered his V-E Day speech, he stated that 'there should be an organization for special feeding to undernourished children and mothers over the whole of Europe, including Germany'. Hoover had proclaimed quite daring words – assisting an enemy, albeit children on the very day of Victory in Europe. Although humanitarian efforts were already underway, convincing the American public to assist the enemy was another problem entirely; one similarly shared on the British home front when advocates such as Victor Gollancz were canvassing local members of parliament to ensure food and sustenance was sent to Germany to aid not only DPs, but the Germans themselves.[22] Hoover lamented that 'infant mortality is very high everywhere on the Continent and unless special supplies are available, it will be still higher. In some areas it is now over fifty per cent.'[23]

There was no real victory to Hoover as a Quaker as even after the Second World War ended, children were still dying, horrifically, needlessly.

Events plummeted during this immediate post-war era with a hectic summer, confusing fall and dreadful winter. Ten months after the end of the Second World War, the world had endured a series of constant end-of-war emergencies with a poor autumn harvest, and many of the world's people now faced 'The Greatest Famine in all History'.[24] At the start of the new year of supposed peace, Truman's concerns accelerated as highlighted in a New York City press statement delivered on 8 February 1946, titled 'On President Truman's Appeal to Save Food', where he spoke of UNRRA's efforts. 'UNRRA is devoting itself largely to helping Eastern Europe', the president noted, 'and while the problem is not one of charity for Western Europe, whose supplies can be financed, yet it is no less urgent that food must be made available.'[25] Soon enough, Hoover had arranged a famine mission, at the request of Truman, in order to assess the extent of the problem in Europe. A group of experts titled the Famine Mission Men, who were chosen by Hoover, would fly to Paris and begin work.

Yet, another evaluative task remained in March before the Famine Mission Men could fly to Paris. Hoover, in conjunction with the Combined Food Board leaders (composed of the United States, United Kingdom and Canada), evaluated sixty-four countries and divided these into three major classifications of food supplies: deficit (45), self-sufficient (15) and major surplus (4).[26] The four countries with major surplus food stocks remained Argentina, Australia, Canada and the United States. The two major arguments for (or against) the four countries' contributions of food supplies, particularly of wheat and rice, then became militarism and humanitarianism. Of the forty-five deficit countries, seventeen were European with a combined population of 305 million, along with almost 30 million people who lived in Africa, the French provinces and South Africa, and seven Asian countries. A combined population total of almost 1 billion people lived with such drastic deficits in food supplies that they were nearing the brink of starvation.[27] The Soviets, however, could not be classified properly by the Combined Food Board due to a lack of available formal information.

The net result of Hoover's global computations proved startling: 313 million people had become 'confronted with the problem of providing overseas food for some 1.4 billion [sic] hungry people in "deficit" countries'. A desperate world now needed 26 million tonnes of cereal for a minimum of 1,500 calories per person. The situation, as Hoover simply stated, looked 'hopeless': 'On the basis of these statistics, it now appeared that we could not prevent mass starvation among over 800 million [sic] people.'[28] Following these initial computations, reassuring but persuasive speeches needed to be made. Hoover, mindful not to be ambiguous, stated 'the inevitable aftermath of war is famine and with famine civilization itself is jeopardized'. He continued, that after this world war, the United States however remained 'the last great reservoir' for aid, furthering:

> There is thrust upon us one of the greatest obligations of these troubled years … It is my belief that the American people will respond again, as they did after the last war. And we cannot fail. If we fail, we shall see a world of disorders which will paralyze every effort at recovery and peace. We shall see the death of millions of fellow human beings. Guns speak the first word of victory, but only food can speak the last word.[29]

This famine mission trip would be fast-paced, serious, complicated, diplomatic, economic, exhausting and exhilarating: every minute of every day – except seven or eight hours to sleep – was filled with work and anxieties. 'This account', Hoover recorded in *An American Epic*, 'is not a travelogue of journeys – of hotels good or bad, of people intelligent or apathetic, or of the incidents of such an unusual mission, [but] a race with a ghastly famine.'[30]

After reaching their first destination of Paris on 19 March, the day began with the never-completely-routine round of meetings with prominent dignitaries, food officials, military men and community leaders as well as observations of the local children's institutions. On 22 March the mission colleagues flew again to Rome for their second stop on this complicated itinerary, which included a vital visit to the Vatican to meet Pope Pius XII. The Pope's smiling yet serious tone added to the gracious hour-long visit, as Hugh Gibson recalled, and filled a serious political and religious void.[31] The Pope's attentive manner to Hoover assured his dedication – along with the often-repeated phrase 'willingly, most willingly' – with the intention to create a powerful, worldwide Catholic message to alleviate famine distress.[32] While Hoover was in Europe conducting his famine survey, UNRRA delegates travelled to Atlantic City's Traymore Hotel in late March to discuss the extreme food crisis which threatened one-fourth of the world's population. The United States had reportedly 'fallen behind on its promised food deliveries'. UNRRA's newly appointed Director-General Fiorello LaGuardia wasted no time in attracting media attention: 'Protocol is off … I want plows, not typewriters … Ticker tape ain't spaghetti … I want fast-moving ships'.[33] LaGuardia may have been a media sensation, but his motives to make UNRRA a more effective global relief organization appeared to be sincere, as the photo caption in *Newsweek* stated, 'Statistics of Death Haunt new UNRRA Chief.' He would also be quoted in the same magazine, declaring the urgency of UNRRA's relief work, saying 'People only die once.'[34]

Surveying the globe: The Pate Reports in twelve countries

Hoover had recruited 'the invaluable Maurice Pate' for this difficult journey as he initiated and directed child feeding operations in several countries during and after the Great War. Pate had proved himself, working long days and travelling extensively to aid the starving in Belgium, and he continued to work with Hoover during the interwar years. Following their first survey visits to France and Italy, Hoover assigned Pate the specific duty of investigating the child problem in each of the thirty-eight countries they visited in 1946. Their publicity work on the famine issue would also be extensive. In Hoover's own words, Pate 'hammered away on this urgent question', compiling research and composing reports, while Hoover delivered speeches both in person and on the radio as well as specific press statements regarding the feeding of children in this traumatic post-war era. He gave a total of twenty-one such speeches and press statements between 4 March and 28 June 1946. 'I was determined', Hoover promised himself, 'to indurate the public mind of the world with the problem'.[35]

Pate would travel the world to develop the famine story and secure food facts, always with the world's children in mind. Could they eat? Were they growing? Did they play? While speaking to a reporter in Paris, Hoover stated, 'here's how I see my job: After the last war I directed food supplies for a large part of Europe. Now I've been called back again like an old family doctor.'[36] Food did equal freedom, but in the immediate aftermath of the Second World War the politics of food grew complex and bitter. At this point, when famine threatened a quarter of the world's population, it was clear that the work conducted by Pate and the Famine Mission Men was crucial to the development of post-war societies, and with it some stability.

To undertake the Famine Mission, Pate would assess children's health and welfare in his characteristic style of short reports of each country's status. Each nation's numbers and statistics would be different – depending on the available 'narrative' of each country's wartime conflict and aftermath. The 'narrative' constructing these reports was often established in each country as Pate sought out and listened to local social workers, teachers, nurses, doctors and relief workers. Although it was a case of whoever may be available during his visit, it was clear from his reports that the insights provided by those he consulted, and the anecdotes of children's lives he gathered, would have a great impact on future consultations of emergency and sustained relief for children. Hoover noted that from 'Mr. Pate's appraisal' on the condition of children in 1946, 'untold numbers' of needy children still existed in Europe, Russia, the Middle East and Asia.[37]

As former Director of Prisoner of War Activities of the American Red Cross, Pate ultimately reported to Hoover that twenty million European children from infancy to early adulthood required supplementary feeding. When their Emergency Famine Mission reached Cairo, Egypt, Pate gathered his summations of children's health conditions for each of the visited European counties to be printed by the US Department of Agriculture and presented to President Truman as well as members of the new United Nations. He simply titled his pamphlet 'The Children Are Hungry'.[38] Pate had very little time in each of the countries to radically assess their dramatic conditions and shortages. Twelve countries thus composed 'The Pate Reports': Poland, Finland, Sweden, Norway, England, the Netherlands, Belgium, Denmark, Germany, Austria, Greece and Yugoslavia. In each country, Pate had collected one- or two-page reports, gathering facts along the Mission survey's route, and he found that of the 40 million children (0–18 years) in the world, 20 million are seriously underfed and 11 million are now orphans or 'half-orphans' due to the Second World War. Pate, like Hoover, wanted to use the dramatic reality of unfathomable numbers to ensure something was done. Although UNRRA provided the necessities for post-war relief, it was unable to then provide additional food and nourishment to help the already stunted bodies of children and adolescents. After the report was submitted, Pate's name carried a new formal title: 'Member of former President Hoover's globe-circling party investigating famine conditions'. Alongside the shocking numbers, Pate's report to Truman and the United Nations formed a proposal entitled 'The Child Feeding Program', a compilation of the nutrition surveys from Poland through Yugoslavia which he had compiled, composed, printed and presented from Cairo.[39]

The Famine Mission had already visited France, Italy, Switzerland and Czechoslovakia initially, but Hoover had not called upon him to specifically start measuring the status of children's health until their Poland visit. He placed an emphasis on school meals as well as the milk, fats, protein, cereals, calories, and rations that children within each country were receiving. Still, most of Europe's children desperately needed more supplies. The different statistics presented within each country offered different facets to the story, and Pate's process depended on what possible information could be gathered within a short time, usually one or two days within each country's visit, combined with reports provided by officials regarding their country's narrative. Pate believed the plight in Poland to be the very worst with over a million orphans and 'half orphans', of which 23 per cent attempted to somehow care for themselves within a drastic post-war environment.⁴⁰ The text demonstrated urgency: 'Herbert Hoover pleads for food for children like these young Poles'. Children's mortality now approached 20 per cent, and Pate would surmise that the Polish people were 'the most poignant human problem in Europe today'.⁴¹

In Finland, adolescents' health grew increasingly more vulnerable as their 'inadequate and unbalanced diet renders them less resistant to illness'. Tuberculosis cases ranked 16 per 10,000, the highest rate of the other Scandinavian countries [Sweden, Norway and Denmark]. Pate described childcare in Finland as 'an heroic effort', with 75 per cent of elementary schools serving modest noon lunches, and within a month of their visit 83 per cent of Finnish children receiving these meals thanks to Quaker and other private charitable initiatives.⁴² He stated that 99 per cent of the money for Finland's food relief came from public government sources, but private efforts pushed 'to carry out the laws for the health and protection of children'. Hoover's press statement in Helsinki on 1 April 1946 spoke of these charitable efforts: 'The American Quakers, the Lutherans, the Red Cross and UNRRA, are giving service to the children and adults in these distressed areas and the refugees. But it is insufficient.'⁴³

Children, aged up to eight years, consumed what was available from the national Finnish milk supply, and 'in spite of noon soup in schools', the 600,000 children within the 8–18-year bracket demanded the most attention, as the 'noon soup' only amounted to 355 calories per serving along with 50 grams of dark bread at approximately 115 calories. Finland's children desperately needed more fats, proteins, sugar and cocoa – 'for morale' – in order to relieve 'a very drab, unchanging diet'.⁴⁴ Children's health conditions varied in the other Scandinavian countries. Of the 6.6 million residents of Sweden, 1.4 million were children (ages 0 to 15). As stated in the first sentence of the Swedish 'The Health and Child Care' report, this country had not experienced a Nazi occupation – its thefts, violence and deprivations – during the Second World War, and had fared best. As reported and observed by Pate, the health in Sweden ranked 'unusually high'. Some rationing existed within the country, but food appeared 'ample'. Milk would not be rationed, and dairy consumption had doubled since 1938. As a consequence, the annual birth rate since 1938 had increased over 50 per cent. The school feeding programme, as Pate determined, had been 'steadily developing' since 1943 when 523,000 pupils received lunches, yet Pate could garner no exact health statistics on the development of school feeding within neutral Sweden after the war years.

Despite the long years of Nazi occupation, Norway's health records would appear in the first full post-war year as 'generally good', but because of their 'insufficient war diet', most Norwegian children measured at least four to five pounds underweight by 1945. No school lunches had yet been planned, but the Norwegian government, however, did reach almost 95 per cent of children by providing free breakfasts of milk, bread, butter, whey cheese, carrots, apples or oranges.[45]

Pate emphatically stated, however, that 'England has the most advanced, extensive, and generous system of supplementary child feeding of any country in the world'. The section of the Pate Reports titled 'Child Feeding in England' earned strong praise by April of 1946 for its country's post-war efforts. With 4.5 million British children of school age, nearly 1.85 million received supplementary meals, and 3.2 million received one or two-third pint containers of milk. From all surveyed British health officials, Pate received word that the health status of English children had never been higher. With new attention placed on social welfare, particularly following evacuation of urban children to safer rural areas, the collective height and weight (even combining all economic classes) for British children's health had reached an 'all-time high'. Pate observed the British children seemed to be 'looking unusually well and round'. A routine school meal now included corned beef, mashed potatoes with gravy, a mixed green salad with mayonnaise sauce, cheese, raw carrots and pudding with sauce. Still, a notation followed: 'No bread is served.' This phrase referred to an initial and rather bitter argument over bread rationing in Britain, unlike in the United States, which would continue until 1953. No British bread rationing had been implemented during the war years, but the aftermath proved dire for the Empire with shortages of wheat and coal in particular.[46]

At the time of the Famine Mission visit, health conditions and the care of children within the Netherlands appeared to be 'generally good'. The critical period of the last six months of the Second World War when the actual individual caloric intake fell to the extreme range of 800 to 1,000 calories per day – starvation conditions – is what the Dutch referred to as 'The Hunger Winter'.[47] Aid came to the Netherlands later that spring, but in 1946 food levels still remained unpredictable. Ironically, a larger number of children in the Netherlands had received school meals during the German occupation, but now this number of assisted children had fallen to a very low level, less than 3,000. Many families did not favour or support post-war child feeding because it required still desperately needed ration coupons that could, perhaps, be better utilized for the entire family.

A sad irony existed within Belgium, the country where Hoover had first developed and practised child feeding during the Great War. Throughout the Second World War, more attention had remained focused on child health, but now in the complicated aftermath Belgium's school feeding programmes had fallen to almost zero per cent by 1946. Only a small amount of government aid existed while children desperately needed more milk and fats. Child mortality statistics, Pate stated, 'tell the story': in 1942, 7.68 per 100; 6.71 in 1943; 7.49 in 1944, but by 1945–6, children's mortality in Belgium had risen to 9.52 per 100 (almost 10 per cent).[48] The health conditions in Denmark, however, remained 'generally sound'. In official observations of children's overall health in each country's urban setting, Pate and Hoover always looked to see if children were playing as a sure sign of well-being, and as he commented on the Danish youth, 'The children were energetically playing games in court yards'. Although UNRRA did not create any form of strict criteria for assessing children's playtime – they were certainly more mindful of linguistic and social development – the general indication to assess a child's progress for many welfare workers was observing whether they could enjoy activities. The laughter which appeared during play appeared to be the most positive sign in a conquered country's recent recovery, as children's laughter implied strength, growth and overall well-being: a sure sign of rehabilitation in more ways than one.

Children's health in Germany remained the most complicated and deficient as infant mortality rates were compounded by diseases such as diphtheria and tuberculosis. In all four German quadrants, the occupying nations had attempted a positive start towards regaining this conquered country's heath and morale.[49] For example, the occupying military units reserved any fresh milk supplies solely for infants. Children's rations often consisted of a very welcome hot soup on 'a dank day', and these patient children, as Pate poignantly observed that April, always appeared 'very grateful'. Yet for these bewildered German children, the 'stunting process of wartime' would continue, unabated, for years to come.[50] Many experts considered Austria to be the country facing the most serious health conditions. In Vienna, their 'Soup to Children' programme consisted mostly of a starch base and lacked any fats or proteins.

While visiting Czechoslovakia, the white tie and tails evening dinner of thirty guests posed problems. 'Everybody was there', explained Hugh Gibson, Hoover's dedicated associate. 'The head of UNRRA for Czech is a Russian, Alexiew who appeared in the whitest tie and the longest tails', Gibson said. His prose went on to demonstrate a bit of awe, then frustration:

He looked like something carved out of hard wood with a dull knife and was very regal. It was idiotic to put him in charge of UNRRA, but our timid old Lehmann [sic] was sure we could not operate unless a Russian was put in charge […] Needless to say, the whole operation has been represented to the Czech people as a work of Russian charity. The trains come in, covered with Russian flags and pictures of Stalin, and the communists make speeches about the brotherly love of Uncle Joe. The new Deputy Director is an American, Winn, and he has secured from the Czechs the printing of new ration cards on which it is printed that the material sent in is the gift of UNRRA, but of course he has not been able to add that we provide over 90% of it and Russia next to none.[51]

Yet, Hoover would speak charitably at a press conference in Prague on 28 March 1946 concerning the food conditions in Czechoslovakia after seven years of German occupation. To avoid complicating the matter, he merely stated that 'without UNRRA, the Czechoslovaks could not have carried on thus far'.[52]

Greece did not fare much better where Pate visited a foundling hospital and discovered 'the vulnerable group' – children, mothers, hospital patients, refugees – in severe condition despite the efforts of a group called *Pikpa* (Patriotic Foundation for Mothers and Children) who had been active for decades and now received UNRRA rations to continue aid contributions.[53] The last country surveyed within the Pate Reports would be Yugoslavia which now faced a sudden influx of refugees with severe crowding conditions. Tuberculosis had increased in children, but few, if any, institutions were available to tend these children as patients. Out of the overall 14.5 million population in Yugoslavia, the Pate Reports stated that 1 million children 'seriously require supplementary feeding'.[54] As tension mounted between the Soviet Union and the United States in 1946, whoever was deemed to be the benevolent supplier of food and supplies would quickly garner public attention and, according to Hoover, Yugoslavia had been 'kept in ignorance by their Communist regime'. He added, 'The fact that we contributed anything to UNRRA or to them is unknown to anyone in Yugoslavia. It is a Communist state, with a completely controlled press … Instead, directly or indirectly, UNRRA was supporting Tito's army. Altogether it is a very sad chapter.'[55]

Within Pate's 'Child Health and Welfare in Egypt', he described the supplementary school feeding programme within a typical village near Cairo where infant mortality remained very high even after the war years. Yet, Pate could not devote much time to collecting Egyptian data as he needed to spend most of his days in Cairo editing and polishing his collection of child health reports which were to be mimeographed at the American Embassy and then delivered to Truman. Pate self-described his continual work as 'the systematic canvass of the condition of the children'.[56] Hoover delivered the first of a four-part radio address on the world's famine conditions from Cairo on 19 April. President Truman, Secretary of Agriculture Anderson and UNRRA Director La Guardia would compose the other three portions. 'The reconstruction of the children is more precious than factories or bridges,' Hoover stated poignantly during his part. 'They will determine the good or evil future of Europe. The food supplied by UNRRA to the nations they serve has been an untold blessing.'[57] The Hoover Famine Mission, however, was nearly cut short by President Truman after they had visited the proposed European countries. Only after a tense but productive long-distance phone call (only two-and-a-half minutes) from Truman in Egypt would Hoover be able to persuade the president to continue their mission.[58] The mission pushed onward to India, China, Korea, Japan and the Philippines, finally landing in Hawaii on 8 May (the anniversary of V-E Day), having travelled in 155.25 flight hours exactly 31,687 miles, circling the globe in fifty-five days.

The birth of UNICEF

Hoover delivered his nationwide radio report on 17 May 1946, from The Sherman Hotel in Chicago, stating

> The further proof is that there are somewhere from twenty to thirty million physically subnormal children on the Continent … After the war in 1919–1920, we gave a good extra meal a day, of 500 or 600 calories of restorative food, to 12,000,000 children. I deplore that this special aid for children has had no counterpart through a wide-spread organization set up after this war.[59]

Hoover then emphasized:

> Civilization marches forward upon the feet of healthy children. It is not too late to stop this most costly retreat and its debacle of endless evil. Our Mission has stimulated some action for children, both in Europe and Asia. It is a primary job for the United Nations Organization, if peace and good-will are to be re-established on earth. UNRRA was intended to focus on almost twenty per cent of the world's food needs.[60]

It was a fantastically improbable task. As Hoover assessed, 20 per cent of UNRRA's supplies were donated by charitable means, mostly from the United States, but many of the hungry people in the world could purchase food if only they had access to these supplies – 'it is the furnishing of supplies which people can buy, yet they are as hungry as the destitute'.⁶¹ Before closing his radio address, Hoover expressed 'tribute to my colleagues on this journey' as well as 'the great army of men and women in every nation over the world who are working unceasingly to save these millions of lives'.⁶²

When the thirty delegates of the United Nations Food and Agricultural Committee met in Washington on 20 May 1946, this meeting 'offered a chance to get something started on by way of organization'. Hoover delivered a nine-point talk, and in point five he noted that the United Nations by 1 September should absorb the food and agricultural activities of UNRRA 'which covers only 20 per cent of the present world problems'. Although Hoover recounts in his memoirs that he was the one 'urging' the delegates that a special organization needed to be setup for the children, declaring 'they agreed with me, and passed a resolution', Dr Ludwik Rajchman is largely credited with suggesting UNRRA's excess expenditure go towards helping a specialist organization for children.⁶³

During his many years as a humanitarian, the former president had learned enough about political institutions to realize that sometimes a good idea needed to be handed off to others. He passed the reins over to Maurice Pate and Arthur Ringland (of the State Department), as well as Congressman Christian Herter. All of whom were important men in Hoover's Second World War relief organization to save 'the Five Small Democracies' at the outbreak of hostilities, and they became the three individuals charged to 'push it'. On 23 August, Ringland crossed out the letterhead, The President's War Relief Control Board, in order to save paper for the Advisory Committee on Voluntary Foreign Aid from the Washington Building in DC. He must have believed Pate would appreciate the cost-saving gesture:

> Dear Maurice: UNRRA has just advised me of the following cable received from Council meeting in Geneva which was concluded August 16th: International children's fund recommended, that funds remaining at completion of UNRRA's work may with Central Committee approval be utilized for children and adolescents, contemplates creation of international children's fund to be supplemented by public and private gifts.

As Ringland concluded his brief but informative letter, 'It is presumed, that the action of the Council is in follow-up of Mr Hoover's suggestion to the UN' to 'push it'.⁶⁴ Hoover believed that from July to December 1946, the American press was inundated with stories of the misuse of appropriations to UNRRA due to inefficiency and corruption. 'These corruptions were ventilated in Congress,' Hoover explained. 'LaGuardia and his publicity bureau did their utmost in denials, but the evidence was overwhelming.' By September 1946, Hoover's press agent Frank Mason jotted some speech notes on 'UNRRA as a political tool'. Hoover would state that he saw UNRRA as 'an instrument of aggression and domination by the U.S.S.R'. He went further with an anecdote, 'The most accurate description was the unintentional typographical error of the New York Herald Tribune on July 27, 1946, when UNRRA was translated as 'the United Nation's Russian Relief Administration.'[65] Although not the first time UNRRA's acronym was altered to sleight the organization, the constant reporting on black-marketeering across the DP camps in Germany quickly led to widespread discontent about how UNRRA's goods were controlled and used.[66]

Although the conception of UNRRA by the United Nations was always considered to be a temporary organization, its end was rough. 'Finally, in December 1946, the American Government determined UNRRA must die'. Hoover's statement was brusque, 'American relief was here after to be undertaken directly by American agencies. The residual funds were turned over to the Children's Fund under the United Nations.'[67] That day was five years after the Pearl Harbour attack. Hoover's words would be softer at a banquet address in New York City to honour His Excellency, the prime minister of Greece, on 16 December when he informed the guests that 'International relief through UNRRA will cease in fifteen days' while simultaneously honouring the Greek commitment in seeking political justice and moral support from the United Nations.[68] Hoover later emphasized that 'Maurice Pate had been an important official in our children's reconstruction organization in Europe after the First World War when we had organized 18 nations for rehabilitation of 12 to 14 million subnormal children'. Within a later memoir, Hoover deliberately contributed significant space to Pate, stating that 'he devoted himself solely to this particular task … He presented me, for each country we visited, a complete report based on his own observations, his own wide experience in Europe, the reports of technicians in those governments and information from the various children's aid organizations.'[69] These reports remained crucial to Hoover and his ability to accurately detail and describe – both factually and symbolically – the stories of famine upon children's lives. 'First, the children in the occupied democracies had come out of the war with all the disabilities we had so often foretold when we were urging relief for them,' lamented Hoover. Mortality was terrible, rising as high as 25 per cent in some regions, and Pate seriously estimated a minimum of 30 million 'subnormal' children in Europe alone.[70] 'The second vital fact which he established', as Hoover sadly concluded, 'was that only sporadic efforts were being made at rehabilitation of the children, mostly by the Swedes.'

Conclusion

On 3 December 1946, Hoover wrote to Truman to thank him for his 'kind note' of 29 November, but also to make a suggestion for the world food situation in the upcoming year. Hoover would go on to enumerate a number of points, but crucially he wished for the distribution of American food to never be under international control again – except for the rehabilitation of children – as 'the experience with UNRRA should be enough'. He also wished to 'coordinate any action that we may take with other governments but not accept any joint control'.[71] Although an understandable position, this was the same basis upon which American participation in UNRRA had been agreed as it was only ever to have American director generals.[72] His second point reiterated his belief that countries should pay for food purchases, 'however insecure the credit may be', and his third point was that the United States should end government charity immediately except for children. His fourth and final point added that 'the United Nations should set up some rehabilitation of European children', but because the United States would certainly be making the majority of the financial contributions, 'the direction should be American'. Although Maurice Pate remained unnamed directly at this juncture, it became predictable his name would be thrown into the ring. President Truman wrote directly back three days later expressing his gratitude for his letter and concluding the suggestions of America's participation in the distribution of food were sound.[73] UNRRA's fate appeared to be sealed. Merely having an American Director General clearly did not satisfy.

UNICEF came into existence in December 1946 in part persuaded by the Pate Reports. The new United Nations Organization's committee delegates considered the different ramifications of such an international organization, or, as Hoover phrased it, 'fiddled with the subject' until a meeting of the Assembly on 7 December 1946, shortly after his exchange with Truman, to ultimately pass a resolution titled 'International Children's Emergency Fund'.

The new committee selected Dr Ludwik Rajchman as UNICEF's first chair of the organization – a former Polish delegate to UNRRA and specialist in public health who had suggested at UNRRA's last meeting that residual funds be transferred to a child feeding programme.[74] Rajchman, a supporter of the new Polish communist government, was not much liked by his American counterparts for his life of excess in the United States, but his apparent commitment to all things communist when back in Poland. As Morris asserts, however, when discussing Rajchman in private papers it was becoming clear that 'Cold War tensions had infiltrated the UN from the start'.[75] For Hoover, the process had swung too far astray, rankling within his organized 'anti-statism' mind. He attempted to intervene to ensure that Pate was put forward as the organization's administrator. Although Rajchman was friendly to Pate and Hoover from the 'old Polish days', Hoover rounded up the votes from the Dutch, Belgian, French, Brazilian and Czechoslovakian delegates on the Children's Fund to formally nominate Maurice Pate as its first executive director. Hoover also spoke directly to the UN Secretary General Trygve Lie, 'emphasizing to him Pate's unique experience in 1919–20 and his familiarity with the situation in 1946'.[76] Maurice Pate had dutifully travelled as special envoy of Hoover's on this worldwide emergency famine tour to assess starvation, disease and other forms of war's destruction in twenty-five countries throughout Europe and Asia. Pate particularly focused on children's wartime aftermath by visiting homes, hospitals, clinics, orphanages, schools, kitchens and refugee camps. He compiled complex statistics, noted calorie levels, counted population demographics, captured emotional photographs, interviewed exhausted caregivers, measured infant mortalities and held little children's hands. His research, 'The Pate Reports', of children's health and welfare in the aftermath of the Second World War emphasized Hoover's final message to President Truman regarding the needs of the world's children in war's aftermath, initiating the formation of UNICEF.

After this extensive expedition visiting thirty-five capital cities and travelling over 35,000 miles while conducting expert reporting during the famine mission of 1946, Maurice Pate's consistent and empathetic work regarding the world's children would be rewarded. On 10 December 1946, the United Nations created UNICEF and Maurice Pate would be nominated to serve as the executive UNICEF director from its initiation in January 1947 until his death in 1965.[77] 'Historically speaking', as Pate would fondly write to his mentor Hoover on 1 November 1954, 'the idea of the inception of the United Nations Children's Fund goes back to 18 March 1946. This is the day we were crossing the Atlantic from Stefansville to the Azores by plane, en route to Paris.' Pate could only begin to have imagined that this journey would be a new phase in his life's work to dramatically improve the status of children's health around the world.

The Director General of another organization, UNESCO, would later write in a pamphlet titled 'Children, War's Victims: The Education of the Handicapped' of war's effect on 'a tragic generation … war-damaged and war-endangered'. He deeply hoped and believed that these European children 'may be liberated from the handicaps of our times and grow up to become courageous, peace-minded young people who will be social minded, cooperative, and ready to accept and defend the responsibilities of freedom'.[78] UNRRA's efforts had fallen somewhat short of ensuring the children in post-war Europe were not only fully fed, but 'rehabilitated' in a number of ways to ensure they could readjust to post-war life. Keith Lowe in his work on post-war Europe would comment, 'for all its failings, UNRRA is often remembered with fierce affection by the DP's [displaced persons] themselves. UNRRA workers were usually the first non-violent foreigners these people encountered, and they provided the one thing that many DP's craved above all else: compassion.'[79]

Hoover certainly recognized the need for an international relief organization following the Second World War, but he believed a long-term agency with a renewed focus on children's food, health, and educational needs with a balanced funding of governmental and private support would be the most effective to save children's lives. Maurice Pate had dutifully and creatively served as UNICEF's executive director until his sudden death in January 1965. 'Later that year', as Morris would conclude, 'UNICEF whose global status and reputation as the most successful child relief aid organization in the world was due largely to Pate's efforts, would be awarded the Nobel Peace Prize'. Indeed, for almost twenty years Pate had consistently served as UNICEF's 'architect and builder'.[80]

Today tens of millions of children have been saved by UNICEF. During its seventy-five-year legacy, and as the UNICEF website proudly proclaims: 'All children deserve to live happy and healthy lives.'[81]

Notes

1 Herbert Hoover, *An American Epic: The Guns Cease Killing and the Saving of Life from Famine Begins, 1939–1963. Volume Four* (The Hoover Institution of War, Revolution, and Peace. Chicago: Henry Regnery Company, 1964), 102–3.

2 J.H. George, Jr., 'Another Chance: Herbert Hoover and World War II Relief', *Diplomatic History*, 16:3 (July 1992), 389–407.

3 The Yalta conference was held between 4 and 11 February 1945 with the 'Big three' in attendance: United Kingdom, United States, and Soviet Union represented by Prime Minister Winston Churchill, President Franklin D. Roosevelt and General Secretary Joseph Stalin.

4 Herbert Hoover Presidential Library-Museum, Post Presidential: Individual. Box 171: O'Laughlin, 1944-O'Laughlin, 1949: File Correspondence, January–February 1945.

5 Hoover, *An American Epic*, 86–7.
6 Jennifer M. Morris, *UNICEF: The Origins of UNICEF, 1946–1953* (New York: Lexington Books, 2015), 16.
7 Bertrand M. Patenaude, *The Big Show in Bololand: The American Relief Expedition to Soviet Russia in the Famine of 1921* (Stanford, CA: Stanford University Press, 2002), 137.
8 For a history of UNICEF, see Morris, *UNICEF*.
9 Hoover, *An American Epic*, 105–9.
10 Ibid.
11 Herbert Hoover, *Addresses upon the American Road, 1945–1948* (New York: D. Van Nostrand Company, Inc., 1949), 10.
12 Hoover Institution, The Hoover Library on War, Revolution, and Peace (hereafter HLWPR), typeset draft of Hoover's memoir, *The Four Horsemen of World War II*, 211–12.
13 HLWPR, *The Four Horsemen of World War II*, 211–12.
14 The National Archives, Kew, London (hereafter TNA), Foreign Office (hereafter FO) 371/59607, 'League Publication: "Food, Famine and Relief, 1940–1946"', cover; United States Department of Agriculture, Office of Information 'Our Hungry World', April 1946, cover.
15 HLWPR, *The Four Horsemen*, 93.
16 Ibid., 94.
17 Ibid.
18 Ibid.
19 Hoover, *An American Epic*, 85–6.
20 HLWPR, *The Four Horsemen*, 101.
21 Ibid., 98, 101 and 102.
22 John E. Farquharson, '"Emotional but Influential": Victor Gollancz, Richard Stokes and the British Zone of Germany, 1945–9', *Journal of Contemporary History*, 22 (July, 1987), 501–19.
23 HLWPR, *The Four Horsemen*, 116.
24 Hoover, *An American Epic, Volume Four,* Section V title.
25 Hoover, *Addresses upon the American Road*, 163.
26 *New York Sunday Times*, 3 March 1946, E5.
27 *Newsweek*, 1 April 1946, 25. 'Food & Peace' by Ernest Lindley.
28 Hoover, *An American Epic*, 120.
29 Hoover, *Addresses upon the American Road*, 167–8.
30 Hoover, *An American Epic*.
31 Hoover Institute, Hugh S. Gibson Papers, Box 70, Food Mission Diary.
32 Hoover Institute, Hugh S. Gibson Papers, Box 70, 23 March 1946; Hoover Presidential Library and Archives, Frank Mason's Papers, *Five-year Diary*, 3/23/46; *The Washington Post*, 24 March 1946, 1.

33 *Washington Evening Star*, 29 March 1946; and *Time*, 8 April 1946, 20.
34 *Newsweek*, 22 April 1946, and 15 April 1946.
35 Herbert Hoover, *An American Epic: The Guns Cease Killing and the Saving of Life from Famine Begins, 1939–1963*, vol. 4 (Chicago: Henry Regnery Company, 1964), 278–9.
36 *Newsweek*, 1 April 1946, 40; and *Newsweek*, 8 April 1946, 19.
37 Hoover, *An American Epic*, vol. 4, 278.
38 Herbert Hoover Presidential Library & Archives, Post-Presidential Papers, Famine Emergency Collection, File: Report on Children – Countries.
39 Princeton University Library, Department of Rare Books and Special Collections, Seeley G. Mudd Manuscript Library, Public Policy Papers. Maurice Pate Papers, 1904–1985 (bulk 1945–1965), MC 103: Reports, 1946. Box 14, Folder 12 (digital copy) (The Pate Reports hereafter), 1.
40 For further reading on displaced children and their experiences in central and east-central Europe, see Tara Zahra, *The Lost Children: Reconstructing Europe's Families after World War II* (New York: Harvard University Press, 2011); Nicholas Stargardt, *Witnesses of War: Children's Lives under the Nazis* (New York: Alfred A. Knopf, 2006).,
41 The Pate Reports, 2.
42 Ibid., 3.
43 Hoover, *Addresses upon the American Road*, 186.
44 The Pate Reports, 3.
45 Ibid., 4.
46 See Ina Zweiniger-Bargielowska, 'Bread Rationing in Britain, July 1946–July 1948', *Twentieth Century British History*, 4:1 (1993), 57–85.
47 *National Geographic*, 'Holland Rises from War & Water', June 1946, 237.
48 The Pate Reports, 5.
49 For more on public health in Germany in the post-war period, see Jessica Reinisch, *Perils of Peace: The Public Health Crisis in Occupied Germany* (Oxford: Oxford University Press, 2013).
50 The Pate Reports, 6–7.
51 Hoover Institution, Hugh S. Gibson Papers, Box 70, 27 March 1946.
52 Hoover, *Addresses upon the American Road*, 179.
53 The Pate Reports, 7.
54 Ibid., 8.
55 Hoover, *Addresses on the American Road*, 22.
56 'The Pate Reports', page 2. 'The attached reports are based not only on statistics but on visits to schools, children's institutions, laborers' and clerks' homes in each country.'
57 Hoover, *Addresses upon the American Road*, 195.

58 Hoover Institute, Hugh S. Gibson Papers, Box 70, 19 April 1946.
59 Herbert Hoover, *Addresses upon the American Road, 1945-1948*, "World Famine Situation", Address under auspices Famine Emergency Committee', Sherman Hotel, Chicago, 17 May 1946, 226.
60 Hoover, *Addresses upon the American Road*, 227.
61 Ibid., 227.
62 HLWPR, *The Four Horsemen*, 171-2.
63 Hoover, *Addresses upon the American Road*, 231; and HLWPR, *The Four Horsemen*, 212.
64 Hoover Institution, Famine Emergency Committee, Boxes 1-31, Digitized Letter #0084.
65 Hoover Institution, Frank Mason Papers, Speeches & Writings, file: 'UNRRA as a political tool', September 1946.
66 See Chapter 1 in this volume by Samantha K. Knapton, and also Ben Shephard, *The Long Road Home: The Aftermath of the Second World War* (London: Bodley Head, 2010).
67 HLWPR, *The Four Horsemen*, 183-4.
68 Hoover, *Addresses upon the American Road*, 267-8.
69 Hoover, *An American Epic,* 175.
70 HLWPR, *The Four Horsemen*, 152.
71 Harry S. Truman Presidential Library and Archives, Papers of Harry S. Truman, General File, Folder: *Hoover, Herbert C. Letters* dated 3 December 1946.
72 The National Planning Association, 'UNRRA: Gateway to Recovery', *Planning Pamphlets* (1944), 16; 'Farewell to U.N.R.R.A', *Social Service Review,* 21 (September 1947), 398-401.
73 Harry S. Truman Presidential Library and Archives, Papers of Harry S. Truman, General File, Folder: *Hoover, Herbert C. Letters* dated 6 December 1946.
74 Morris, UNICEF, 35.
75 Ibid., 39.
76 HLWPR, *The Four Horsemen*, 213.
77 Hoover, *An American Epic*, 279-82.
78 Doc.Ost, File: UNRRA, United Nations Relief & Rehabilitation Assoc. (1940s), pamphlet: 'Children, War's Victims: The Education of the Handicapped.' Publication of UNESCO.
79 Keith Lowe, *Savage Continent: Europe in the Aftermath of World War II* (New York: St. Martin's Press, 2012), 108.
80 Morris, *UNICEF*, 131.
81 This popular phrase is recounted across all of UNICEFs modern social media – see: www.unicef.org or Twitter: @UNGeneva, 11 December 2020.

8

The UNRRA: The ambiguity of 'rehabilitation', suppressed discourses, and unlearned lessons from FDR's post-war assistance operation

Dan Plesch and Grace Schneider

Introduction

The United Nations Relief and Rehabilitation Administration (UNRRA), which delivered everything from insecticide to locomotives, remains the world's largest multilateral post-conflict organization that operated from Belarus to Beijing with contributions from states as large as the United States and as small as Liberia and Haiti, all contributing 1 per cent of their GDP. In contrast, the United States alone funded the Marshall Plan to Western Europe from 1949 with 2 per cent of its GDP. Led by Franklin Delano Roosevelt (FDR) and his officials, UNRRA was discarded as their successors ousted his New Deal approach at home and abroad.

After seven decades, this volume is part of a fresh attempt to reassess UNRRA. What did the now obscure term 'rehabilitation' mean in the 1940s, and what overall might be UNRRA's legacies for the international community in twenty-first century post-conflict environments? The purpose of this chapter is not to hold up UNRRA as a perfect model for today. It barely touched on issues of race, for example, and the United Nations Information Organization (UNIO) Women's committee critiqued the exclusion of women from UNRRA debate 'expressing regret over the fact that few women were included in the national delegations to the UNRRA Conference'.[1] Nevertheless UNRRA, enriches our understanding of the 1940s and has implications for scholarship and practice in the twenty-first century.

To begin, what was the function of the term 'rehabilitation'? Tony Judt in his acclaimed history of Europe since 1945 has a chapter entitled *The Rehabilitation of Europe*.[2] Although he gives credit to UNRRA's efforts in famine relief and disease control, Judt does not unpack the term 'rehabilitation'. In 1944, however, British official Richard Law explained what 'rehabilitation' meant to the British government:

> So far as rehabilitation, that is to say the supply of spare parts, machinery and so on, is needed for that purpose, then UNRRA will assist in rehabilitation; but it is laid down clearly in Resolution 12, Paragraph 9, that UNRRA is not itself an organ of world reconstruction […] It would clearly be impracticable for this piece of United Nations machinery, which already has this formidable task before it, to take on in addition the task of a world economic conference.[3]

UNRRA was never intended to be permanent, yet many regarded its end in 1947 as premature. UNRRA's opponents in the United States considered this not a moment too soon to shut what they regarded as a profligate example of the 'globaloney' New Deal policies of the Roosevelt era. UNRRA's effective 'one-world' internationalism is largely absent from the literature on post-conflict reconstruction and development as well as wider considerations of realist and liberal internationalisms. This chapter builds on prior research into the UN alliance of the Second World War as well as UNRRA-specific studies, contributes to the discussion on rehabilitation and offers suggestions about how a fuller consideration of UNRRA can enrich policy-oriented study today.[4]

UNRRA: As part of the wartime UN alliance

When, in the spring of 1942 the US State Department circulated a proposal on post-war relief, the British reaction was rooted in an understanding of the necessity of a comprehensive international policy supported by American public opinion. Anthony Eden, the Foreign Minister, wrote to his colleagues:

> It must be obvious that for the success of any post-war relief scheme the contribution of the United States will be all-important. For that reason alone we should be well advised to fall in with the American proposals. But I fancy that there is much more than post-war relief in question. The United States Administration appear to be acting on the thesis that the more international machinery that can be got into operation with their participation before the end of the war, the greater the likelihood of American public opinion being ready to continue international co-operation after the war. It would perhaps be putting it too high at this stage to say that the Administration definitely intend to try and establish under the aegis of the 'United Nations' the embryo of the international organization of the future. American post-war co-operation in the

international sphere being so vitally important, I submit that we must play up to any scheme of theirs tending to turn the United Nations into an operative piece of machinery.[5]

Thus, from its inception, UNRRA had a forward-looking role in building a global system of liberal institutionalism that was far broader than its immediate mission. Like US foreign policy today, the United States was powerful enough to easily make bilateral arrangements and select alliances according to its will. FDR's policy was to create a fully international agency which provided a collective forum for developing policy and sharing the burden of provision while ensuring that US power and its desires prevailed.

The United States called a conference to create UNRRA for the autumn of 1943 with Dean Acheson as leading diplomat for the United States. Acheson later remarked that UNRRA was 'the John the Baptist of the Marshall Plan'.[6] UNRRA formed a central part of the intra-war development of FDR's planning and should be considered together with the UN Information Organization, the UN War Crimes Commission of 1943–8, the Interim UN Food and Agriculture commission of 1943–5, the UN Monetary and Financial Conference at Bretton Woods in 1944, and the UN Conference on International Organization in San Francisco in 1945.[7] As Eden indicated, part of the value of the UN organizations and conferences was to build habits of cooperation. Acheson was joined at the UNRRA conference by future diplomatic stars, including Jean Monnet of France, Lester B. Pearson of Canada and Oliver Franks of Great Britain.[8]

What is often today described as 'the US-led-post-war-liberal-order' had radically different phases. UNRRA and its 'Rehabilitation' was a term and a practice born of the prevailing political interactions that shaped the creation of the present international system in its early 'one world' phase. Elsewhere, Acharya and Plesch have deconstructed the false unity of the Western liberal order, while Plesch and Weiss discuss the realist necessity of multilateralism.[9] The initial period of one-world socialistic, social democratic policies became by the late twentieth century a neoliberal policy arena that would have been unrecognizable as 'liberal' to actors in the mid-1940s. At this time, a strong state and global management to prevent mass unemployment and poverty were very widely considered to be essential to international peace and security.

That the UN alliance preceded the charter agreed at San Francisco and that that meeting itself was a UN Conference had vanished until twenty-first-century research. Yet, the pre-Nuremberg UN War Crimes Commission's work has been unknown to generations studying Allied responses to the Holocaust and the development of International Criminal Law. The overlooking, or suppression, of UNRRA is also part of a wider amnesia of the wartime United Nations, as this formative period was set aside as somehow utopian or against US national interest. To support this argument in the arena of UNRRA we can see how, while it was operational, the UN itself promoted UNRRA in its public information operations, and how UNRRA's occurrence in the academic literature shows a precipitous decline from the early 1950s until indications of revival in the early twenty-first century.[10]

UN member states used the United Nations' public information operation to publicize UNRRA and their national view on its operation. As such, the UN Information Organization was the first multilateral organization to bear the UN name.[11] It bridged the wartime UN from 1942 to the popularly known UN created by the Charter of 1945.[12] Within the archival material of the UNIO, UNRRA features in over 1,000 instances across more than 100 documents. Discussions of rehabilitation, aside from its use in the organization's name, occur more than 400 times in over 100 documents. These, and numerous public information films, amplified the broad meaning of rehabilitation across the various sectors of UNRRA's work as a phase of operations supplemental to immediate relief. Thus, the Allied nations' public information organization was disseminating intra-allied debates on rehabilitation even prior to the creation of UNRRA.

Missing UNRRA

A search for UNRRA in digital academic resources shows that UNRRA was discussed extensively in the later 1940s with a precipitous drop off in the early 1950s.[13] Of the 5,000 results over the past eighty years, more than half of those results were published at the time of UNRRA's operation and in the half decade after its closure. After that point, reference to UNRRA ceased almost entirely until the early 2000s, as illustrated in Figure 8.1 Dan Plesch and Jessica Reinisch's contributions opened up the field of UNRRA studies with important contributions focused on refugees by Silvia Salvatici, Peter Gatrell, Laura J. Hilton and Laure Humbert, alongside those discussed in the present volume.[14] This restorative archaeology in historical scholarship, however, is not found in wider development studies and political science. For example, UNRRA is absent both from a leading survey of non-governmental organizations (NGOs) and Institutional Organizations over two centuries in development and in a critique of this study.[15]

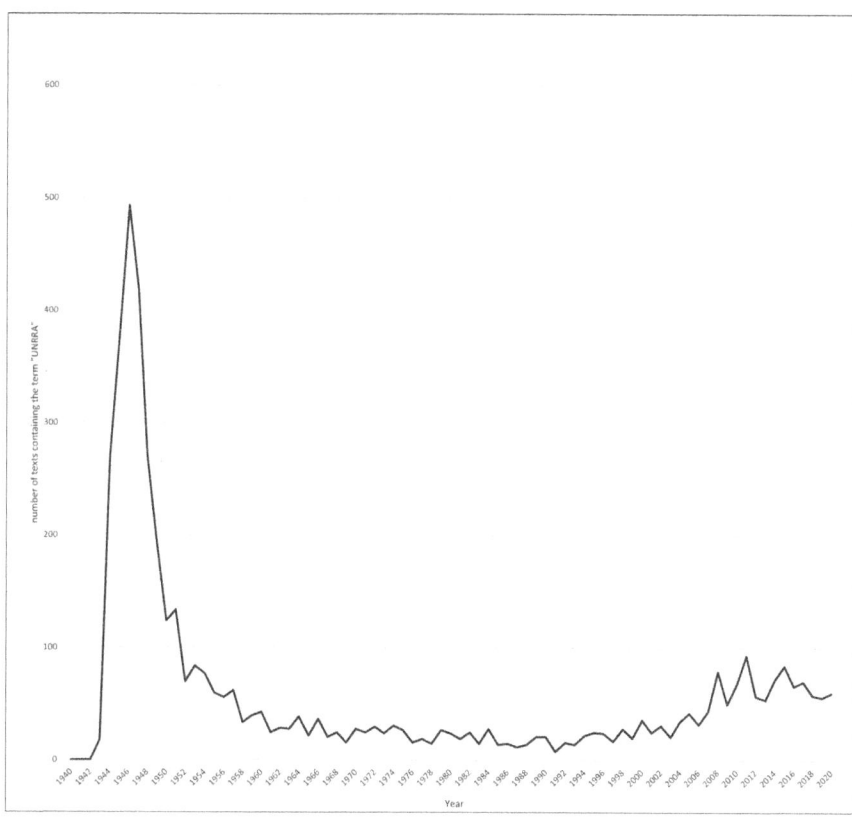

Figure 8.1 Number of publications in JSTOR containing the phrase 'UNRRA' (in title, body and/or citations) from 1940 through 2020.

The omission of UNRRA from twentieth-century scholarship is most obvious in post-conflict reconstruction and development. Known under a variety of names and descriptors, this field deals with challenges posed in the process of transitioning a society away from violent conflict to long-term peace. A shift in this literature can be observed in the last decade of the twentieth century, as the framework for 'post-conflict' responses changed from the traditionally dominant framework of 'national security' to one centred around the needs of people in evaluating the transition to peacetime

As such, historical understandings of post-conflict recovery overwhelmingly revolve around responses from individual states. Tasks often involved deliverance of immediate humanitarian relief, rebuilding war-torn infrastructure and establishing new institutions for peacetime. These activities, usually referencing the US Marshall Plan and interventions in Japan, Germany and Korea in the post-war years, are collectively referred to as 'nation-building'. The RAND

Corporation's 2008 study exemplifies this continuing discourse. Even though FDR is in the title of the study, UNRRA, his creation, has no place in RAND's pantheon of US post-war achievements.[16] 'Nation-building', therefore, took on a more critical connotation beginning with the Vietnam War. Interventions and policy practices previously deemed successful, specifically those undertaken by the United States, were increasingly called into question in the academic literature. A combination of internal critiques, as well as allegations of neocolonialism by the Soviet Union and unaligned 'Third World' nations, resulted in the term 'losing favour' in academic literature. It was the end of the Cold War, in fact, that brought back discussions of post-conflict 'nation-building', although this time under a new name and featuring new players. In the 1990s, studies did seek to learn from the past and move beyond old notions of 'nation-building'. Two key frameworks were introduced in this time period: 'post-conflict reconstruction' and 'human security'. The latter, introduced in the 1994 United Nations Development Progamme (UNDP) report, called for a change from prioritizing the security of nations, as past 'nation-building' efforts had done, to instead centre on the security of individuals.[17] 'Human security', as defined by the UNDP, encompassed seven dimensions: economic, food, health, environmental, personal, community and political.[18]

According to the 1994 UNDP Report, the ideas underpinning human security have been recognized by the UN and the United States since 1945. The report emphasizes that the founders of the UN had always given equal importance to people's security and to territorial security. As far back as June 1945, the US secretary of state reported this to his government on the results of the San Francisco Conference:

> The battle of peace has to be fought on two fronts. The first is the security front where victory spells freedom from fear. The second is the economic and social front where victory means freedom from want. Only victory on both fronts can assure the world of an enduring peace ….No provisions that can be written into the Charter will enable the Security Council to make the world secure from war if men and women have no security in their homes and their jobs.[19]

There is no hint in the UNDP report, however, that these sentiments had already been translated into a global programme through UNRRA. UNDP as an organization of record should not omit such an important area of work and more than that, would its work not be enhanced if it reminded its own stakeholders of UNRRA's work?

Two exemplary instances of 'missing out UNRRA' by officials and scholars in the present century are Robert Orr, who edited *Winning the*

Peace: An American Strategy for Post-Conflict Reconstruction while at the influential Centre for Strategic International Studies, and Carol Lancaster, author of *Foreign Aid: Diplomacy, Development, Domestic Politics*, who argued for stronger and more effective US engagement in world issues, both unilaterally and through the UN.[20] Neither draws on the precedent set by the American creation of UNRRA. For Orr, the genesis of US post-conflict experience is the occupation of Japan under General MacArthur, remarking that the Japanese experience 'helped to solidify a particularly American attitude that societies coming out of war could and should be rebuilt by the United States'.[21] The UNRRA experience, on the other hand, was that such work should and could be done when the United States shared the burden effectively collectively through the UN, and UNRRA was structured so that the USSR had no veto.

Lancaster sees the genesis of US foreign aid in the Marshall Plan, regarding UNRRA as solely concerned with relief and a natural product of the US experience in providing relief to Belgium under the occupation of the Kaiser's Army and to famine-hit Russia in the 1920s. For Lancaster, the Marshall Plan is the start of the United States' more complex post-conflict assistance. With over 1,000 citations in Google Scholar, Lancaster's views continue to shape the discourse. Unfortunately, although Lancaster places aid within its domestic context the omission of UNRRA from precisely these dynamics, as Eden outlined and we develop further, reduces the value of her conclusions. In particular, the use of the term 'rehabilitation' to enable activity between relief and reconstruction would enrich the analysis.

A rare mention of UNRRA in the 2013 Overseas Development Institute (ODI) working paper *A History of the Humanitarian System: Western Origins and Foundations* gives barely a column to UNRRA and as much space to the work of NGOs.[22] For example, the work of what became OXFAM was of importance in the 1940s, but the nation states and their formal interactions were far more significant. UNRRA's rehabilitation role does not trouble the ODI report's authors.

UNRRA and rehabilitation

From the Atlantic City conference onwards, rehabilitation in its many facets was central to the assistance planned and implemented in the nations that had suffered Axis occupation. However, Congressional approval of UNRRA, accepted by its Council, included the provision that 'it is understood that the task of rehabilitation must not be considered as the beginning of reconstruction – it is coterminous with relief.'

By 1946, UNRRA operations had gathered momentum worldwide. From Headquarters at Dupont Circle in Washington DC, its director Herbert Lehman organized divisions to help with Displaced Persons, Health, Welfare, Food, Clothing and Textiles, as well as Agricultural and Industrial Rehabilitation and Medical and Sanitary supplies. By mid-1945, UNRRA had some 7,500 employees in purchasing offices across Latin America, the Middle East, the Indian subcontinent, and aid operations from China to Denmark. While the majority of the resources came from nations, financing was mobilized from a variety of other sources. At the time Eire was neutral and was outside the UN but nevertheless sent 285 tonnes of bacon and 8,000 beef cattle.[23] Indeed, NGOs also made contributions to UNRRA amounting to several million dollars-worth of commodities.[24]

Rehabilitation had meaning across these operations, whether psychological with refugees disorientated after years as slave labourers or as rehabilitating infrastructure with cranes and bulldozers imported by UNRRA.[25] In China, by March 1947, despite the civil war, 400 miles of the Yellow River had been protected from flooding in a process enabled by Canadian-supplied tree trunks sunk side by side to depths of forty feet along the river bank which provided a frame for stone and concrete fencing.[26] Nevertheless, UNRRA's functions were contentious from the start, with recipients seeking a wider brief than some parts of the donor governments. This Congressional view is more restrictive than that given by Law, and more important given the funding Congress provided.

Pieter Kerstens, the Netherlands Economic Minister expressed the 'disappointment displayed by the delegates at Atlantic City that the concept of "rehabilitation" had been so strictly limited both in space and time'. He explained 'rehabilitation' was understood to encompass the supplies and projects necessary to establish a minimum level of economic self-sufficiency. He gave the following example in an attempt to clarify the definition whilst recognizing the nuance of the objective:

> For the Netherlands, under rehabilitation is meant the most rapid provision of artificial fertilizers and cattle food because these two groups contribute immediately towards relieving hunger, in the first place, in the Netherlands, and probably also in neighboring countries.

> Self-sufficiency in this respect would in the shortest time save the necessity of bringing this overseas, hence would save shipping space, which is a most valuable factor.
>
> Under the heading of rehabilitation there are no raw materials for the cosmetic industry, not even for reasons of fighting unemployment, although in borderline cases this might contribute to an affirmative decision, but the luxury trade does not fall under this.[27]

The creation and operation of UNRRA's Industrial Rehabilitation Division further illuminates the rehabilitation debates in a sector far from the social welfare application of rehabilitation. James Colbert, a senior official in the Division wrote an analysis of its operations where he develops the argument that the use of the word 'rehabilitation' and the absence of the word 'reconstruction' was in part intended to meet the concerns of some members of the US Congress who were opposed to US investment in post-war reconstruction efforts around the world.[28] US funding by Congress came in several annual budgets each accompanied by conditions. Thus, the delivery of US assistance was a function not merely of demand and supply dynamics but the political interactions between UNRRA and its Divisions, the State Department and the Committees of Congress. Colbert's argument concerning industrial operations is particularly relevant as deliveries of machinery, livestock and even buildings were contested as reconstruction or development in a way in which food and medicine were not.

Colbert details the intense bureaucratic interactions as UNRRA and State Department officials sought to maximize the speed and scope of UNRRA's industrial rehabilitation work. These instrumental political concerns may have been as relevant to the choice and use of the term 'rehabilitation', as theoretical debates on accurate social science terminology. Rehabilitation was at times a deliberate sleight of hand encompassing reconstruction and even development, but also at times an honest tautology. Rehabilitation was not only a bridge between relief and reconstruction, but also a very broad usage across culture and education to agriculture and industry. For advocates of a maximal approach to post-war action, rehabilitation was a highly constructive ambiguity, while for others its use was obstructive.

We have seen, however, that the architects of the wartime UN who designed a transitional system, created within UNRRA, envisaged the international community's work through UNRRA would transition into economic development work by the International Monetary Fund and European Bank for Reconstruction and Development. The work of UNRRA should be used more fully in contemporary discussion of post-conflict reconstruction and international aid.

UNRRA and lessons for twenty-first century post-conflict reconstruction and development

The following examples cannot, in the scope of this chapter, be comprehensive; rather, they support the idea that UNRRA offers useful lessons for today, not least in the spectrum of activities it called rehabilitation. UN agencies and development researchers often identify the gap that is sometimes filled by 'rehabilitation' but are oblivious to a large body of work by and on UNRRA decades ago. To illustrate the breadth offered by the UNRRA experience, we simultaneously introduce discussions focused on the 'soft power' issue of 'rehabilitation' through addressing psychological problems of victims in a post-conflict environment, and the 'hard power' issues of finance to achieve this, before signposting other areas for further study.

The ODI study from 2014, 'Remaking the case for linking relief, rehabilitation and development' missed the opportunity to draw on UNRRA.[29] It dates the origins of rehabilitation to the 1980s but argues that the idea has never been applied in practice. Indeed, UN agencies themselves continue to struggle to bridge the gap between aid and development. Two further reports illustrate the continuing problem as the UNDP and the UN Office for the Coordination of Humanitarian Affairs (UNOCHA) seek means of interim measures.[30] The use of democratic practices in the field as a means to ameliorate demoralization may address some of the concerns identified by ODI, UNDP and UNOCHA. This might also be considered as existing across the relief and development policy areas. Here might be a topic where UNRRA experience contributes to the gaps identified.

Democracy in the administration of relief and rehabilitation was a key part of the success of the process which enabled people freed from Nazi rule to regain control over their lives. Here, rehabilitation is psychological, a meaning closer to twenty-first-century usage. For instance, UNRRA-administered DP camps which operated under a system of self-government. Such policy is not a core function of the twenty-first-century UNHCR. Part of UNRRA's work was assistance to the millions of displaced persons across Europe at the end of the war, and the organization's official history claims that UNRRA was successful in ensuring that its camps were self-governing with elected councils, courts, and fire services that would not 'have been possible if UNRRA had pursued a policy of efficient command'.[31] Building on contemporary field reports, UNRRA's official historian George Woodbridge notes, 'although many leaders had been appointed at the beginning of the operation by UNRRA or military officials, by the summer of 1946 almost all had been elected by the camp residents'.[32] According to Woodbridge, it was, 'no exaggeration to say that [self-governance] was the goal toward which all activities were pointed'.[33] The policy came from both the US Army and UNRRA. General Dwight D. Eisenhower's Headquarters' 'Guide to the Care of Displaced Persons in Germany' stated that 'displaced persons should be encouraged to organize themselves as much as is administratively possible'.[34] As Woodbridge points out:

> In each camp there was usually a camp committee elected by the entire population, either at large, by nationality (if in a mixed camp), by area or block within the camp, or by some other means. This committee usually selected the camp a chairman or camp leader, although in some cases he was directly elected. This committee supervised all activities and represented the population in all dealings with outside authorities.[35]

This was the ideal, but practice was slow and imperfect. Later, in 1946 and afterwards, the political character of the camps became part of both the emerging Cold War and the attempt of Jews to immigrate to Israel. It should not be considered radical that the principle of fundamental democratic empowerment was part of the practice of international assistance to refugees. This democratic policy formed part of a broader recognition of the psychological tasks epitomized in the UNRRA slogan of 'Helping People Help Themselves'. There was clear recognition of the need to prevent a welfare dependency. A Czech minister in exile in London spoke of the need for post-war assistance to recognize the 'moral humiliation' inflicted by the Nazis and avoid assistance being presented as charity rather than good neighbourliness. And indeed, his country was donating sugar to UNRRA by 1947.[36]

If democracy is at the heart of the values that underpin international post-conflict activity, then funding drives the amount of activity that can be undertaken. Low levels of funding continue to hamper relief and development and by extension any attempt to fill the rehabilitation gap. It is well known today that the UN has a target for developed states to contribute 0.7 per cent of GDP to international development. This particular metric was put forth in the seminal 1969 World Bank report, *Partners in Development*, the product of a commission headed by the former Canadian prime minister Lester B. Pearson.[37] Pearson's report credits the inspiration of the 0.7 per cent recommendation to a 1958 proposal from the World Council of Churches that recommends nations contribute assistance equalling 1 per cent of GDP.[38] This citation appears to inform the orthodox history of the 0.7 per cent recommendation as reported by the UN, World Bank and OECD.[39]

These organizations, and the narrative about the codification of development assistance, do not reference UNRRA's 1 per cent objective. Pearson himself chaired an UNRRA supply committee yet neglected to make any mention of the 1 per cent metric that funded UNRRA.[40] The fault lies not only in him; the handful of explicit mentions of the UNRRA origin by his contemporaries appears to have been entirely ignored in favour of Pearson's narrative. Robert Jackson, another former-UNRRA-official-turned-UN-consultant, explicitly cites UNRRA as the origin of the 1 per cent formula in his 1969 'Capacity Study' for the UNDP.[41]

This 1 per cent solution was put forward by Harry White, a US Treasury official who was also involved in the financial discussions that reached fruition at the UN Monetary and Financial Conference held at Bretton Woods.[42] The White Plan had the advantage that everyone was contributing what they could so that it was not simply a matter of US taxpayers subsidizing the world. The system had an obvious equality and a clear limit that helped prevent disagreements over who supplied how many tonnes of what foodstuffs, while still accommodating the realities of US wealth. The adoption of this contribution system by the UNRRA Council imposed a non-binding obligation on governments, one that placed peer pressure on member states while convincing US taxpayers that while they were paying the most, others were paying a fair share.

The US contribution was over $2.6 billion of the $3.6 billion global cost of the programme – $1 billion, however, was supplied by other countries, mainly Britain and Canada who contributed $617 million and $138 million respectively as well as in smaller quantities by forty other members of the United Nations.[43] The Dominican Republic increased its export tax, transferring the revenue to UNRRA. Brazil made the fifth largest contribution, with forty million dollars, nearly double the requested 1 per cent of National Income.[44] Lauding rather than suppressing the UNRRA 1 per cent can reinforce efforts to implement the 0.7 per cent today. Some states, such as those in the EU, benefitted from UNRRA and such history can create increased moral pressure to live up to today's goals. Furthermore, the example of the effectiveness of the formula in the 1940s in creating concrete relief with equitable contributions has the potential to have a positive impact internationally.

UNRRA was to set the conditions for successful economic development, as Richard Law explained in the introduction.[45] While by the 1950s economic development largely focused on GDP, a measure of production, the overriding objective of economic development in the 1940s was to serve international security policy by ensuring that mass unemployment did not fuel extremism. The UNIO records government statements from the middle of the 1940s making this argument and connecting it to post-war relief and rehabilitation.[46] At the level of bureaucratic structure UNRRA had at least two features of value identified by Karetny and Weiss.[47] The first is a sunset clause designed to ensure that the organization could not last forever, a problem they consider with some UN organizations, while the second is the delivering of the 'One UN' concept introduced by Kofi Annan in 2005.[48] Here too, UNRRA precedents can help UN reform today.

UN practitioners and scholars may consider that their work can be enhanced by considering whether UNRRA provides a sounding board and comparison for the global operation of a unified UN. Furthermore, UNRRA's administrative costs were low in comparison to today, as expenses were 1.18 per cent.[49] In comparison, the US Agency for International Development and associated economic development programmes had (in 2020) the administrative expenses of nearly double the administrative cost of UNRRA. This provides a useful example of the historic efficiency of multilateral organizations. A deeper dive into the rationale of differing cost structures might be beneficial, but the headline difference is of a type that is often used to shape public debate.

Additional areas of interest for current policy where we offer pointers to further debate and study include UNRRA structures, global economic strategy, political-psychological rehabilitation strategies, and the idea of voluntary contributions being tied to percentage of GDP.

Conclusion

By the end of UNRRA's mandate, the political outlook had changed. Only Stalin remained of the three wartime leaders, and confrontation between the Communist and Western world was escalating. In the United States itself, FDR's New Dealers were out of favour. In September 1947, US President Harry Truman's Secretary of State James F. Byrnes, once Roosevelt's right-hand man, explained: 'We wish to give relief as the United States, not as a member of an international organization in which a committee composed of other governments determines the allotment of the relief given by us.'[50] Gone was the recognition that UNRRA had been created with the United States controlling the formal strategy – but through a multilateral process.

A vitriolic critic of Truman's new policies in Germany and towards UNRRA was Ira Hirschmann, an experienced UNRRA official with a record of helping Jews escape the Holocaust. In his 1949 book, *The Embers Still Burn*, Hirschmann attacks the rebuilding of Germany, the neglect of refugees, the encouragement of Nazi-associated anti-communist militia, the invitation to extreme right-wing Europeans to settle in the United States, and what he called the 'killing of UNRRA'.[51] But it was Dean Acheson's verdict on UNRRA, in his, for many, definitive memoir of the post-war settlement that was influential, rather than Hirschmann's. Acheson wrote that the United States sought closure of UNRRA because of the Republican landslide in the 1946 Congressional elections, its ineffectiveness, its role in black markets, its support for communist regimes who used it 'to entrench themselves', and that its staff had been weak and its leadership weaker.[52]

One lasting material impact of the success of Acheson's verdict provides an important context to the focus of the UNRRA-focused studies on refugees. A key function of UNRRA from 1945 was an International Tracing Service for missing persons – not least those caught up in the Holocaust. This thirty million-page archive was classified until 2011, robbing survivors, scholars and prosecutors alike of a vital source of Holocaust and refugee studies – loudly echoing Hirschmann's concerns but still absent from most discussions of UNRRA's refugee work.[53]

As a US unilateral initiative, the Marshall Plan committed some 2 per cent of GDP to Western Europe over a four-year period. In 1945–7, UNRRA dispensed half of that percentage of GDP but from some thirty states and to recipients in all the previously Axis-occupied countries. Its budget, geographic reach and variety of activities all justify its restoration alongside the Marshall Plan. Sadly, however in the World Bank's public briefing paper 'Lessons of the Marshall Plan' UNRRA is invisible.[54] Given UNRRA's rehabilitation work in much of Western Europe, this leaves the false impression of the efficacy of unilateral US action and the absence of the multilateral, providing a false and distorted history on which countless officials and members of civil society have founded their thinking.

The recognition of UNRRA's significance is long overdue. This chapter is a restorative archaeology of knowledge that brings UNRRA out from under the poured concrete of Cold War ideology that continues to underpin much of twenty-first-century scholarship and practice.⁵⁵ This form of internationalism should be set alongside both the Marshall Plan and early-twentieth-century relief efforts as a core source in any primer on post-conflict reconstruction. At a minimum UNRRA's successor organizations the UN High Commission for Refugees, UN World Health Organization, UNICEF and OCHA should draw on the work of their ancestor.

The practical implementation practiced by UNRRA is highlighted by the remarks of Canadian Prime Minister Mackenzie King:

> The service of relief and rehabilitation in times of strain is the moral equivalent of military service in time of war […] We are members one of another. The doctrine of mutual aid is the antithesis of the doctrine of force […] it signifies brotherhood, not fratricide. It considers human need, rather than human greed. […] Men and nations must substitute co-operation for coercion. Mutual aid must become the guiding principle of international relationship […] The hope of the future lies in the universal recognition of our common humanity.⁵⁶

Notes

1. 'Minutes of the 87th Meeting of the United Nations Information Board' in folder United Nations Informational Organization (hereafter UNIO) S-0537-0003-0004, 15. Available at https://search.archives.un.org/minutes-of-meetings-of-inter-allied-information-committee-united-nations-information-board-and-their-sub-committees-dec-1943-dec-1945.
2. Tony Judt, *Post-war; A History of Europe since 1945* (New York: Penguin, 2005), 63–99.
3. War and Peace Aims No. 4 Page 12, Richard Law MP, Minister of State, House of Commons, 25 January 1944. UNIO. Folder S-0537-0010-0004.
4. Jessica Reinisch, *The Perils of Peace: The Public Health Crisis in Occupied Germany* (Oxford: Oxford University Press, 2013); Dan Plesch and Thomas G. Weiss, '1945's Forgotten Insight: Multilateralism as Realist Necessity', *International Studies Perspectives*, 17:1 (February 2016), 4–16, Available at https://doi.org/https://doi.org/10.1093/isp/ekv013; Dan Plesch and Thomas G Weiss, *Wartime Origins and the Future United Nations* (London: Routledge, 2015); Amitav Acharya and Dan Plesch, 'The United Nations: Managing and Reshaping a Changing World Order', *Global Governance: A Review of Multilateralism and International Organizations*, 26:2 (2020), 221–35. https://doi.org/10.1163/19426720-02602001.
5. The National Archives, London, UK (hereafter, TNA), Cabinet Papers (Cab)/66/24/42 W.P. (42) 212, Anthony Eden. 20 May 1942.

6   Cited in Robert L. Beisner, *Dean Acheson* (Oxford: Oxford University Press, 2006), 18.
7   Dan Plesch, *America, Hitler and the UN: How the Allies Won World War II and Forged a Peace* (London: I.B. Tauris, 2010).
8   Alex, Danchev and Oliver Franks, *Founding Father* (Clarendon Press: Oxford, 1993).
9   Plesch and Weiss, '1945's Forgotten Insight', 4–16, https://doi.org/https://doi.org/10.1093/isp/ekv013; Acharya and Plesch, 'The United Nations', 221–35, https://doi.org/10.1163/19426720-02602001.
10 The Official UN website: https://www.un.org/en/site-search?query=UNRRA accessed 11 June 2022.
11 United Nations Archives and Records Management Section: Fonds AG-037-United Nations Information Organization (UNIO) (1940–1945). The authors would like to thank Greg Chaffin for his work on making a digital copy of the wartime archives of the UNIO.
12 The UNIO archive consists of a variety of internal communications and committee minutes (which warrant an exploration in their own right) as well as an extensive collection of external publications that inform the research in this chapter. Of particular note are the *UNIO News Bulletins* from the London office and the bimonthly *United Nations Review* out of New York. (The latter publication includes a series of supplemental issues that provide a curated collection of public speeches, radio broadcasts and talks from influential actors across all member nations. These supplements in particular are a powerful source of contemporary attitudes and discussions about UNRRA.)
13 The authors have used JSTOR to conduct this research.
14 Silvia Salvatici, '"Help the People to Help Themselves": UNRRA Relief Workers and European Displaced Persons', *Journal of Refugee Studies*, 25:3 (September 2012), 428–51, Silvia Salvatici, *A History of Humanitarianism, 1755–1989: In the Name of Others* (Manchester: Manchester University Press, 2019), Silvia Salvatici, 'Fighters without Guns': Humanitarianism and Military Action in the Aftermath of the Second World War, *European Review of History: Revue européenne d'histoire*, 25:6 (2018), 957–76; Laura J. Hilton, 'The Reshaping of Jewish Communities and Identities in Frankfurt and Zeilsheim in 1945', in Avinoam J. Patt and Michael Berkowitz, Laura J. Hilton, *We Are Here: New Approaches to Jewish Displaced Persons in Post-war Germany* (Detroit, MI.: Wayne State University Press, 2010); Peter Gatrell, *The Unsettling of Europe: The Great Migration, 1945 to the Present* (London: Penguin Books, 2019); Laure Humbert, *Reinventing French Aid: The Politics of Humanitarian Relief in French-Occupied Germany, 1945–1952* (Cambridge: Cambridge University Press, 2021). Yael Sandra Siman Druker, *Entre politica y humanitarismo: el papel de la Administracion de las Naciones Unidas para el Auxilio y la Rehabilitacion*

(UNRRA) ante la crisis de los desplazados judios en la Europa de la posguerra/Between politics and humanitarianism: the role of the United Nations Relief and Rehabilitation Administration (UNRRA) facing the crisis of Jewish displaced persons in post-war Europe. Relaciones Internacionales, 132 (2018) 67+.

15 Steve Charnovitz, Two Centuries of Participation: NGOs and International Governance, *Michigan Journal of International Law*, 18:2 (1997) and David Lewis, 'Individuals, organizations and public action: trajectories of the "non-governmental" in development studies', in Uma Kothari, *A Radical History of Development Studies* (London: Bloomsbury, 2005), 200–221.

16 James Dobbins, Michele A. Poole, Austin Long and Benjamin Runkle, *After the War, Nation-Building from FDR to George W. Bush* (Santa Monica, CA: Rand Corporation, 2008).

17 Shahrbanou Tadjbakhsh and Anuradha M. Chenoy, *Human Security: Concepts and Implications* (London: Routledge, 2007).

18 *Human Development Report* (New York: Oxford University Press for the United Nations Development Programme [UNDP], 1994), 24–5.

19 Ibid.

20 Carol Lancaster, *Foreign Aid: Diplomacy, Development, Domestic Politics* (Chicago: Chicago University Press, 2006).

21 Robert C. Orr (ed.), *Winning the Peace: An American Strategy for Post-Conflict Reconstruction* (Washington, DC: Center for Strategic & International Studies, 2004), 86.

22 Eleanor Davey, with John Borton and Matthew Foley, 'A History of the Humanitarian System: Western Origins and Foundations', *Humanitarian Policy Group* working paper 2013: https://odi.org/en/publications/a-history-of-the-humanitarian-system-western-origins-and-foundations/, Accessed May 2022.

23 Woodbridge, *The History of UNRRA, Vol. 1*, 125 and Woodbridge, *The History of UNRRA, Vol. 3*, 502–3.

24 Woodbridge, *The History of UNRRA, Vol. 3*, 504.

25 Woodbridge, *The History of UNRRA, Vol. 2*, 252.

26 Woodbridge, *The History of UNRRA, Vol. 2*, 424–37.

27 Radio broadcast by Pieter A. Kerstens, *Netherlands Minister of Economic Affairs over Radio Orange, Free Netherlands Station in London on 5 February 1944 'The United Nations Review Vol. IV – No. 3'* (New York: The United Nations Review, 1944). The United Nations Review: A Monthly Summary of Documents on the Allied Fight for Freedom. UNIO. Folder S-0537-0008-0007.

28 James Colbert, *The Industrial Rehabilitation Program of UNRRA, Doctoral Thesis* (New York: Columbia University, 1950), 18–21, 42 (Congressional rider) 50–1; 158; 218–20; 227; 360–71.

29 Irina Mosel and Simon Levine, 'Remaking the Case for Linking Relief, Rehabilitation and Development', Humanitarian Policy Group Overseas

Development Institute (April, 2014), available: https://odi.org/en/publications/remaking-the-case-for-linking-relief-rehabilitation-and-development/. Accessed 3 August 2021.
30 *UNDP and OCHA chiefs renew call for new way of working*, available: https://www.undp.org/africa/news/undp-and-ocha-chiefs-renew-call-new-way-working, accessed June 2022; OCHA, UNDP, and DOCO, *Lessons Learned and Good Practice Tool: Adapting Coordination Mechanisms to Support National Transitions* (2012), available: https://www.humanitarianresponse.info/sites/www.humanitarianresponse.info/files/documents/files/ocha_undp_doco_joint_lessons_learned_and_good_practice_tool_adapting_coordination_mechanisms_oct_2012.pdf, accessed 5 Jun. 2022.
31 Woodbridge, *The History of UNRRA, Vol. 2*, 523–4.
32 'U.S. Zone History Report, Camp Self-Government,' Appendix A, R.Taylor, 'Camp Self-Government, District I'; and Appendix B, Virgil Payne, 'Camp Self-Government, District III'; cited in Woodbridge, *The History of UNRRA, Vol. 2*, 523–4.
33 Woodbridge, *The History of UNRRA, Vol. 2*, 523.
34 Supreme Headquarters Allied Expeditionary Force, Headquarters 'Guide to the Care of Displaced Persons in Germany', May 1945 revision, Part 1, Section 1; cited in Woodbridge, *The History of UNRRA, Vol. 2*, 522.
35 Woodbridge, *The History of UNRRA, Vol. 2*, 523.
36 Article from the *New York Times* (17 September 1944) by the Czech Reconstruction Minister Frantisek Nemec, quoted in 'War and Peace Aims: Special Supplement No. 5 to the United Nations Review'. 1945. New York. War and Peace Aims. UNIO. Folder S-0537-0010-0005, Page 8. Section *CZECHOSLOVAKIA*. Nemec refers to UNRRA under the name of the Allied relief organization.
37 Lester B. Pearson, *Partners in Development: Report of the Commission on International Development* (New York: Praeger, 1969), 152.
38 Ibid. 144.
39 'The 0.7% ODA/GNI Target – a History.' OECD. Organization for Economic Co-operation and Development. Accessed 3 August 2021. https://www.oecd.org/development/stats/the07odagnitarget-ahistory.htm.
40 For reference, see notes of the 86th Extraordinary Meeting of the United Nations Information Board (UNIO).
41 See footnote on page 4 of: Jackson, Robert. 'A Study of the Capacity of the United Nations Development System Vol. 2.' Geneva: United Nations Publications, 1969. UNA Folder S-0290-0005-07. For more information on the roles Jackson held in UNRRA, see Appendix One: WHO'S WHO IN UNRRA in Woodbridge, *The History of UNRRA, Vol. 3*, 3–18.
42 TNA, *Treasury papers* (T)247/89, Treasury papers of John Maynard Keynes, 1938–1949. Reel 12, Vol. 5, 77 (additionally pages 75–6 of same document for a more detailed version of White's plan).

43 Woodbridge, *The History of UNRRA, Vol. 3*, 500.
44 Ibid.
45 See quote associated with footnote 3.
46 For example, see Law's comments on debt relief (page 13) and Wallace's paragraph on full employment (page 101) in 'War and Peace Aims: Special Supplement No. 4 to the United Nations Review'. 1944. New York. War and Peace Aims. UNA, UNIO. Folder S-0537-0010-0004. Additionally, in 'War and Peace Aims: Special Supplement No. 5 to the United Nations Review'. 1945. New York. War and Peace Aims. UNA, UNIO Folder S-0537-0010-0005, pages 7 through 9 discuss the economic implications of surpluses, the potential for triggering rapid inflation, and the role UNRRA could play in managing the supply of goods. For a discussion on trade, UNRRA, and government regulations, see Acheson (page 41) in the same issue (War and Peace Aims No. 5).
47 Eli Karetny and Thomas Weiss, 'UNRRA's Operational Genius and Institutional Design', in *Wartime Origins and the Future United Nations* (Abingdon, Oxon: Routledge, 2015).
48 For more details, see https://www.un.org/en/ga/deliveringasone/.
49 Woodbridge, *The History of UNRRA, Vol. 3*, 523.
50 Quoted in Ira A. Hirschmann, *The Embers Still Burn: An Eye-Witness View of the Post-war Ferment in Europe and the Middle East and Our Disastrous Get-Soft-With-Germany Policy* (New York: Simon and Schuster, 1949), 147.
51 For greater detail, see Chapter 11 of Hirschmann, *The Embers Still Burn*, 134–54.
52 Acheson, *Present at the Creation*, 201.
53 https://www.theholocaustexplained.org/survival-and-legacy/survivors-and-dp-era/the-international-tracing-service/ Website of the Wiener Holocaust Library, accessed 15 July 2022.
54 Barry Eichengreen, *Lessons of the Marshall Plan*, World Development Report, 2010. https://web.worldbank.org/archive/website01306/web/pdf/wdr_2011_case_study_marshall_plan_1.pdf accessed May 2022.
55 Rebecca Adami, Dan Plesch and Amitav Acharya, 'Commentary: The Restorative Archaeology of Knowledge about the role of Women in the History of the UN – Theoretical implications for International Relations', in Rebecca Adami and Dan Plesch (eds.), *Women and the UN: A New History of Women's International Human Rights* (Abingdon, Oxon: Routledge, 2021). Available: https://library.oapen.org/viewer/web/viewer.html?file=/bitstream/handle/20.500.12657/49539/9781000418767.pdf?sequence=1&isAllowed=y.
56 See page 9 of War and Peace Aims No. 5 Special Supplement to the United Nations Review. In folder S-0537-0010-0005.

Afterword
UNRRA: An overview

Peter Gatrell

UNRRA was not much loved at the time either by those who brought it into being and kept its operations running or by those who were its intended beneficiaries. Cynical and dismissive views abounded.[1] Along with unresolved tensions between military and civilian administration, critical comments were made – and rebutted – about the organization's high overhead costs, its failure to prevent racketeering and the generation of endless paperwork. Other fundamental issues came to the fore after the dust settled. Doubts and cynicism bred neglect. Did its claims to embody a spirit of post-1945 internationalism inevitably come to grief on the rock of national self-interest? How far did it enlist local actors, or did it instead ride roughshod over them by asserting the primacy of foreign expertise? With a handful of notable exceptions, noted below, UNRRA has enjoyed scant attention from historians and political scientists interested in genealogies of humanitarian intervention, as pointed out by the editors of this volume, Samantha K. Knapton and Katherine Rossy. At best, UNRRA has become a footnote in accounts of post-war rebuilding and in histories of humanitarianism. Disparaged at the time, abruptly terminated and neglected ever since, this is a damning verdict on an organization that had immense financial, material and human resources at its disposal and that produced an enormous archive.

In one sense, UNRRA was the victim of the Cold War, which derailed wartime aspirations of sustained international engagement between East and West to address post-war problems. Although in 1943–4 the wartime alliance between the United States, the United Kingdom, and the Soviet Union was firmly entrenched as UNRRA began to take shape, the rival political and social systems nevertheless meant that cooperation rested on fragile foundations. One consequence was that UNRRA's operations in Eastern Europe, especially in Ukraine and Belarus, disappeared from view. In the Soviet Union, Poland, Czechoslovakia, and Yugoslavia, the emphasis shifted to national state-building, social and economic transformation, and to socialist internationalism even though, according to some observers, UNRRA propped up communist Yugoslavia. The contempt in which it came to be held ensured that the historiography duly followed suit.

In this afterword I concentrate on some of the key issues that were at stake at UNRRA's inception and what significance attaches to its practices and its legacy. The first point to remember is that elements of UNRRA bore pre-war hallmarks in terms of ideas, practices and personnel. Member states of the League of Nations had addressed a range of issues and cooperated in relation to international health and the movement of refugees.[2] Under its auspices, relief workers were sent to Greece to assist refugees following the 1923 population exchange between Greece and Turkey; they would return after the country's liberation. Other relief agencies, notably the American Relief Administration (ARA) and Near East Relief, intervened in Russia and the Balkans to deal with the aftermath of war as well as with famine and infectious disease. The American Jewish Joint Distribution Committee (JDC) was another key actor and indeed Herbert H. Lehman operated as an influential figure in the JDC before taking up his post in UNRRA. These and other agencies exposed American-trained agronomists, engineers, nurses, nutritionists and others to unfamiliar settings where they could apply the techniques they had learned at home. UNRRA's presence also raised questions about the status of international relief efforts in relation to existing domestic provision in Europe and especially in China. More fundamentally, the pre-1914 and interwar preoccupation of aid workers and missionaries with the need to 'civilize' parts of Europe and the Far East, morphed into ideas around 'modernization' without losing the connotation that Anglo-American ideas and practices were inherently superior to 'backward' parts of the globe.[3] I return to this point later.

Planning also meant addressing structural problems, with technical expertise playing an enhanced role.[4] One such element in post-1945 thinking concerned anxieties over global food security and whether they should be addressed at a national or international level. US plans for a dedicated organization to provide food relief to Europe were already well advanced by 1944.[5] Related debates took place about 'over-population' in Italy, Greece and elsewhere, and whether it required organized efforts to resettle people overseas.[6] Kenneth Brooks suggested opening up areas for resettlement, such as in South America. In language that would have been familiar to the League of Nations, he concluded that 'it will be as impossible to repatriate as to colonise [sic] without capital for development or rehabilitation'.⁷ Although UNRRA did not concern itself directly with global migration issues, they were never far from the surface of post-war debates.

The creation of UNRRA needs to be placed alongside other plans for redesigning Europe in the aftermath of the Second World War. Allied cooperation took various forms, some of them insidious. Beyond their preoccupation with the relief and rehabilitation of victims of war, other post-war initiatives launched by the Allies included settling scores with former enemies. Retribution included the orchestrated mass expulsion of Germans from East-Central Europe whose support became the sole responsibility of a defeated and divided Germany. These expellees did not qualify as victims and UNRRA's architects chose to ignore them. But orchestrated expulsions and population transfers belonged to post-war planning no less than schemes for improving food output or investing in fixed capital in war-damaged countries.⁸

UNRRA's vision of the post-war world took concrete form in countless projects. It was one thing to talk of the emergency relief of suffering civilians, but what did rehabilitation actually mean? In so far as it equated to replacing damaged infrastructure, rehabilitation implied economic recovery and restoration. On the other hand, rather than being retrospective, might rehabilitation envision a bright future of purposeful international cooperation together with the application of new technologies and new approaches to social welfare? These questions were debated from the outset without any clear conclusion being reached, as Samantha K. Knapton's chapter shows. Nevertheless, Herbert Lehman attempted to instil in his team the belief that UNRRA was a pioneer in international cooperation and in coordinating operations in different countries. Whether imposing price controls or washing babies, its field-based staff needed to be adaptable in handling all manner of tasks.⁹

Other questions also arose. Which countries would be targeted for relief and rehabilitation? In addition to war-torn Europe, UNRRA identified China as a key target to boost food production in the medium and long term in pursuit of broader economic development. Other parts of the world were excluded, such as South Asia, sub-Saharan Africa and Europe's colonial possessions. What did it imply for a country to be the recipient of relief? Rana Mitter has argued that China needed (and secured) foreign assistance but insisted on cementing and retaining its sovereignty – hence, the need for a separately constituted but parallel agency. With the Chinese National Relief and Rehabilitation Administration, or CNRRA, in place, China would not admit foreign aid workers who answered to an external authority. Instead, the Nationalist leadership planned to build a reinvigorated state.¹⁰

Who would be responsible for relief and rehabilitation? In terms of relief, UNRRA worked in parallel with the Allied military whilst relying by prior agreement upon national governments to manage the day-to-day distribution of food, clothing and medical supplies.[11] An impressive recruitment drive encouraged numerous individuals to enlist, many of them with experience of relief work stretching back to the First World War. This included volunteers fired with Quaker ideals, such as Francesca Wilson, who embraced – and hoped to live – the ideals of international cooperation, having been disappointed by its miserable results after 1918.[12] Others, such as Mabel Geldard Brown, had a background in wartime relief (in her case, in Egypt, Greece and Italy) but, like Phoebe Bannister, were additionally trained in US social work and welfare, inspired by New Deal principles.[13] As Joshua Thew points out, other US genealogies can be traced through the experience of 'managing' first-nation people, urban immigrants and colonial subjects. Although staffers received training at the hands of UNRRA, their prior experience counted for a great deal more, since it had already instilled in them a belief in planned intervention rather than charity.[14]

The acceptance of military oversight and the insistence on the application of technical expertise in a variety of fields encouraged UNRRA to adopt a top-down approach to emergency relief as well as preventive measures against starvation and disease. Again, some insiders cast a critical eye on the implications. As early as September 1942, the experienced Canadian welfare worker Mary Agnes McGeachy warned that 'relief' expressed an unequal relationship between the individual donor and the recipient, such that 'human relations between benefactor and beneficiary tend to deteriorate'.[15] Spurgeon Keeny, a veteran of the anti-typhus campaign in post-1918 Poland who endorsed UNRRA's efforts against the mass outbreak of epidemic disease, stressed the need to respect and to draw upon local knowledge.[16] In a preparatory document on 'the psychology of refugees and displaced persons' (see below), American social psychologist Kimball Young advised relief workers: 'do not try to order and forbid and not explain ... provide a sense of participation of refugees and displaced persons in their own movement'. He added, 'if badly handled this anxiety may turn to frustration and aggression'.[17] Yet, as contributors to this book point out, patronizing and top-down approaches prevailed. Caroline Reeves adds that unequal power relations manifested themselves in China, where prevailing images of suffering went hand in hand with the depiction of victims as the grateful beneficiaries of Chinese Red Cross efforts to alleviate distress.

The geography of UNRRA disclosed a hierarchy of international concern. The main operating regions were Europe, the Middle East and the Far East, including the Philippines and Korea. In practice, the European cockpit (where the European Regional Office played a key role) meant Italy, Poland and Greece, but it also extended to Ukraine and Belarus, where plans for industrial and agricultural rehabilitation took second place to famine relief in 1945–6, a task later handed over to staff responsible for implementing the Marshall Plan.[18] Elsewhere, as in the Middle East, rehabilitation meant something different: UNRRA took over refugee camps previously administered by the Middle East Relief and Refugee Administration (MERRA) in Egypt, Palestine and Syria that housed Greek refugees who fled enemy invasion and occupation in 1942 along with former Yugoslav partisans who arrived in 1944. As Thew explains, refugee camps such as Camp Nuseirat became key sites of relief and immanent rehabilitation, preparing Greek refugees for repatriation.[19]

As Knapton and Rossy state in their Introduction, rehabilitation amounted to an immensely ambitious project.[20] In particular, the mass displacement of military personnel and civilians attracted close attention, and of course mattered hugely to families that had been wrenched apart by the war. Whilst pointing to the need to distribute emergency food supplies fairly to avoid starvation and 'prevent pestilence [and] "restore to a normal, healthy and self-sustaining existence" people in the oppressed countries', US President Franklin D. Roosevelt argued that these measures would 'thereby enable our own boys overseas to come home'.[21] In another early intervention addressing specifically the situation of civilians, Kenneth Brooks advocated that DPs should be assembled in 'national groups [to] facilitate feeding and clothing and enable the work of tracing families to be done', helping to pave the way for mass repatriation.[22] SHAEF (the *Supreme Headquarters Allied Expeditionary Force*) itself insisted on these measures, because 'self-repatriation' risked DPs forming 'roving bands of vengeful pillaging looters on trek to their homes'.[23]

All this belonged to the realm of short-term planning, but in the longer term more ambitious objectives took place. There was no uniform template in managing DPs, as Silvia Salvatici notes, but the wider ramifications of relief and rehabilitation were inescapable even as UNRRA trumpeted its 'non-political' remit.[24] Specifically, it was committed to a world of 'democratic peoples', as expressed by bacteriologist Charles-Edward Winslow (1877–1957), a key figure in American public health who wrote in 1944: 'relief inevitably merges into rehabilitation, rehabilitation into reconstruction, and reconstruction into the welfare of the permanent society of autonomous, democratic, cooperating peoples which is the object of our post-war planning'.[25]

George Woodbridge, the official historian of UNRRA, wrote that it was in the 'field of human rehabilitation that the Administration made its contribution to the care of the displaced persons'. In a revealing comparison, he went on to state that 'any mother who has tried knows that when she first teaches her children how to perform simple household tasks … [and] it requires far more time to teach the children to do such work and to supervise their doing than to do such work herself'.[26]

What, precisely, were DPs expected to learn? According to Eleanor Roosevelt, who reported after visiting DP camps in Germany, 'charity is a wonderful thing, but it does not give one that sense of security. What is important is rehabilitation … The sooner these people can be taken where they can become citizens and feel that they are actually building a new life, the better it will be for the whole world.' Citizenship in turn required developing self-reliance as an antidote to 'dependency'.[27] No stone was to be left unturned. As Silvia Salvatici explains, the supply of food went hand in hand with the cultivation of good eating habits among refugees and DPs. Sick and damaged people living in filthy and overcrowded conditions needed to be shown that the route to recovery and rehabilitation meant following lessons in civilized conduct. Katarzyna Nowak adds that children, teenagers and young mothers in DP camps were a particular object of attention. This was not straightforward. In echoes of what she described as the 'positive approach' adopted previously by the League of Nations, Mary McGeachy, appointed Director of UNRRA's Welfare Division, suggested that rehabilitation included the formulation of 'a constructive approach to the problem of rehabilitation into normal life [of] the women and girls whom the enemy has condemned to forced labour or prostitution'. The term was capable of elastic interpretation, but the path led to citizenship in democratic society.[28]

The influential Inter-Allied Psychological Study Group mused on rehabilitation in relation to displacement as a whole. In a memorandum prepared in June 1945, the team spoke of 'a haze of mysterious benevolence [that] hangs round this word, and indeed this subject'. The authors proceeded to argue that 'the process of rehabilitation is essentially psychological and sociological … [involving] recovery from losses of health, skills, valued social relationships and of social connections'. Along with DPs and refugees, attention needed to be paid to prisoners of war, military veterans, and even colonial repatriates whose 'psychological suffering and dislocation' required close attention, 'for men do not live by bread alone'. In each case, rehabilitation meant 'a regaining of independence and a tolerance of certain deprivations'.[29]

As Plesch and Schneider point out, UNRRA's publicity machine soon went into overdrive in support of its ambitious agenda. In UNRRA's own words:

> The truth of the matter is that the public reacts well, or ill, very much in proportion as the facts are properly brought to its attention. If the great tasks of the post-war period are offered with apology and timidity, the public will begrudge even the little that is asked. If, however, they are portrayed in their true magnitude, as the right and proper continuation of the struggle against tyranny and for the establishment of a just and prolonged peace, then men and women will respond with all their mind and heart.[30]

The soundtrack of the UNRRA-backed film *Seeds of Destiny* (1946) adopted bodily metaphors that referred to 'the plasma of peace', 'the pulse of rehabilitation and restoration', 'the human heart, stronger than the atomic bomb'.[31]

As indicated above, UNRRA held state intervention on the global stage to be essential. But what kind of state did UNRRA envisage and what limits were to be imposed on the state's sphere of action? Kimball Young wrote in 1944 of the need to exercise caution in promoting reconstruction, lest 'the state comes to stand for the parent'. He noted the 'contrast of totalitarian and democratic state forms [the former resting upon] fixed class structure, hierarchy of power top to bottom, complete domination of every phase of life, Gleichschaltung', and waxed lyrical on a vision of 'democratic, free men, brother relations, father image in representatives freely chosen ... positive elements, symbol of kingship and stable government in exile, now returned'. He warned of the 'dangers of the Fascist-minded in every community who may try to seize the new forms of authority'.[32] Here, once more, the rehabilitation of displaced people constituted a vital field of intervention, to enable them to participate in democratic state-building.

Research by Jessica Reinisch and Silvia Salvatici has established that a key strand that ran through the UNRRA project and that proved a point of contention was the rival claims of nationalism and internationalism in framing relief efforts. While enthusiastic American proponents of New Deal internationalism found their voice, others took the view that its status as the primary contributor of funds meant that national economic self-interest and sovereignty trumped other considerations. To be sure, some observers saw no contradiction: in 1944, Francis B. Sayre, appointed as diplomatic adviser to UNRRA, spoke of the need to ship fertilizer, seeds and spare parts to Europe in the shortest possible time, since 'our nation cannot remain prosperous in a world of bankrupt customers'.[33] Nevertheless, by 1947, as Reinisch notes, Washington announced that any economic and especially political gains that might have accrued to the United States had not materialized, and UNRRA's money and personnel had instead helped sustain the emerging Soviet bloc. American interests dictated a different approach.[34]

Rehabilitation also exposed the fault line between nationalism and internationalism. In Italy, Silvia Salvatici traces the difficulty of imposing an external programme of modernization, endorsed by international experts on an existing social welfare system that Italian traditionalists were keen to protect. No less assertively, as already mentioned, China resisted external interference and asserted its sovereignty with a view to following its own path of rehabilitation. Francesca Wilson described UNRRA as an 'international civil service', and other relief workers embraced the internationalist spirit.[35] Sir Frederick William Leith-Ross, chair of the Inter-Allied Committee, insisted to Mary McGeachy that 'it is obviously desirable for us to show that, for example, Catholic and Jewish workers can cooperate for the common aim of relief work without distinction of race or creed [and] that all personnel are employed as "relief workers", not as members of particular societies'.[36]

What happened when UNRRA field workers imbued with that philosophy came face to face with DPs? Will Arnold-Foster welcomed the prospect of not only working 'in a multi-national team' but also encountering 'people differing in nationality but alike in having suffered much'.[37] His expectations were largely dashed. As mentioned already, SHAEF's assembly centres worked on the basis of gathering DPs according to nationality. Voluntary agencies had no choice but to fall into line. More to the point, DPs harnessed their fortunes to that of the nation-state. Like her fellow Quaker relief workers, Francesca Wilson lamented the abortive attempt to develop trust between people of different nationalities. Instead, Margaret McNeill confirmed, 'competitive nationalism' took a strong hold on DPs in the refugee camp. It did not take long for expressions of national identity to become associated with the condition of exile.[38]

No less important than nationalist sentiment in the light of mass population displacement were the questions concerning the relationship between rehabilitation and another term capable of various interpretations, namely 'planning'. The renowned American social caseworker Cora Kasius (1897–1984) made a radical connection between social welfare, full employment and rehabilitation. Describing her work with concentration camp survivors, she explained that the initial aim had been to enable them to recover from starvation and typhus, but thereafter rehabilitation became 'much more inclusive'. With 'widening social interests in the larger community, the healing influences of work, wages and social acceptance were obvious at every hand'. This was an ambitious and progressive agenda that specified an important role for state intervention and planning to ensure full employment and security for all in capitalist society.[39]

After being wound up in 1947, albeit with a sense that it still had unfinished business, UNRRA was reassembled in other institutional forms, as Katherine Rossy and Lisa Payne Ossian explain. The newly established International Refugee Organization (IRO) assumed responsibility for the repatriation of DPs and the resettlement of those who refused to return to homes now under communist control. UNRRA's tracing bureau morphed into the International Tracing Service. The disposition of its assets demonstrated the link between UNRRA and other new UN organizations, notably UNICEF, to which UNRRA's Council transferred its residual assets, with the proviso that half of the funds be used to support Arab and Jewish refugees eligible for its assistance.[40] Some UNRRA personnel likewise channelled their efforts into UNICEF, such as John Alexander-Sinclair (1906–88), a British diplomat who was seconded to UNRRA's mission in France before becoming vice-chair of UNICEF. Subsequently, he took up posts with the Office of the UN High Commissioner for Refugees (UNHCR), the Food and Agriculture Organization and the World Health Organization. As a survey in 1960 noted, all of these inter-governmental organizations 'engaged to some degree in rehabilitation programmes'.[41]

UNRRA came and went, but global conflicts, civil wars, famine and epidemic diseases persisted. Many of the issues and complaints around UNRRA continued to bedevil relief efforts. How should the consequences of mass population displacement be managed, and by whom? Where did humanitarian relief end and rehabilitation begin? New sites of crisis encouraged proliferation of knowledge and practice. A striking echo of UNRRA doctrine and practice was the adoption of relief and rehabilitation in India following the demographic upheaval of Partition. The independent state insisted on the need for tutelage from above to assist several million refugees, particularly from East Bengal, and established a Ministry of Rehabilitation dedicated to that purpose. It is worth noting that Prime Minister Jawaharlal Nehru invited two UNRRA staffers to share their experiences.[42] Ultimately, 'rehabilitated' refugees would demonstrate through their own efforts that they had earned the right to be recognized as citizens.[43] Similar ideas inflected the UN Korean Reconstruction Agency, whose top-down efforts to relieve and rehabilitate refugees reproduced tensions between the military and civilian administration.[44]

The doctrine of rehabilitation also found fertile ground in the Middle East after Palestinian refugees were forced to flee in 1948. The UN Relief and Works

Agency (UNRWA) provided food rations and then financed education, training and employment schemes designed to help them to 'integrate'. But Palestinian refugees had no interest in this kind of rehabilitation: they wanted to return to their homeland, not to be granted citizenship in host states. Meanwhile, rehabilitation continued to offer career opportunities, exemplified by Burnell Vickers, a relief worker in Poland in 1945 who was quickly snapped up by UNRRA in Germany. After being transferred to the IRO, he moved to Gaza as a field programme officer working for UNRWA, later on serving as a legal adviser in Beirut.[45] In India, Korea and the Middle East, rehabilitation posed difficult questions about the rights and expectations of refugees and about the role of the state and intergovernmental organizations, core questions that had confronted UNRRA.[46]

As mentioned above, UNRRA faced administrative and ethical difficulties in relation to the management and repatriation of DPs. Those difficulties persist. In more recent times, UNHCR has backed purportedly voluntary repatriation deals in sub-Saharan Africa and South-East Asia and has confronted the same dilemmas around arranging or facilitating the return of refugees without adequately consulting the people most directly affected. One is reminded of Quaker relief workers in the field who protested the compulsory repatriation endorsed by the Allies and UNRRA breached the rights of DPs.[47] Other so-called durable solutions likewise echo post-war practices that emphasized the need to rehabilitate refugees in order to equip them with the 'appropriate' attitudes and behaviour preparatory to repatriation or resettlement.[48]

New organizations appeared on the scene, posing questions about external intervention, expert knowledge and state sovereignty. Intergovernmental organizations coexisted with new non-governmental organizations (NGOs), such as CARE (initially the acronym for Cooperative for American Remittances to Europe), which delivered food parcels to post-war Europe.[49] In relation to refugees, NGOs continued to handle operations on the ground at the behest of intergovernmental organizations such as UNHCR which channelled funds in their direction accordingly. They invested in training programmes for personnel, they prized technical expertise, and they insisted on the need to collect, retain, and process data. As their predecessors had done, they travelled the world.[50] Specialized casework in mental health carried on where UNRRA left off. At the same time, volunteering lost none of its attraction as new campaigns gathered momentum, notably the UN campaign for World Refugee Year (1959–60) and Freedom from Hunger, enlisting young women and men imbued with internationalist ideals.[51]

The chapters in this book shed new light on the proponents and practitioners of relief and rehabilitation during the UNRRA years. Adopting a longer view allows us to detect continuity and change in discourse and practice, against the backdrop of recurrent conflict and crisis. By way of conclusion, I shall mention one notable shift, namely the substitution of 'development' for rehabilitation. Like the cognate term 'modernization', this keyword gained fresh traction in the second half of the twentieth century.[52] This was not accidental. Beyond the connotation of fundamental social and economic transformation, the mantra of development had profound implications for refugees. Projects of economic development were endorsed by host countries to accommodate large numbers of refugees fleeing war and persecution. In addition to flows of aid from wealthy countries, these programmes served the interests of states in the Global North in enabling host states to contain or repatriate refugees rather than resettling them, the favoured option in the late 1940s and 1950s.[53] It is a reminder that political leaders today, like their counterparts in the era of UNRRA, ultimately impose their own interests on the world's most vulnerable populations.

Notes

1. In one of her letters, relief worker Kathryn Hulme wrote that 'All life you see reduces to supply lines. One talks airily of rehabilitation! I read the circulars and scream with ironic mirth. Just to keep these thousands fed and housed is a job of such titan dimensions, a word like rehabilitation flutters around like a piece of useless lace under the wheels of our supply trucks'. Quoted in Ben Shephard, *The Long Road Home: The Aftermath of the Second World War* (London: Bodley Head, 2010), 173.
2. Marta Aleksandra Balińska, 'Assistance and Not Mere Relief: The Epidemic Commission of the League of Nations', in Paul Weindling (ed.), *International Health Organizations and Movements, 1918–1939* (Cambridge: Cambridge University Press, 1995), 81–108; Claudena M. Skran, *Refugees in Inter-War Europe: The Emergence of a Regime* (Oxford: Clarendon Press, 1995).
3. Davide Rodogno. *Night on Earth: A History of International Humanitarian Relief and Rehabilitation in the Near East (1918–1930s)* (Cambridge: Cambridge University Press, 2021). For an earlier treatment, see Frank A. Ross, C. Luther Fry and Elbridge Sibley, *The Near East and American Philanthropy: A Survey* (New York: Columbia University Press, 1929).
4. Jessica Reinisch, 'Relief in the Aftermath of War', *Journal of Contemporary History*, 43:3 (2008), 371–404,384–5.
5. Grace Fox, 'The origins of UNRRA', *Political Science Quarterly*, 65:4 (1950), 561–84; Arnold Toynbee and Veronica Toynbee(eds.), *The Realignment of Europe*

(Oxford: Oxford University Press, 1955), 53–66. See also Sunil Amrith and Patricia Clavin, 'Feeding the World: Connecting Europe and Asia, 1930–1945', *Past and Present*, Supplement 8 (2013), 29–50; Elizabeth Borgwardt, *A New Deal for the World: America's Vision for Human Rights* (Cambridge, MA: Harvard University Press, 2005), 116–18.

6   Irene B. Taeuber, 'Population Displacements in Europe', *Annals of the American Association of Political and Social Sciences*, 234 (1944), 1–12.
7   Kenneth G. Brooks, 'The Re-establishment of Displaced Peoples', in Julian Huxley et al., *When Hostilities Cease: Papers on Relief and Reconstruction Prepared for the Fabian Society* (London: Gollancz, 1943), 99–124.
8   Tony Judt, 'The Past Is Another Country: Myth and Memory in Post-war Europe', in István Deák, Jan T. Gross and Tony Judt (eds.), *The Politics of Retribution in Europe: World War II and Its Aftermath* (Princeton: Princeton University Press, 2000), 293–323. In the middle of the war, the National Planning Administration regarded German children as being of particular concern, since 'the hungry German children of 1919 are the Storm Troopers of today'. *Relief for Europe: the First Phase of Reconstruction*, National Planning Association (NPA) Pamphlet 17, Washington, DC, 1942, 2.
9   Philipp Weintraub, 'UNRRA: An Experiment in International Welfare Planning', *The Journal of Politics*, 7:1 (1945), 1–24; Library and Archives of Canada (hereafter LAC), Mabel Geldard-Brown Papers, MMG30-E497, Vol. 3, file 1. Herbert Lehman, 'Remarks by the Director General, UNRRA at training school', Maryland, 8 June 1944.
10 Rana Mitter, 'Relocation and Dislocation: Civilian, Refugee, and Military Movement as Factors in the Disintegration of Post-war China, 1945–49', *Itinerario*, 46:2 (2022), 193–213.
11 According to Humfrey Gale, who transferred from SHAEF to become the personal representative of UNRRA's director-general in Europe, army logistics was relatively simple – 'you figuratively press a button and know that something will happened quickly' – whereas 'in UNRRA you have not always got the buttons to press, and it is not always certain that if you do press them they will do what you want'. Humfrey Gale, 'The Strategy of Relief', *The Listener*, 34:881 (29 November 1945), 607–8.
12 Francesca M. Wilson, *In the Margins of Chaos: Recollections of Relief Work in and between Three Wars* (London: John Murray), 1944.
13 On Bannister, see the chapter by Silvia Salvatici. For further details of Geldard Brown's career, see Susan Armstrong-Reid and David Murray, *Armies of Peace: Canada and the UNRRA Years* (Toronto: University of Toronto Press, 2008).
14 William Arnold-Forster, 'UNRRA's Work for Displaced Persons in Germany', *International Affairs*, 22:1 (1946), 1–13; Richard Titmuss, *Problems of Social Policy* (London: HMSO, 1950), 476, 480; Silvia Salvatici, *A History of Humanitarianism, 1755–1989: In the Name of Others* (Manchester: Manchester University Press, 2019), 118.

15 LAC, McGeachy Papers, R9369, Vol. 3, file 7. 'Proposals for the Organization of Voluntary Organizations for International Service in Europe after the War', 29 Sep. 1942.
16 Jessica Reinisch, 'Auntie UNRRA' at the crossroads', *P&P*, Supplement 8 (2013), 70–97, 76, 83.
17 Wellcome Library Archives (hereafter WLA), H. V. Dicks Papers. PP/HVD/B/1/5, 'Notes from a Talk to Civil Affairs Training School', 18 July 1944.
18 'UNRRA's Work in Europe: The Human Side of International Relations', *The Listener*, 38:964, 17 July 1947, 85–6.
19 MERRA merged with UNRRA at the end of January 1944, when its head, Sir William Matthews, became chief of the UNRRA Balkan Mission with a headquarters in Cairo. This marked 'the effective beginning of UNRRA in action since MERRA administered refugee camps and procured supplies (Egyptian cotton) on UNRRA's behalf'. Toynbee and Toynbee, *The Realignment of Europe* (Oxford: Oxford University Press, 1955), 65, 103.
20 Helen Leland Witmer, 'A Theoretical Basis for Foreign Relief and Rehabilitation Operations', *Smith College Studies in Social Work*, 14:3 (1944), 273–310.
21 Quoted in Woodbridge, *UNRRA*, vol. 1, 3–4.
22 Brooks, 'The Re-establishment of Displaced Peoples', 116.
23 Malcolm J. Proudfoot, *European Refugees, 1939–1952: A Study in Forced Population Movements* (London: Faber and Faber, 1957), 116–17.
24 The first meeting of UNRRA's council in November–December 1943 asserted the principle that relief work was not 'political'. Woodbridge, *UNRRA*, vol. 1, 29. Compare Reinisch, 'Auntie UNRRA' at the crossroads', 74.
25 Quoted in James A. Gillespie, 'Europe, America and the Space of International Health', in Susan G. Solomon, Lion Murard and Patrick Zylberman (eds.), *Shifting Boundaries of Public Health: Europe in the Twentieth Century* (Rochester: University of Rochester Press, 2008), 114–37, 117.
26 Woodbridge, *UNRRA*, vol. 2, 523.
27 Quoted in G. Daniel Cohen, *In War's Wake: Europe's Displaced Persons in the Postwar Order* (New York: Oxford University Press, 2012), 66.
28 LAC, McGeachy Papers, vol. 3, file 2. UNRRA-Welfare Division reports. Memo on social welfare, 24 April 1945.
29 WLA, H.V. Dicks Papers, GC/135/B1/1-4, Service Psychiatry Monographs, no.6. 'Psychological problems of displaced persons' (Inter-Allied PSG), June 1945. It is fascinating to read that colonial repatriates 'may complain of marked psychological disturbances and in particular of feelings of unreality, of restlessness or apathy or irritability until they have settled down'. See also Laure Humbert, *Reinventing French Aid: The Politics of Humanitarian Relief in French-Occupied Germany,*

1945–1952 (Cambridge: Cambridge University Press, 2021), 204–18; Stella Maria Frei, 'For Men do not Live by Bread Alone: Conceptualizing UNRRA's Psychosocial Rehabilitation Approach for Displaced Persons in the Immediate Post-war Months', in Nikolaus Hagen (ed.), *Displaced Persons-Forschung in Deutschland und Österreich: Eine Bestandsaufnahme zu Beginn des 21. Jahrhunderts* (Berlin: Frank & Timme, 2022), 199–224.

30 *UNRRA: Gateway to Recovery* (Washington, DC: National Planning Association, 1944), 610.
31 https://archive.org/details/SeedsofDestiny [accessed 22 March Mar. 2023].
32 WLA, H. V. Dicks Papers, PP/HVD/B/1/5. 'Notes from a talk to Civil Affairs Training School', 18 July 1944.
33 American Friends Service Committee archives (hereafter AFSCAr), Address by Francis B. Sayre, diplomatic adviser, UNRRA, to the annual luncheon of Women's America ORT, New York City, 10 May 1944. Philadelphia, Foreign Service, 1944, Committees and Organizations. See Roosevelt's remarks, cited in Borgwardt, *A New Deal for the World*, 136.
34 Reinisch, 'Auntie UNRRA' at the Crossroads', 88–90, 97.
35 Francesca Wilson, *Aftermath: France, Germany, Austria, Yugoslavia, 1945 and 1946* (London: Penguin Books, 1947), 19.
36 LAC, McGeachy Papers, vol. 3, file 1. Leith-Ross to McGeachy, 23 February 1944.
37 Arnold-Forster, 'UNRRA's work for Displaced Persons in Germany', 5.
38 Francesca M. Wilson, *Advice to Relief Workers* (London: John Murray, 1945), 641–2. McNeill is quoted in Jennifer Carson, 'The Society of Friends and Displaced Persons (DPs) in Post-war Europe', unpublished PhD dissertation, University of Manchester, 2009, 145. The latest study of this topic is Katarzyna Nowak, *Kingdom of Barracks: Polish Displaced Persons in Allied-Occupied Germany and Austria* (Montreal-Toronto: McGill-Queen's University Press, 2023).
39 Cora Kasius, 'Editorial', *Journal of Social Casework*, 29:7 (1948), 279–80.
40 UN Career Records Project (hereafter UNCRP) at Bodleian Library, Oxford. MS. Eng. C. 4655, folder 206. 'Notes on UNICEF finance, 1947–48', Papers of John Alexander Sinclair (1906–1988). See also Reinisch, 'Auntie UNRRA' at the crossroads', pp. 94–5; Salvatici, *A History of Humanitarianism*, 133–4.
41 Howard A. Rusk and Donald V. Wilson, 'New Resources for Rehabilitation and Health', *Annals of the American Association of Political and Social Sciences*, 329 (1960), 97–106, 98.
42 They were Molly Flynn, who later transferred from UNRRA to UNRWA, and Everett Barger, who went on to work for UNESCO.
43 Joya Chatterji, 'Right or Charity? The Debate over Relief and Rehabilitation in West Bengal, 1947–1950', in Suvir Kaul (ed.), *The Partitions of Memory*

(Delhi: Permanent Black, 2001), 74–110; Uditi Sen, *Citizen Refugee: Forging the Indian Nation after Partition* (Cambridge: Cambridge University Press, 2018).

44 Peter Gatrell, 'Korean Refugees and Aid Work in International Perspective', in Agnes Bresselau von Bressendorf (ed.), *Über Grenzen: Migration und Flucht in globaler Perspektive seit 1945* (Göttingen: Vandenhoeck and Ruprecht, 2019), 275–91.

45 'The broad purpose of rehabilitation should be to reintegrate refugees into the economic life of the Near East [and to enable refugees] to work rather than remain idle, thereby preserving their skills, aptitudes or morale [and] to enable refugees to acquire knowledge or skills or experience of such a kind as to fit them better for life in a more normal community.' 'Memo on Rehabilitation Policy – a basis for discussion', UNCPR, MS. Eng. C.4706, folder 79. 4 February 1956 from Field Program Officer Gaza [i.e., Vickers] to UNWRA Representative, Gaza, D. Burnell Vickers Papers (1922–1983).

46 Ilana Feldman, *Life Lived in Relief: Humanitarian Predicaments and Palestinian Refugee Politics* (Berkeley: University of California Press, 2018).

47 Carson, 'The Society of Friends and Displaced Persons', 207, quoting Yvonne Marrack. See also Richard Black and Khalid Koser (eds.), *The End of the Refugee Cycle? Refugee Repatriation and Reconstruction* (Oxford: Berghahn, 1999); Arthur Helton, *The Price of Indifference: Refugees and Humanitarian Action in the New Century* (New York: Oxford University Press, 2000), 177–81.

48 Aihwa Ong, *Buddha Is Hiding: Refugees, Citizenship, the New America* (Berkeley: University of California Press, 2003), 277. See the remarks of UNHCR High Commissioner Sadako Ogata in 1995, cited by the editors in their Introduction, where she connected rehabilitation to repatriation and 'reintegration'. Tellingly, Ogata spoke of the 'requirements' of refugees, rather than their wishes.

49 Heike Wieters, 'Of Heartfelt Charity and Billion-dollar Enterprise: From Post-war Relief to Europe to Humanitarian Relief to "Everywhere": CARE Inc. in search of a New Mission', in Marc Frey, Soenke Kunkel and Corinna Unger (eds.), *International Organizations and Development, 1945 to 1990* (Basingstoke: Palgrave Macmillan, 2014), 220–39.

50 Uma Kothari, 'From Colonialism to Development: Continuities and Divergencies', *Journal of Commonwealth and Comparative Politics*, 44:1 (2006), 118–36; Bertrand Taithe, 'The Cradle of the New Humanitarian System? International Work and European Volunteers at the Cambodian Border Camps, 1979–1993', *Contemporary European History,* 25:2 (2016), 335–58.

51 Peter Gatrell, *Free World? The Campaign to Save the World's Refugees, 1956–1963* (Cambridge: Cambridge University Press, 2011); Anna Bocking-Welch, 'Imperial legacies and internationalist discourses: British involvement in the United Nations Freedom from Hunger Campaign, 1960–70', *The Journal of Imperial and Commonwealth History*, 40:5 (2012), 879–96.

52 Nick Cullather, *Hungry World: America's Cold War Battle against Poverty in Asia* (Cambridge, MA: Harvard University Press, 2010); Marc Frey, Soenke Kunkel and Corinna Unger (eds.), *International Organizations and Development, 1945 to 1990* (Cambridge: Cambridge University Press, 2014).

53 B. S. Chimni, 'From Resettlement to Involuntary Repatriation: Towards a Critical History of Durable Solutions to Refugee Problems', *Refugee Survey Quarterly*, 23:3(2004), 55–73.

Select bibliography

Convegno per studi di assistenza sociale Tremezzo. *Atti del Convegno per Studi di Assistenza Sociale*. Milano: Marzorati, 1946.

Acheson, Dean. *Present at the Creation: My Years in the State Department*. New York: W. W. Norton, 1969.

Adami, Rachel, Dan Plesch and Amitav Acharya (eds.). *Women and the UN: A New History of Women's International Human Rights*. Abingdon, Oxon: Routledge, 2021.

Armstrong-Reid, Susan and David M. Murray. *Armies of Peace: Canada and the UNRRA Years*. Toronto: Toronto University Press, 2008.

Arnold-Forster, William. 'UNRRA's Work for Displaced Persons in Germany'. *International Affairs* 22, no. 1 (1946): 1–13.

Balint, Ruth. *Destination Elsewhere: Displaced Persons and Their Quest to Leave Post-war Europe*. New York: Cornell University Press, 2021.

Betts, Paul. *Ruin and Renewal: Civilising Europe after the Second World War*. London: Profile Books, 2020.

Borgwardt, Elizabeth. *A New Deal for the World. America's Vision for Human Rights*. Cambridge, MA, and London: Belknap Press of Harvard University Press, 2005.

Brooks, Kenneth G. 'The Re-establishment of Displaced Peoples'. In *When Hostilities Cease: Papers on Relief and Reconstruction Prepared for the Fabian Society*, edited by Julian Huxley et al., 99–124. London: Gollancz, 1943.

Brown-Fleming, Suzanne. *Nazi Persecution and Post-war Repercussions: The International Tracing Service Archive and Holocaust Research*. Lanham: Rowman & Littlefield, 2016.

Carson, Jennifer, 'The Society of Friends and Displaced Persons (DPs) in Post-war Europe'. PhD Diss., University of Manchester, UK, 2009.

Ciampani, Andrea (ed.). *L'Amministrazione per Aiuti Internazionali. La ricostruzione dell'Italia tra dinamiche internazionali e attività assistenziali*. Milano: Franco Angeli, 2002.

Cohen, Gerard Daniel. *In War's Wake: Europe's Displaced Persons in the Post-war Order*. New York: Oxford University Press, 2012.

Cohen, Gerard Daniel. 'Between Relief and Politics: Refugee Humanitarianism in Occupied Germany 1945–1946'. *Journal of Contemporary History* 43, no. 3 (2008): 437–49.

Fox, Grace. 'The Origins of UNRRA'. *Political Science Quarterly* 65, no. 4 (1950): 561–84.

Frank, Matthew and Jessica Reinisch (eds.). *Refugees in Europe, 1919–1959: A Forty Year Crisis?* London: Bloomsbury Academic, 2017.

Frei, Stella Maria. '"For Men Do Not Live by Bread alone": Conceptualizing UNRRA's Psychosocial Rehabilitation Approach for Displaced Persons in the Immediate Post-war Months'. In *Displaced Persons-Forschung in Deutschland und Österreich: Eine Bestandsaufnahme zu Beginn des 21. Jahrhunderts*, edited by Nikolaus Hagen, Markus Nesselrodt, Philip Strobl and Marcus Velke-Schmidt, 199–224. Berlin: Frank & Timme, 2022.

Frey, Marc, Soenke Kunkel and Corinna Unger (eds.). *International Organizations and Development, 1945 to 1990*. Cambridge: Cambridge University Press, 2014.

Gardikas, Katerina, 'Relief Work and Malaria in Greece, 1943–1947'. *Journal of Contemporary History* 43, no. 3 (2008): 493–508.

Gatrell, Peter. *The Making of the Modern Refugee*. New York: Oxford University Press, 2013.

Gatrell, Peter. *The Unsettling of Europe: How Migration Reshaped a Continent*. New York: Basic Books, 2019.

Giorgi, Chiara and Ilaria Pavan. *Storia dello Stato sociale in Italia*. Bologna: Il Mulino, 2021.

Glasman, Joël. *Humanitarianism and Quantification of Human Needs: Minimal Humanity*. London & New York: Routledge, 2020.

Harper John, Lamberton. *America and the Reconstruction of Italy, 1945–1948*. Cambridge: Cambridge University Press, 1986.

Healy Lynne, M. *International Social Work. Professional Action in an Independent World*. Oxford: Oxford University Press, 2008.

Hoeschler, Christian, Henning Borggräfe and Isabel Panek. *Tracing and Documenting Nazi Victims Past and Present*. Berlin: DeGruyter, 2020.

Holborn, Louise. *The International Refugee Organization: A Specialized Agency of the United Nations: Its History and Work, 1946–1951*. Oxford: Oxford University Press, 1952.

Holian, Anna. *Between National Socialism and Soviet Communism: Displaced Persons in Post-war Germany*. Michigan: University of Michigan Press, 2011.

Hooever, Herbert. *An American Epic: The Guns Cease Killing and the Saving of Life from Famine Begins, 1939–1963*. Vol. 4. Chicago: Henry Regnery Company, 1964.

Humbert, Laure. *Reinventing French Aid: The Politics of Humanitarian Relief in French-Occupied Germany, 1945–1952*. Cambridge: Cambridge University Press, 2021.

Inaudi, Silvia. 'Assistenza e povertà infantile negli anni dell'inchiesta sulla miseria'. In *Infanzia e povertà. Storie e narrazioni nell'Italia del dopoguerra (1945–1950)*, edited by Clara Allasia, Bruno Maida and Franco Prono, 47–60. Avellino: Edizioni Sinestesie, 2019.

Inaudi, Silvia. 'L'assistenza nel secondo dopoguerra tra continuità e mancate riforme. Note a margine del dibattito storiografico'. *Storica* XVI, no. 46 (2010): 79–99.

Knapton, Samantha K. *Occupiers, Humanitarian Workers, and Polish Displaced Persons in British-Occupied Germany 1945–1951*. London: Bloomsbury Academic, 2023.

Lin, Yi-Tang, Thomas David and Davide Rodogno. 'Fellowship Programs for Public Health Development: The Rockefeller Foundation, UNRRA, and WHO (1920s–1970s)'. In *Global Exchange. Scholarships and Transnational Circulations in the Modern World*, edited by Ludovic Tournès and Giles Scott-Smith, 140–55. New York-Oxford: Berghahn, 2017.

Malkki, Liisa, 'Speechless Emissaries: Refugees, Humanitarianism, and Dehistoricization'. *Cultural Anthropology* 11, no. 3 (1996): 377–404.

Marrus, Michael. *The Unwanted: European Refugees in the Twentieth Century*. Oxford: Oxford University Press, 1985.

Mazower, Mark. 'Reconstruction: The Historiographical Issues'. *Past & Present* 210, supplement 6 (2011): 17–28.

Mazower, Mark. *Inside Hitler's Greece: The Experience of Occupation, 1941–44*. New Haven: Yale University Press, 1993.

Mitter, Rana. 'Imperialism, Transnationalism, and the Reconstruction of Post-war China: UNRRA in China, 1944–47'. *Past & Present* 218, supplement 8 (2013): 51–69.

Morris, Jennifer. *The Origins of UNICEF, 1946–1953*. Maryland: Lexington Books, 2015.

Nasaw, David. *The Last Million: Europe's Displaced Persons from World War to Cold War*. New York: Penguin Press, 2020.

Nowak, Katarzyna. *Kingdom of Barracks: Polish Displaced Persons in Allied-Occupied Germany and Austria, 1945–1952*. Montreal: McGill-Queen's University Press, 2023.

Paulmann, Johannes (ed.). *Dilemmas of Humanitarian Aid in the Twentieth Century*. Oxford: Oxford University Press, 2016.

Plesch, Dan. *America, Hitler and the UN: How the Allies Won World War II and Forged a Peace*. London: I.B. Tauris, 2011.

Plesch, Dan and Thomas G. Weiss, '1945's Forgotten Insight: Multilateralism as Realist Necessity'. *International Studies Perspectives* 17, no. 1 (2016): 4–16.

Proudfoot, Malcolm J. *European Refugees, 1939–1952: A Study in Forced Population Movements*. Evanston: Northwest University Press, 1956.

Reeves, Caroline. 'Developing the Humanitarian Image in Late Nineteenth- and Early Twentieth-Century China'. In *Humanitarian Photography: A History*, edited by Heidi Fehrenbach and Davide Rodogno, 115–39. New York: Cambridge University Press, 2015.

Reinisch, Jessica. '"Auntie UNRRA" at the Crossroads'. *Past & Present* 218, supplement 8 (2013): 70–97.

Reinisch, Jessica. 'Introduction: Relief in the Aftermath of War'. *Journal of Contemporary History* 43, no. 3 (2008): 371–404.

Reinisch, Jessica. '"We Shall Build Anew a Powerful Nation": UNRRA, Internationalism and National Reconstruction in Poland'. *Journal of Contemporary History* 43, no. 3 (2008): 451–76.

Reinisch, Jessica. *Perils of Peace: The Public Health Crisis in Occupied Germany*. Oxford: Oxford University Press, 2013.

Rodogno, Davide. *Night on Earth: A History of International Humanitarianism in the Near East, 1918–1930*. Cambridge: Cambridge University Press, 2021.

Sackley, Nicole. 'The Village as Cold War Site: Experts, Development, and the History of Rural Reconstruction'. *Journal of Global History* 6, no. 3 (2011): 481–504.

Salvatici, Silvia. *A History of Humanitarianism: In the Name of Others, 1755–1989*. Manchester: Manchester University Press, 2019.

Salvatici, Silvia. 'Between National and International Mandates: Displaced Persons and Refugees in Post-war Italy'. *Journal of Contemporary History* 49, no. 3 (2014): 514–36.

Salvatici, Silvia. '"Help the People to Help Themselves": UNRRA Relief Workers and European Displaced Persons'. *Journal of Refugee Studies* 25, no. 3 (2012): 428–51.

Salvatici, Silvia. 'Sights of Benevolence: UNRRA's Recipients Portrayed'. In *Humanitarian Photography: A History*, edited by Heidi Fehrenbach and Davide Rodogno, 200–222. New York: Cambridge University Press, 2015.

Shephard, Ben. *The Long Road Home: The Aftermath of the Second World War*. London: Bodley Head, 2010.

Toynbee, Arnold and Veronica Toynbee (eds.). *The Realignment of Europe*. Oxford: Oxford University Press, 1955.

Woodbridge, George. *UNRRA. The History of the International Relief and Rehabilitation Administration (Vol. I-III)*. New York: Columbia University Press, 1950.

Wyman, Mark. *DPs: Europe's Displaced Persons, 1945–1951*. New York: Cornell University Press, 1989.

Zahra, Tara. *The Lost Children: Reconstructing Europe's Families after World War II*. New York: Harvard University Press, 2011.

Zurndorfer, Harriet. 'Wartime Refugee Relief in Chinese Cities and Women's Political Activism, 1937–1940'. In *New Narratives of Urban Space in Republican Chinese Cities: Emerging Social, Legal and Governance Orders*, edited by K. L. So Billy and Madeleine Zelin, 65–91. Leiden: Brill, 2013.

Index

A

Acropolis 79
Adolf Hitler 31, 39, 84, 98, 100, 190, 212
Agricultural rehabilitation 2, 22, 58, 112
Alcide De Gasperi 57
Allied Control Council 59, 136
Allied War Crimes Commission 141
Allied-occupied Germany 4, 15, 37, 38, 135, 207, 212
Allies 5, 9, 14, 21, 24, 31, 32, 58, 133, 136, 141, 190, 196, 203, 212
American Red Cross 76, 81, 98, 131, 201
Amministrazione per gli Aiuti Internazionali 12, 57, 67, 68, 71, 210
Anthony Eden 176, 189
Arthur Rothstein 113–115, 129
Assembly centres 39, 46, 54, 144, 201
Atlantic City 2, 139, 199
Atlantic Charter 29
Austria 4, 5, 10, 15, 32–33, 37–38, 41–42, 45, 53–55, 147, 160, 163, 207, 212
Axis occupation 74, 78, 84, 181

B

Balkan Wars 73
Bergen-Belsen 142
Big Three 152
Bretton Woods 177, 186
British Mandate of Palestine 88, 91
British Red Cross 33, 135, 148
Buchenwald 141

C

Cairo Agreement 79
Canada 12, 15, 34, 150, 157, 177, 186, 205, 210
Central Tracing Bureau 7, 11, 12, 133–136, 141–150
Child Search Bureau 12, 142–143
Children xiii, 3, 5, 8, 11, 14–15, 30, 33, 37, 41, 43–44, 48–49, 59, 63–67, 77, 81, 84–86, 92–95, 103, 115, 117–118, 122, 124, 126, 134, 139, 142–147, 149, 151–173, 199, 205, 213

China vi, x, 3, 5, 15, 128, 129, 130, 131, 133, 134, 135, 136, 137, 138, 139, 140, 141, 142, 144, 145, 146, 148, 149, 150, 151, 152, 154, 155, 156, 157, 158, 159, 160, 195, 208
Chinese National Relief and Rehabilitation Administration 1, 129, 133
Christian Democratic Party 70
Cold War 6, 9, 14, 17, 29, 57, 73, 75, 78–80, 87–88, 92, 94–96, 98–99, 105, 169, 180, 185, 188, 194, 209, 212–213
Collaborators 4, 147
Communist 9, 12, 74, 79–80, 90, 92, 94–95, 105, 108–109, 164, 168, 187–188, 195, 202
Concentration camp 37, 48, 137, 141–142, 144, 201
Cyclades 83, 92

D

DDT 8, 42, 44, 89, 92–93, 114
Dean Acheson 18, 21–22, 29, 31, 35, 155, 177, 188, 190, 193, 210
Denazification 9
Deutsches Museum 27, 133
Displacement 1–3, 7, 12–14, 33, 35, 50, 52, 87, 104–105, 127, 198–199, 201–202, 205
Documentary intelligence 137, 140–142
DP camps 6–7, 10, 23–28, 30, 33, 37–55, 138, 144, 154, 167, 184–185, 198–199
DP 12, 3–4, 6–13, 17, 19, 22–35, 37–39, 37–55, 58–59, 107, 133, 138–139, 141, 144, 154, 156, 167, 170, 184, 198–210, 213
Drought 110

E

Eglantyne Jebb 7, 118, 130
Emilie Willms 75, 77, 86–87, 100
Epidemic 18, 21, 45–46, 51, 197, 202, 204

Ernest Bevin 22, 32
Europe 1, 3–4, 6, 7–8, 11–15, 17–25, 31–35, 38–41, 46, 51–57, 59, 62, 67, 69, 70, 73, 78–79, 86–88, 94, 97, 104–108, 111, 127, 143–149, 151, 153–158, 160–161, 165–173, 175, 183–184, 188–208
European Division of Health 10, 38–39, 52–55, 182, 199, 206
European Regional Office 20, 35, 66–67, 71–72, 106, 148–149, 198
Expellees 4, 196
Eyre Carter 141, 149

F
Famine 4, 8–9, 11, 14, 32, 78, 80, 84, 104, 109–112, 116–120, 122–123, 129–130, 151–173, 175, 181, 195, 198, 202, 211
Famine Mission Men 157, 159–160, 162, 169
Farm Security Administration 12, 113
Fiorello LaGuardia 31, 158, 166
First World War 7, 18, 73, 94, 118, 159, 163, 167, 197
Food and Agriculture Organization 12, 96, 202
Foodstuffs 3, 64, 186
Francesca Wilson 23, 28, 33, 35, 197, 201, 205, 207
Franklin Delano Roosevelt 12, 19, 58, 78–79, 113, 154–155, 170, 175–175, 187, 198–199, 207
Frederick E. Morgan 20–21, 25–26, 32, 34, 136, 138, 148
Friends Ambulance Unit 12, 33, 88

G
German Red Cross 136
Germany 3–6, 10–11, 14–15, 21, 23, 25, 28, 31–34, 37–39, 43, 45–47, 52–56, 86, 107, 133–138, 141, 143–148, 156–157, 160, 163, 167, 171–172, 179, 185, 188–193, 196, 199, 203, 205–206, 210–212
Gestapo 141
Great Britain 32, 58, 62, 146, 155
Great War 7, 14, 151–152, 155, 159, 163
Greece 7–8, 10, 73–101, 107, 160, 164, 167, 195, 197–198, 211–212
Greek Civil War 74, 78–80, 94

H
Harry Truman 154, 157, 160, 165, 168, 169, 173, 187–188
Herbert H. Lehman 2–3, 13, 24, 31, 35, 59, 78, 164, 182, 195–196, 205
Herbert Hoover 9, 11, 151–173
Holocaust 9, 141, 146, 177, 188, 193, 210
House of Commons 19, 31, 189
Humanitarianism 2–10, 12–15, 29, 31–33, 37, 58, 62, 67–69, 97–98, 108, 117, 123, 127, 130–131, 144, 146, 150, 152, 155, 157, 190–191, 194, 205, 207, 210–213
Hygiene 7, 10, 37–38, 40–43, 45, 47–51

I
Immunization 42, 45, 55
Imperialism 4, 127–129, 212
Intergovernmental Committee on Refugees 12–13
International Committee of the Red Cross 166, 167, 181, 184
International Refugee Organization 5, 13, 19, 28–30, 35, 38–39, 52, 145
International Tracing Service 12, 134, 145–146
Ira Hirschmann 188, 193
Iron Curtain 4
Israel 91, 185
Italy 10, 57–72, 106, 159–160, 195, 197–198, 201, 211, 213

J
Jewish Committee for Relief Abroad 33
Jiang Tingfu 106–108, 128
Joint Distribution Committee 195

K
Kathryn Hulme 27–28, 34–35, 204

L
League of Nations 13–14, 20, 29, 33, 35, 76, 98, 118, 130, 195, 199, 204
Lira fund 62–63, 66, 70

M
Mackenzie King 189
Malaria 81, 92–93, 101, 211
Malnutrition 44, 92
Manchuria 109

Marshall Plan 11, 52, 57, 175, 177, 179, 181, 188–189, 193, 198
Marvin Klemmé 28, 35
Marxism 109
Maurice Pate 30, 153, 159, 166–170, 172
Mauthausen 142, 149
Memory of the World Register 146
Middle East Relief and Refugee Administration 12, 78, 80, 82–83, 87–88, 90–91, 100–101, 198, 206
Montreal 3, 12, 33
Moses Wells 88

N
National Planning Association 12, 18, 31, 81–82, 99, 173, 205, 207
Nazi 58, 133–135, 141–150
Near East Foundation 7, 10, 73–76, 84–85, 94, 96, 99–101
New Deal 10, 23, 67, 72, 109, 113, 139, 155, 173, 176, 187, 197, 200
Nordhausen 141
Nuremberg 141, 177
Nuseirat 8, 88–92, 100–101, 198

O
Oedema 92
Orphanage 63, 84, 140, 169
Ottoman Empire 73, 97
Overseas Branch of Office of War Information 42

P
Peace 2, 11, 15, 24, 31, 33–35, 41–42, 51–52, 55, 73, 154, 157–158, 165, 170–172, 177, 179–181, 189–193, 200, 205
Philanthropy 61–62, 73–77, 81, 84, 94, 96–101, 119, 120, 130–131, 204
Phoebe Bannister 60–64, 69–70, 197, 205
Poland 15, 34, 48, 59, 106, 137, 148–149, 151, 160, 168, 194, 197–198, 203, 212
Polish Red Cross 137, 148
Pontificia Commissione di Assistenza 63
Public health 1, 5, 10, 15, 26, 31, 37–38, 42–46, 52, 54, 65, 70–71, 76–77, 82, 98, 168, 172, 189, 198, 206, 212

Q
Quisling 4

R
Refugee 1, 3–7, 11–14, 19–20, 30–31, 33–35, 38, 50, 52, 58–59, 68, 76–78, 83, 87–91, 97–98, 100–101, 103–105, 107, 109–131, 135, 137–138, 140, 145, 148, 161, 164, 169, 178, 182, 185, 188–190, 195, 197–199, 201, 202–206, 208–209
Refugee Settlement Commission 76
Rehabilitation 1–15, 17–35, 37–42, 46, 48, 50–54, 57–64, 67–68, 73–100, 103–112, 125–129, 133–135, 138–140, 144–146, 151–156, 163, 167–173, 175–178, 181–192, 196–208
Relief workers 8, 15, 27, 33, 38, 44, 46, 51–52, 97, 140, 159, 190, 195, 197, 201, 203, 207, 213
Repatriation 2–3, 10, 18, 21–22, 24, 26–30, 32, 34, 38–39, 52, 70–71, 127, 133, 135, 138–139, 198, 202–203, 208–209
Resettlement 2, 9, 28, 30, 110, 133, 138–139, 195, 202–203, 209
Resocialization 139–140
Rockefeller Foundation 70, 76, 85, 93, 98–99, 101, 212

S
Sadako Ogata 1, 12, 208
San Francisco Conference 113, 177, 180
Save the Children 8, 33, 118
Second Sino-Japanese War 104, 109, 118
Second World War 1–3, 7, 13–15, 17, 24, 37, 53, 73–74, 77, 83, 92, 103–104, 109, 111, 126–127, 138, 140, 151, 153–155, 157, 159–163, 166–167, 169–170, 173, 176, 190, 196, 204, 210, 213
Security 2, 25, 61, 80, 90–92, 95–96, 113, 177, 179, 180, 187, 191, 195, 199
Sir Frederick Leith-Ross 19–21, 35, 201, 207
Soviet Union 3, 6, 110, 120, 163, 191, 195
Stalag 142
State Department 31, 166, 176, 183, 210
Supreme Headquarters Allied Expeditionary Force 33, 135, 192, 198
Susan Pettiss 26–28, 34–35

T
T. V. Soong 106
Tick fever 92

Tracing 3–4, 8, 11, 133–150, 188, 193, 198, 202, 210–211
Truman Doctrine 96
Tuberculosis 46–47, 92, 161, 163–164
Typhoid 42, 45, 89
Typhus 42–43, 45, 89, 197, 201

U

UN Information Organization 32, 175, 177–178, 189–190
UN Office for the Coordination of Humanitarian Affairs 188
UN War Crimes Commission 141, 149, 177
UNESCO 1, 146, 169, 173, 207
UNICEF 1, 5, 7, 9, 11, 13, 15, 17, 30–31, 35, 66, 68, 151–153, 165, 168–173, 189, 202, 207, 212
United Nations High Commissioner for Refugees 1, 5, 12, 17, 20, 30–31, 184, 202–203, 208
United States 3, 11, 19–20, 24, 29, 42, 58–60, 62, 65, 68–69, 71, 73, 78–81, 83, 86–87, 92–93, 95–101, 104, 106, 127, 129, 146, 148–149, 153, 155, 157–158, 162, 164–165, 168, 170–171, 175–177, 180–181, 187–188, 194, 201
UNRRA Central Committee 106
UNRRA Council 3, 29, 35, 59
UNRRA Nutrition Conference 65

V

Vaccination 45, 51, 89–90
Veneral disease 38, 46–48, 51–52
Volksdeutsche 4, 147

W

War criminals 4, 141, 147
War Department 154
Wehrmacht 4, 147
Welfare Division 10, 60–61, 63, 65, 69–71, 88, 148, 199, 206
Wildflecken 27
Winston Churchill 14, 19, 31, 79, 155, 170
World Bank 185–186, 188
World Council of Churches 186
World Health Organization 1, 5, 9, 31, 96, 189, 202

Y

Yalta Conference 52, 151, 170
Yugoslavia 33, 59, 107, 142, 160, 164, 195, 207

Z

Zonal bureaux 11, 136–137, 141

www.ingramcontent.com/pod-product-compliance
Lightning Source LLC
Chambersburg PA
CBHW052107300426
44116CB00010B/1568